The Early American Republic

A HISTORY IN DOCUMENTS

The Early American Republic

A HISTORY IN DOCUMENTS

Reeve Huston

New York   Oxford
OXFORD UNIVERSITY PRESS
2011

For Isaac, who loves history and knows what's important

General Editors

Sarah Deutsch
Professor of History
Duke University

Carol K. Karlsen
Professor of History
University of Michigan

Robert G. Moeller
Professor of History
University of California, Irvine

Jeffrey N. Wasserstrom
Professor of History
University of California, Irvine

Cover: The Erie Canal, 1825.

Frontispiece: "Life of George Washington—the farmer," 1853.

Title page: President's Levee, or All Creation Going to the White House by Robert Cruikshank, 1829.

Oxford University Press, Inc., publishes works that further
Oxford University's objective of excellence
in research, scholarship, and education.

Oxford   New York
Auckland   Cape Town   Dar es Salaam   Hong Kong   Karachi
Kuala Lumpur   Madrid   Melbourne   Mexico City   Nairobi
New Delhi   Shanghai   Taipei   Toronto

With offices in
Argentina   Austria   Brazil   Chile   Czech Republic   France   Greece
Guatemala   Hungary   Italy   Japan   Poland   Portugal   Singapore
South Korea   Switzerland   Thailand   Turkey   Ukraine   Vietnam

Published by Oxford University Press, Inc.
198 Madison Avenue, New York, New York 10016
www.oup.com

Oxford is a registered trademark of Oxford University Press

Library of Congress Cataloging-in-Publication Data
Huston, Reeve.
The early American republic : a history in documents / by Reeve Huston.
   p. cm.
   ISBN 978-0-19-533824-9 (pbk. : alk. paper) — ISBN 978-0-19-510812-5 (hard-
cover : alk. paper) 1. United States—History—1783–1815—Sources. 2. United
States—History—1815–1861—Sources. 3. United States—Politics and govern-
ment—1783–1865—Sources. 4. Political culture—United States—History—18th
century—Sources. 5. Political culture—United States—History—19th century—
Sources. 6. United States—Economic conditions—To 1865—Sources. 7. United
States—Territorial expansion—Sources. 8. Mexican War, 1846–1848—Sources.
I. Huston, Reeve, 1960–
   E301.E135 2010
   973.4—dc22
                                                                2010016616

1 3 5 7 9 8 6 4 2
Printed in the United States of America
on acid-free paper

Contents

What Is a Document?

To the historian, a document is, quite simply, any sort of historical evidence. It is a primary source, the raw material of history. A document may be more than the expected government paperwork, such as a treaty or passport. It is also a letter, diary, will, grocery list, newspaper article, recipe, memoir, oral history, school yearbook, map, chart, architectural plan, poster, musical score, play script, novel, political cartoon, painting, photograph—even an object.

Using primary sources allows us not just to read *about* history, but to read history itself. It allows us to immerse ourselves in the look and feel of an era gone by, to understand its people and their language, whether verbal or visual. And it allows us to take an active, hands-on role in (re)constructing history.

Using primary sources requires us to use our powers of detection to ferret out the relevant facts and to draw conclusions from them; just as Agatha Christie uses the scores in a bridge game to determine the identity of a murderer, the historian uses facts from a variety of sources—some, perhaps, seemingly inconsequential—to build a historical case.

The poet W. H. Auden wrote that history was the study of questions. Primary sources force us to ask questions—and then, by answering them, to construct a narrative or an argument that makes sense to us. Moreover, as we draw on the many sources from "the dust-bin of history," we can endow that narrative with character, personality, and texture—all the elements that make history so endlessly intriguing.

Cartoon

This political cartoon addresses the issue of church and state. It illustrates the Supreme Court's role in balancing the demands of the 1st Amendment of the Constitution and the desires of the religious population.

Illustration

Illustrations from children's books, such as this alphabet from the *New England Primer*, tell us how children were educated and also what the religious and moral values of the time were.

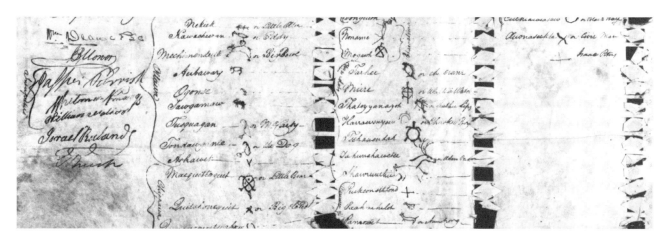

Treaty

A government document such as this 1805 treaty can reveal not only the details of government policy, but also information about the people who signed it. Here, the Indians' names were written in English transliteration by U.S. officials; the Indians added pictographs to the right of their names.

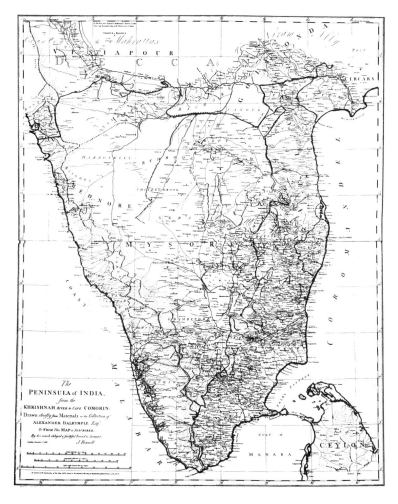

Map

A 1788 British map of India shows the region prior to British colonization, an indication of the kingdoms and provinces whose ethnic divisions would resurface later in India's history.

Object

In this fifteenth-century ewer, both the physical materials of brass and silver and the iconic depiction of heaven as a forest display the refinement of the owner, an Egyptian sultan's wife. Objects, along with manuscripts and printed materials, provide evidence about the past.

How to Read a Document

Documents can tell us a little if we passively absorb information from them, but they can tell us a *lot* if we actively interrogate them. Who wrote the document? What were the writer's class, race, gender, religion, and political commitments? How might his or her social position and commitments have shaped his or her ideas and interpretation of events? For example, slave owners tended to have a very different understanding of slavery than slaves did. What situation was the author responding to? What was he trying to accomplish? How might his agenda have shaped what he said? Authors tend to leave out information that detracts from their aim, and highlight or exaggerate those facts that serve it, much as a teenager away from home does not e-mail her parents about *everything* she's doing.

What information does the document convey? Given who the author is and what his purpose is, how reliable is that information? What does the document say or imply about the author's attitudes, beliefs, and agendas, about the situation he is confronting, and his relationship to other historical actors? The text will directly answer some of these questions, but often you need to read between the lines to get at them. If you ask a specific, well-defined question of a document—Who counts as a citizen, according to this author? What does she see as the proper relationship between men and women? What is her notion of the proper relationship between representatives and constituents?—you can often get an answer that you would never get by reading it passively.

Context

The first half of the nineteenth century witnessed a revolution in communication, as printed material became cheaper and more abundant. This revolution was part of a broader process of democratization, and mobilization for reform movements. The war with Mexico (1846–48) was a major media event—the first war in which newspapers sent paid correspondents to report from the front. Richard Caton Woodville's *War News from Mexico*, painted in 1848, depicts a group of people at a hotel learning war news from a newspaper.

Placement and relationships of figures

In Woodville's painting, the men are all responding to the same news and share the same emotional response. The young man on the right is loudly repeating the war news to the old man on his left—none in this central group is left out of the group experience. The white men are all at the center of Woodville's painting, on the hotel porch. The woman at far right and the black man and boy at bottom right are also interested in the news, but are at the margins of the central group and ignored by its members. Nor do they share in the intense emotions experienced by the white men.

Clothing and material items

The men at the center of the painting are all dressed in middle-class clothing. They are divided by style, however. While most of the white men are dressed in mainstream clothes, the figures on the left and right of the group are dressed like young men of fashion. The black people at bottom right, by contrast, wear ragged clothing.

Context

This is a song sung at patriotic occasions in 1794 by an emerging popular opposition to the administration of George Washington. At that time, the supporters of Washington (known as Federalists) argued that American citizens had a duty to obey the constitutionally elected and appointed authorities under all circumstances. Federalists saw the French Revolution as dangerously radical and a source of chaos; they sought close ties to monarchical England instead.

Source and Tone

The author wrote new words about killing kings and queens to the most famous English song in praise of the king. The author of this song was aiming at parody: he was turning a monarchical ritual upside down.

Symbolism

The guillotine symbolizes the killing of the monarch, and its use here symbolizes the most radical phase of the French Revolution.

Influence

The author of the song celebrates how the example of the guillotine spread from France around the world. The people who sang it in the streets did not share the Federalists' sympathy for monarchical England; they hoped for world revolution.

God Save the Guillotine

Tune: "God Save the King."

GOD save the Guillotine,
Till England's King and Queen,
Her power shall prove:
'Till each anointed nabob
Affords a clipping job,
Let no vile halter rob
The Guillotine.

Fame, let thy trumpet sound,
Tell all the world around
How Capet fell;
And when great GEORGE'S poll
Shall in the basket roll,
Let mercy then controul
The Guillotine.

When all the sceptre'd crew
Have paid their homage due
The Guillotine.
Let Freedom's flag advance,
'Till all the world, like France,
O'er tyrant's grave shall dance,
And peace begins.

We the Ladys
of Edenton do
hereby Solemnly
Engage not to Conform
to that Pernicious Custom
of Drinking Tea, or that we the
aforesaid Ladys will not promote y̔ wear
of any Manufacture from England
untill such time that all Acts
which tend to Enslave this our
Native Country shall be Repealed.

Introduction

The American Revolution brought numerous excluded groups into politics, a fact which horrified many observers. Literate women were among the newly politicized. *A Society of Patriotic Ladies* portrayed politically active women as ugly and unfeminine, reflecting widespread fears that women's involvement in politics would unsex them. The neglected child under attack by the dog, which is urinating on the floor, and the man attempting to seduce the lady, who seems pleased by his attentions, represented the fear of many men that women's political activism would create domestic chaos.

In June 1789, James Madison, the main architect of the new Constitution of the United States, wrote to his friend Thomas Jefferson. Madison was nervous. The United States was something new: a nation created by the active decision of its leaders and people, with a government formed through conscious deliberation and political struggle. Nobody had tried it before. "We are in a wilderness without a single footstep to guide us," he wrote.

Madison's nervousness was understandable. Creating a new nation is an uncertain, dangerous enterprise. Look at the new nations of the twentieth century—Ghana, Zimbabwe, South Africa, Vietnam, Cambodia, China, Nicaragua, Cuba. At the moment when each of these nations freed itself from colonial rule or from less formal foreign domination, several fundamental decisions had to be made quickly: foreign alliances, economic policies, the structure of the government, the membership of the leadership class, the role of different social groups in politics, the degree to which dissent would be tolerated. And they frequently had to be made under the pressure of rebellions, factional rivalries, and external threats. Things often went wrong. Political instability or civil war; economic dependency or, worse, economic collapse; military defeat or economic suffocation at the hands of a powerful enemy—all of these are common in the history of new nations.

The United States was the first modern postcolonial nation, and in many ways it became a model for later efforts at creating a coherent political community out of the wreckage of monarchy or colonialism. It was the first modern republic—that is, the first political community to be governed by representatives of "the people." It was also the first political movement to create a modern nation—a widely shared sense of peoplehood and a state that claimed to represent that people. Nobody knew how it would turn out.

By the time the federal Constitution was ratified, some basic outlines of the new country's character were clear. The United States would be a republic. Governmental power would be shared between states and the federal government, and among a legislative, executive, and judicial branch at each level. James Madison had promised that basic civil liberties such as freedom of speech, the right to assemble and petition one's representatives, and the right to a trial by jury would be guaranteed, and Congress fulfilled that promise in 1791. Beyond these certainties, everything was up for grabs. Would the United States have a mixed economy, or one largely limited to agriculture and overseas trade? How much power would financiers have over the economy and over the government? What would be the precise balance between the power of the state and federal governments? What role would ordinary citizens play in politics? To what extent would dissent be tolerated? Would the relationships between men and women, European Americans and African Americans, whites and Indians, rich and poor be maintained or changed? What would happen to slavery?

Poor and middling people were deeply politicized during the Revolution, including by military service. A watercolor by a French officer in the Continental Army depicts the variety of people who enlisted, including an African American infantryman and a Virginia frontiersman in buckskin.

This book provides a glimpse into the ways in which the first three generations of Americans grappled with these questions and, in the process, defined the character of the United States. It presents this story through primary sources—letters, diaries, newspaper accounts, contemporary cartoons and paintings. It begins its story in 1789, when the federal Constitution was ratified and the first federal elections were held, and closes in 1848, with the close of the Mexican-American War and the annexation of half of that country's territory. In the sixty years between these two events, many of the social, political, legal, and economic institutions, practices, ideas, and relationships were established that contemporaries believed made the United States such a remarkable society and political community.

A republican culture of equality emerged during the Revolution and exerted a powerful influence on popular thought, social relations, and politics throughout the period. American egalitarianism was a centerpiece of Americans' self-image by the early nineteenth century and dominated foreign ideas about Americans. It also provided a set of ideals that radicals used to challenge relations of gender, racial, and class domination throughout the period. The early republic witnessed the halting and bitterly contested emergence of two-party democracy—a development that transformed American politics and provided a model (both positive and negative) for the rest of the world.

During this period, the United States dramatically expanded its territory. In 1789, the United States consisted of thirteen states hugging the Atlantic seaboard; in 1848 it was a continental power stretching from Maine to California, with many Americans agitating for the annexation of part or all of the Caribbean and South America. This expansion made possible the long-term prosperity of both independent family farmers and slave owners; it rested on the dispossession of the Indians and Mexicans.

Territorial expansion led to the dramatic expansion of slavery. At the end of the Revolution, plantation slavery was limited to the Atlantic seaboard and a few river valleys in the East. In many areas it was faltering economically and under political attack; many thought its days were numbered. By 1848, the system had spread to Louisiana and Texas. It was under even fiercer attack, but it was flourishing economically. The northern states also experienced dramatic economic growth during the early republic but did so while gradually abolishing slavery. Even more than in the South, economic growth brought significant change: new farming techniques, a new ethos of economic innovation and market engagement, the rapid expansion of wage labor, and new ideals and practices of family life.

The different trajectories of economic development in the North and South led to the deepening of

In this engraving, a family on the New York frontier taps maple trees for their sap and boils it down to make maple sugar, which can be sold. Most migrants arrived in their new homes with little in the way of equipment, furniture, or cash. What they did have was labor, and their success depended on using that labor to turn the natural resources around them into property that they could keep or sell. *Women Visiting a Maple Sugar Camp in the Woods* also shows that settlers mixed work with visiting and play—a constant feature of preindustrial life.

economic, social, and cultural differences between them, and to the politicization of those differences in a series of increasingly bitter sectional disputes. Alongside the emergence of sectional conflict and the expansion of slavery, a powerful ideology of white supremacy emerged and white Americans' racial practices hardened. Even as the United States spread across the continent, underwent industrialization, and forged a democratic political order, Americans experienced a widespread and dramatic surge of Protestant evangelism during the early nineteenth century. Evangelical revival transformed American culture, influenced American politics, and unleashed a wave of reform movements. In the process, it informed many of the other developments of the era, especially sectional conflict and the creation of new gender and class relations in the North.

This painting from the 1844 presidential campaign portrays one of the hallmarks of electoral democracy that emerged during the early republic: grassroots organizing. Democratic Party activists visit a voter in his home.

The political and social order that coalesced during the early republic—democratic, largely white supremacist, expansionist, Christian, divided between wage labor, family labor, and slavery—did not develop in quiet consultation and consensus. All of the major changes of the era emerged out of fierce conflict. Democratic politics was born of a long struggle among gentlemen, self-made political activists, and humble white men. The new industrial wage-labor system in the Northeast was shaped by fierce struggle between workers and employers. The expansion of slavery marked the defeat of enslaved people, free African Americans, and radical whites who sought to destroy the institution. New familial ideals and practices in the North were resisted by many women and men. The territorial expansion of the United States came only by crushing the Indians who sought to hold on to their own territory.

These conflicts shaped the institutions, relationships, ideas, and practices that, in the eyes of most Americans and foreign observers, made the young republic such a distinct and exciting place. Just as important, they created the most important tradition in

American public life, one that has spread to much of the world: a democratic tradition of public struggle over the future of the nation. The defining feature of American public life has long been free-ranging conflict over what the United States is and should be. Originating in the revolutionary struggle, that tradition became an accepted part of national life through the social and political conflicts of the early republic.

Note on Sources and Interpretation

The work of historians consists less of discovering facts than of making meaning out of those facts. Although there are plenty of wrong interpretations, there is rarely only one correct one for any problem or issue: the historical record is too diverse and too rich with shades of meaning to be amenable to only one interpretation. Historians who are equally attentive to evidence and careful in their interpretations frequently assign dramatically different meanings to the same events. The best historians (and the best students of history) are those who are open to multiple interpretations and try to synthesize as many diverse readings of the evidence into their own interpretations. The world has always been a complicated place; why should our interpretations be simple?

The history of the early American republic has often been a subject of controversy. Until the late 1960s, many historians placed national political leaders or intellectuals at the center of their interpretations, on the assumption that powerful white men like Washington and Jefferson, Jackson and Clay shaped their era profoundly and embodied its ethos. Others studied intellectuals, almost always from the upper classes, in the belief that they represented the thinking of most Americans, or at least the best and most important thinking. Since the 1960s, many historians have studied history "from the bottom up," seeking to understand the early republic through the experiences, ideas, and efforts of particular social groups: enslaved people, working-class women, the urban poor, northern farmers, the urban middle class, southern planters. Out of the hundreds of studies that have been written about different groups, a different understanding of politics and society has emerged. Social historians tend to see all groups of society having one degree or another of influence over events. They believe that great men do not define their eras on their own but often respond to the initiatives and demands of those they wish to rule, and often find that their options are limited by those efforts and demands. Social historians also tend to see history as being driven by interactions, and often conflict, between different social or cultural groups. For example, historians of slavery tend to agree that masters did not alone determine the character of the slave regime; it was the constant negotiation and conflict between slaves and masters, as each side tried to gain the most advantage, which determined its character.

The "new social history," as this kind of history is called, has many challengers. Recently, the study of the founding fathers has made a comeback. Many biographers of the founders dismiss studies of poor people as trivial and insist that the era is best understood by studying the character and actions of great leaders. Many historians of culture, religion, and politics eschew social historians' focus on social groups. Their studies often show that some of the most important developments of the era—religious revivalism, political partisanship, nationalist rituals, consumerism—inculcated identities and beliefs that united people from different classes, genders, even sometimes races while dividing each social group into different camps.

Other disagreements abound. Some historians argue that the period between 1815 and 1848 was marked by a revolutionary transformation of the economy, one that for the first time brought a majority of Americans into the world of market exchange, wage labor, and modern credit. The "Market Revolution," they insist, transformed Americans' beliefs, identities, and daily lives, created new social divisions, and drove dramatic changes in religion and politics. These historians tend to see widening market exchange and wage labor as a largely negative development, one that brought wrenching social dislocation and deepened inequalities in its wake. Others see the idea of a market "revolution" as overblown. Sure, market exchange grew, they argue, but Americans had been exchanging their goods in markets for a long time, and wage labor remained a minority experience. The economic change that occurred was simply an acceleration of already existing trends toward greater market production and consumerism. These historians argue that the economic changes of the era were overwhelmingly positive, as rising standards of consumption and a revolution in transportation and communications brought in their wake widespread prosperity, a wide dissemination of ideas, and a democratic flowering of political innovation and social reform. They deny that class or other economic conflicts were important in the early republic: the real conflicts of the era, they argue, were religious, ethnic, and sectional in nature.

Finally, some historians depict Andrew Jackson and his Democratic Party as advocates of democracy and as ushering in unprecedented political power for ordinary white men. Others see Jackson and the Democrats in a darker light, emphasizing Jackson's policy of Indian removal and arguing that the Democrats were staunch defenders of slavery.

The greatest advantage of primary sources like those in this book is that they allow readers to assess historians' arguments for themselves. No doubt the selection of the documents has been influenced by my interpretations of events—and here I should declare that I have been deeply influenced by the new social history. It would be entirely appropriate to emphasize other important developments

BORN TO COMMAND.

OF VETO MEMORY.

HAD I BEEN CONSULTED.

KING ANDREW THE FIRST.

Dressed in royal robes, Andrew Jackson holds in one hand a scepter and in the other a scroll titled "Veto"—a presidential power he used frequently. At his feet lie the federal Constitution in tatters and a torn document titled "Internal Improvements" and "U.S. Bank," legislation Jackson had vetoed. Whigs were united in their insistence on the supremacy of the legislative branch and in their opposition to Jackson's expansion of presidential power, satirized in this political cartoon.

during the early republic—technological development, foreign policy, the emergence of a distinct national literature and philosophy. My own choice of themes rests on a belief that social relations and political conflict had a greater impact on how people lived and saw their world than technology, foreign policy, or high intellectual developments. Still, I have sought to offer rich documents that are open to multiple interpretations, and a wide enough variety of documents that students can make their own interpretations of the era.

The early republic gave rise to fierce political, religious, and social conflict. This fact was a source of distress to many contemporaries, but it is a boon to historians. Every conflict left behind a treasure trove of newspapers and pamphlets, thanks to an ongoing revolution in publishing that made printed materials increasingly cheap and abundant. Of course, such sources need to be interpreted with care, because they are polemical: they sought to win converts to a cause, not to provide unbiased information.

Sources on the social experience, ideas, and beliefs of elites are abundant for the North and South, as wealthy and powerful men and women tended to be literate and to communicate frequently through letters, as well as often keeping diaries. Letters and diaries are equally abundant for middling people in the North, where literacy rates were high. Literacy rates were lower in the South, and the middle class was smaller, so there are fewer surviving letters and diaries for middling people from that region. In addition, the United States was a major attraction for European travelers, most of them from the upper classes, who were curious to see the American experiment in republican government and republican equality. These travelers tended to spend their time with wealthy Americans, and sometimes with middling ones. They often published books about their travels, a major source of information and insight into the lives, beliefs, and practices of wealthy and middling Americans.

Documents that reveal the lives and ideas of the poor and powerless are less plentiful and trickier to interpret. Many workers and poor farmers and most free African Americans and enslaved people were illiterate. Those sources that were written by them were often polemical. Perhaps the richest source written by former slaves are slave narratives—autobiographies published by abolitionists in order to promote the abolitionist cause. Most sources documenting the lives of poor and powerless people were written not by them, but about them by their superiors. The authors filtered the actions and statements of their subordinates through their own worldview and preoccupations. English travelers emphasized what was color-ful and outrageous in the behavior of the American lower class; masters interpreted everything that slaves said and did through their preoccupation with gaining obedience and their belief in slaves' inferiority. When reading these sources, one must set aside the authors' own interpretation of their inferiors' behavior. These interpretations provide great evidence about the authors' attitudes but only distort our interpretation of the behavior of the powerless. Readers need to distill just the facts of poor people's behavior and words and interpret those words and that behavior for themselves. In addition, readers should remain sensitive to the possibility that an author's preoccupations and beliefs led him or her to misrepre-sent the facts themselves, embellishing, omitting, or outright lying about what his or her subordinates did.

E. Tisdale del.

et Sculpt.

The TORY'S Day of JUDGMENT.

CHAPTER 1

The People Rule—But Who Are the People?

A crowd of revolutionaries, in the dress of poor and middling people, lift a Loyalist up a liberty pole by his breeches while a member of the crowd plucks a goose to tar and feather him. The American Revolution brought poor and middling white men into political life in unprecedented ways, convincing them that they were crucial actors in the making of a new nation.

William Cooper was not a humble man. Although born poor, he had married a wealthy woman and, with help from his new father-in-law, become a prosperous storekeeper outside Philadelphia. He began reading widely, introducing himself to the world of history, politics, and literature. In 1786, he bought twenty-seven thousand acres of wilderness land in western New York and began selling it to settlers. With the money from his lands, he built an enormous and elegant mansion, equipped it with the best furnishings from Philadelphia and Europe, and began wearing fine clothes with lace ruffles and brass buttons. At the same time, he cultivated the friendship and support of some of the most powerful men in New York. Like many other men, Cooper was trying to remake himself into a gentleman —a man who was recognized as superior to poor and middling people because of his wealth, learning, refinement, and alliances with powerful men and women. Like other gentlemen, he expected poorer men and women to treat him as a superior. When he met with them, he counted on them to take off their hats and speak in humble tones. He assumed that they would seek out his help and advice. And he expected them to humbly follow his advice and, above all, vote the way he directed them.

James Moore had other ideas. He was one of the settlers on Cooper's lands. Like other settlers, he probably bought his land on credit and owed Cooper a great deal of money. Cooper counted on Moore's financial dependence as an incentive to vote the way he directed. But Moore refused to be controlled. During the governor's election of 1792, Cooper treated his settlers to liquor, bantered playfully with them, and pressed ballots, marked with the name of his ally John Jay, into their hands. When Cooper put a ballot in Moore's hands, Moore opened the ballot, looked at it, and said, "Judge Cooper, I can not vote so, for if I do vote for Governor, I would wish to vote clearly from my own inclination, as I [do] not mean to be dictated to by any person." Cooper flew into a temper, retorted, "You are a fool, young man, for you cannot know how to vote as well as I can direct you," and stomped off.

Confrontations like the one between Moore and Cooper were common occurrences in the decades after the Revolution. During the colonial era, most people had acknowledged that gentlemen were a "better sort" of human being and deserved the obedience of their inferiors. They also accepted that poor people, women, and African Americans would know some degree of control by others. Enslaved people, of course, experienced the most dependence and control, but apprentices, indentured servants, even wage earners were not fully autonomous. The gentlemen who led the revolutionary movement expected that the old social order would be preserved in an independent America—that enslaved people, women, and the "meaner sort" would continue to know their place. But revolutions have a way of shaking up the rules of a society. People who had long been dependent and obedient—poor white men, African American slaves, women of all colors—participated in the conflict. Large numbers of enslaved people fought for the British because they had been promised their freedom for doing so. For them, the Revolution strengthened their commitment to winning their emancipation. Others joined in on the side of independence. They participated in political debates and began to think of themselves as important political actors. They learned to apply the ideology of the Revolution to their own situation, coming to believe that they too were "endowed by their creator with certain inalienable rights" and that "among these rights are life, liberty, and the pursuit of happiness." In the years after the Revolution, white women, African Americans, and ordinary white men fought to destroy or limit their subordination to husbands, masters, and gentlemen. They fought to extend to themselves the "liberty" that the Revolution had promised. In the process, the United States grew into a society divided into two sections—a "free" North and a slave South.

The Founders' Social Vision

We are usually taught that the founding fathers fought the Revolution to establish an egalitarian political order, and this is true. Even so conservative a revolutionary as Alexander Hamilton cherished "the equality of political rights exclusive of all *hereditary* distinction." But elite revolutionaries sought to establish a limited kind of equality: political equality between propertied white men, equal economic opportunity, and freedom from hereditary privileges. Beyond that, most defended inequality. In a 1776 letter to James Sullivan, a revolutionary activist from Maine, John Adams explained his opposition to a universal application of revolutionary political theory. Adams's sentiments continued to dominate gentry thought in the decades after the Revolution.

It is certain, in theory, that the only moral foundation of government is, the consent of the people. But to what an extent shall we carry this principle? Shall we say that every individual in the community, old and young, male and female, as well as rich and poor, must consent, expressly, to every act of legislation? No, you will say, it is impossible. How, then, does the right arise in the majority to govern the minority, against their will? Whence arises the right of the men to govern the women, without their consent? Whence the right of the old to bind the young, without theirs? ... Why exclude women?

You will say, because their delicacy renders them unfit for practice and experience in the great business of life, and the hardy enterprises of war, as well as the arduous cares of state. Besides, their attention is so much engaged with the necessary nurture of their children, that nature has made them fittest for domestic cares. And children have not judgement or will of their own. True. But will not these reasons apply to others? Is it not equally true, that men in general, in every society, who are wholly destitute of property, are also too little acquainted with public affairs to form a right judgment, and too dependent upon other men to have a will of their own? If this is a fact, if you give to every man who has no property a vote, will you not make a fine encouraging provision for corruption, by your fundamental law? Such is the frailty of the human heart, that very few men who have no property have any judgment of their own. They talk and vote as they are directed to by some man of property, who has attached their minds to his interest. ...

Depend on it, Sir, it is dangerous to open so fruitful a source of controversy and altercation as would be opened by attempting to alter the qualifications of voters; there will be no end of it. New claims

The fine clothing of Robert R. Livingston, a special American envoy to Paris, advertises his wealth and taste, while his posture displays his magisterial bearing. On the table is evidence of his public service: a copy of his "Plan for establishing an Academy of Fine Arts in New York" and a letter addressed to "Robt. R. Livingston, Minister Plenipotentury from the United States of America, Paris." Most wealthy gentlemen had such portraits painted, trumpeting their claims to social superiority.

will arise; women will demand a vote; lads from twelve to twenty-one will think their rights not enough attended to; and every man who has not a farthing will demand an equal voice with any other, in all acts of state. It tends to confound and destroy all distinctions, and prostrate all ranks to one common level.

Few founding fathers enjoy a greater reputation for egalitarianism than Thomas Jefferson. And with good reason: his Republican party sought a greater political equality for propertied white men than Federalists like John Adams were willing to accept. In some respects, his vision of equality extended to African Americans as well. Like most revolutionary leaders, he opposed slavery as a violation of natural rights. In his *Notes on the State of Virginia*, written in 1781 and 1782, Jefferson offered a devastating natural-rights criticism of American slavery.

A 1798 watercolor, *Overseer Doing his Duty*, portrays an overseer leisurely smoking a pipe while two women hoe their owner's tobacco field. The scene was familiar to Americans from Pennsylvania southward: African Americans working under the command of a white person.

Amor patriae
Amor patriae is Latin for "love of country."

There must doubtless be an unhappy influence on the manners of our people produced by the existence of slavery among us. The whole commerce between master and slave is a perpetual exercise of the most boisterous passions, the most unremitting despotism on the one part, and degrading submissions on the other. Our children see this, and learn to imitate it. . . . The parent storms, the child looks on, catches the lineaments of wrath, puts on the same airs in the circle of smaller slaves, gives loose to his worst of passions, and thus nursed, educated, and daily exercised in tyranny, cannot but be stamped by it with odious peculiarities. . . . And with what execration should the statesman be loaded, permitting one half the citizens thus to trample on the rights of the other, transforms those into despots, and these into enemies, destroys the morals of the one part, and the *amor patriae* of the other. . . . And can the liberties of a nation be thought secure when we have removed their firm basis, a conviction in the minds of the people that these liberties are the gift of God? Indeed I tremble for my country when I reflect that God is just: that his justice cannot sleep for ever: that considering numbers, nature and natural means only, a revolution of the wheel of fortune, an exchange of situation, is among possible events: that it may become probable by supernatural interference! The Almighty has no attribute which can take side with us in such a contest. . . . I think a change already perceptible, since the origin of the present revolution. The spirit of the master is abating, that of the slave rising from the dust, his condition mollifying, the way I hope preparing, under the auspices of heaven, for a total emancipation, and that this is disposed, in the order of events, to be with the consent of the masters, rather than by their extirpation.

Jefferson's opposition to slavery did not spring from a belief in the equality of Americans of European and African ancestry. In a different chapter of *Notes on the State of Virginia*, he offered his views on African Americans' characteristics, capacities, and destiny. After describing a proposed law that would emancipate Virginia's slaves but forcibly send them to another land, Jefferson wrote:

It will probably be asked, Why not retain and incorporate the blacks into the state . . . ? Deep rooted prejudices entertained by the whites; ten thousand recollections, by the blacks, of the injuries they have sustained; new provocations; the real distinctions which nature has made; and many other circumstances, will divide us into parties, and produce convulsions which will probably never end but in the extermination of one or the other race.—To these objections . . . may be added others, which are physical and moral.

 The first difference which strikes us is that of color. . . . And is the difference . . . the foundation of a greater or less share of beauty in the two races? Are not the fine mixtures of red and white, the expressions of every passion by greater or less suffusions of color in the one, preferable to that eternal monotony, which reigns in the countenances . . . of the other race? Add to these, flowing hair, a more elegant symmetry of form, their own judgement in favour of the whites, declared by their preference of them, as uniformly as is the preference of the Oranootan [orangutan] for the black women over those of his own species. . . . Their existence appears to participate more of sensation than reflection. . . . In memory they are equal to the whites; in reason much inferior, as I think one could scarcely be found capable of tracing and comprehending the investigations of Euclid; . . . in imagination they are dull, tasteless, and anomalous. . . . Never yet could I find that a black had uttered a thought above the level of plain narration; never see even an elementary trait of painting or sculpture. . . . Their inferiority is not the effect merely of their condition of life. We know that among the Romans, about the Augustan age especially, the condition of their slaves was much more deplorable than that of the blacks on

"Rules of Civility and Decent Behavior"

26th: In Pulling off your Hat to Persons of Distinction, as Noblemen, Justices, Churchmen, &c make a Reverence, bowing more or less according to the Custom of the Better Bred, and Quality of the Person. . . .

29th: When you meet with one of Greater Quality than yourself, Stop, and retire especially if it be at a Door or any Straight place to give way for him to Pass. . . .

37th: In Speaking to men of Quality do not lean nor Look them full in the Face, nor approach too near them at least Keep a full Pace from them. . . .

40th: Strive not with your Superiors in argument, but always submit your Judgment to others with Modesty.

—From an English etiquette manual, copied by George Washington, age 15, into his diary the continent of America. . . . Yet notwithstanding these and other discouraging circumstances among the Romans, their slaves were often the rarest artists. They excelled too in science. . . . Epictetus, Terence, and Phaedrus, were slaves. But they were of the race of whites. It is not their condition, then, but nature, which has produced the distinction. . . . Among the Romans emancipation required but one effort. The slave, when made free, might mix with, without staining the blood of his master. But with us a second is necessary, unknown to history. When freed, he is to be removed beyond the reach of admixture.

Poor White Men's Bid for Equality

Whether or not they owned property, most poor and middling white men rejected Washington's and other gentlemen's belief that they were inferior to men of great wealth and distinguished families. During the political and military mobilizations of the Revolution, they had embraced the doctrine that all legitimate political power derives from the people. Rejecting gentlemen's belief that physical labor was degrading, they came to regard useful labor as a badge of honor, and they came to see their labor and their political participation as the main support of the new republican government. On July 4, 1788, when Philadelphians celebrated the ratification of the federal Constitution, the artisans of the city—small property owners and propertyless workers who manufactured goods with their hands—paraded behind their wealthier fellow citizens. Their banners and floats asserted the importance and dignity of their role in the new republic. Francis Hopkinson, the genteel chairman of the Committee of Arrangements for the celebration, published a detailed description of the parade in the *Pennsylvania Packet and Daily Advertiser*, a city newspaper.

The verse on the silk banner of the Society of Pewterers, flown in New York's federal procession in 1788, ties the crafts to the well-being of the republic: "The Federal Plan Most Solid & Secure / Americans Their Freedom Will Ensure / All Arts Shall Flourish in Columbia's Land / And All Her Sons, Join as One Social Band." Manual labor, once seen as degrading, became a source of pride after the Revolution.

On Friday, the 4th day of July, 1788, the citizens of Philadelphia celebrated the declaration of independence made by the thirteen united states of America . . . and the establishment of the constitution or frame of government by the late general convention, and now solemnly adopted and ratified by ten of those states. . . .

About half after nine o'clock, the grand procession began to move; of which the following is as correct a detail as could be procured. . . .

XLI. Bricklayers. . . . A flag with the following device: the bricklayers' arms; the federal city rising out of a forest, workmen building it, and the sun illuminating it. Motto, *"both buildings and rulers are the work of our hands."* . . . Ten master bricklayers, with their aprons on, and their trowels and plumb-rules in their hands—followed by fifty-five masters and journeymen, in their aprons, and carrying trowels in their hands.

XLVIII. Black-smiths, white-smiths, and nailers. A machine drawn by nine horses, representing the federal blacksmiths', white-smiths', and nailers' manufactory, being a frame of ten by fifteen feet, and nine feet high, with a real chimney. . . . In front of the building three master blacksmiths . . . , supporting the standard, elegantly ornamented with the smiths' arms.—Motto: *"by hammer in hand, all arts do stand."* The manufactory was in full employ during the procession.—Mr. John Mingler, and his assistant, Christian Keyser, blacksmiths, completed a set of plough-irons out of old swords, worked a sword into a sickle, turned several horse-shoes, and performed several jobs on demand. Mr. John Goodman, Jun., whitesmith, finished a complete pair of plyers, a knife, and some machinery, with other work on demand. Messrs. Andrew Fessinger and Benjamin Brummel forged, finished and sold a considerable number of spikes, nails, and broad tacks. The whole . . . was followed by two hundred brother black-smiths, white-smiths and nailers. . . .

LI. Hatters, Led by Mr. Andrew Tybout. The standard . . . on a white field a hat in hand . . . the crest, a beaver—Motto . . . —*"with the industry of the beaver, we support our rights;"* followed by one hundred and twenty hatters. . . .

Urban artisans were not the only group of poor and middling Americans to assert their authority. Americans were notorious among upper-class Europeans for their "impertinence"—that is, for their habit of stepping out of the inferior role that their superiors wished them to adopt. Charles William Janson, a wealthy Englishman who visited the United States around 1806, discovered with outrage that Americans of low status refused to give to their social superiors the deference and the social distance that George Washington's "Rules of Civility" advised them to. Janson reported his experience in a book about his travels.

I shall now shew the reader . . . what must sometimes be endured from the manners and customs of the people. . . .

The federal city
The federal city referred to Philadelphia, which was capital of the United States at the time.

Arrived at your inn, let me suppose, like myself, you had fallen in with a landlord, who at the moment would condescend to *take the trouble* to procure you refreshment after the family hour and that no *pig*, or other trifling circumstance called off his attention, he will sit by your side, and enter in the most familiar manner into conversation; which is prefaced, of course, with a demand of your business, and so forth. He will then start a political question (for here every individual is a politician), force your answer, contradict, deny, and, finally, be ripe for a quarrel, should you not acquiesce in all his opinions. When the homely meal is served up, he will often place himself opposite you at the table, . . . drinking out of your glass, and of the liquor you are to pay for, belching in your face, and committing other excesses still more indelicate and disgusting. . . . If you arrive at the dinner-hour, you are seated with "mine hostess" and her dirty children, with whom you have often to scramble for a plate, and even the servants of the inn; for liberty and equality level all ranks. . . .

The arrogance of domestics in this land of republican liberty and equality, is particularly calculated to excite the astonishment of strangers. To call persons of this description *servants*, or to speak of their *master* or *mistress*, is a grievous affront. Having called one day at the house of a gentleman of my acquaintance, on knocking at the door, it was opened by a servant-maid, whom I had never before seen, as she had not been long in his family. The following is the dialogue, word for word, which took place on this occasion:—"Is your master at home?"—"I have no master." "Don't you live here?"—"I stay here."—"And who are you then?"—"Why, I am Mr. _____'s *help* I'd have you to know, *man*, that I am no *sarvant*; none but *negers* are *sarvants*."

Middle- and Upper-Class Women's Bid for Intellectual Equality

At the same time that ordinary white men and women asserted their equality with their social superiors, white women of the educated classes began to call for a greater equality between men and women. American society was patriarchal. Law and public opinion viewed women not as autonomous individuals or as men's equals but as dependent members of their husband's or father's household. Sir William Blackstone's *Commentaries on the Laws of England*, which American lawyers and judges

accepted as a foundational text in American law, explained the subordinate legal status of married women.

By marriage, the husband and wife are one person in law: that is, the very being or legal existence of the woman is suspended during the marriage, or at least is incorporated and consolidated into that of her husband: under whose wing, protection, and *cover*, she performs every thing; and is therefore called in our law-french a *femme covert* . . . is said to be *covert-baron*, or under the protection and influence of her husband, her *baron*, or lord; and her condition during her marriage is called her *coverture*. . . . A man cannot grant any thing to his wife, or enter into covenant with her: for the grant would be to suppose her separate existence. . . . If the wife be indebted before marriage, the husband is bound afterwards to pay the debt; for he has adopted her and her circumstances together. If the wife be injured in her person or her property, she can bring no action for redress without her husband's concurrence, and in his name, as well as her own; nor can she be sued, without making the husband a defendant. . . .

[A]ll deeds executed, and acts done, by her, during her coverture, are void, except it be a fine, or the like matter of record. . . .

The husband also . . . might give his wife moderate correction. For, as he is able to answer for her misbehaviour, the law thought it reasonable to intrust him with this power of restraining her, by domestic chastisement, in the same moderation that a man is allowed to correct his apprentices or children. . . . The courts of law will still permit a husband to restrain a wife of her liberty, in case of any gross misbehaviour.

[E]ven the disabilities, which the wife lies under, are for the most part intended for her protection and benefit. So great a favourite is the female sex of the laws of England.

White women of the middle and upper class did not challenge their legal disabilities or their special duties as mothers and caretakers of the household. Instead, they sought recognition of women's intellectual equality with men and demanded an end to men's personal "tyranny" over women. In 1791, an anonymous contributor to *The Universal Asylum and Columbian Magazine* used the language of the Revolution to assert women's physical and intellectual equality with men and to call for radical reform in the relations between men and women.

On the Supposed Superiority of the Masculine Understanding

The mind of man no sooner expands itself into action, than it is impressed with the passions of vanity, and a love of power. An indulgence of these passions, . . . aided by a tame submission to whatever receives the authority of hereditary usage, have combined to sanction absurdities, and establish laws which nature never designed.— However inconsistent the hypothesis, if it flatters ambition, or promises dominion, it will have its votaries, and be handed down by the ignorant and designing, until it becomes sacred by prescription.

From these . . . circumstances, we may trace the source of that assumption of superiority, by which the men claim an implicit obedience from our sex: a claim which they support on the vain presumption of their being assigned the most important duties of life, and being intrusted by nature with the guardianship and protection of women. . . .

Some middle- and upper-class women used the egalitarian ideals of the Revolution to challenge inequalities in marriage. An anonymous writer to the Lady's Magazine, and Repository of Entertaining Knowledge *challenged the widespread belief that wives had a duty to obey their husbands.*

I object to the word *obey* in the marriage service . . . because it is a general word, without limitation or definition. . . . Where I have sworn, or even promised to obey any man, . . . I have bound myself to be his *slave*. . . .

The obedience between man and wife, I conceive, is, or ought to be mutual. And it ought to be mutual for the sake of their happiness; for . . . whatever miseries arise in the marriage state, arise from the assumption on one side or other of absolute power. Marriage ought never to be considered as a contract between a superior and inferior, but a reciprocal union of interest, an implied partnership of interests, where all differences are accommodated by conference. . . . Separate privileges there may be on both sides; but like the houses of lords and commons, tenacious as they are of their privileges, they should, in all disputed points, meet each other half way.

The daily follies committed by men, leave it unnecessary to prove the imbecility of their *minds*; and as to what strength of *body* they possess superior to women, this may be chiefly attributed to the exercise permitted and encouraged in their youth; but forbidden to us, even to a ridiculous degree.

Nothing gives muscular strength but exercise. In the nursery, strength is equal in the male and female. Education soon draws on those distinctions with which nature is charged. A boy no sooner goes to school than his fellows dare him to fight: he has no alternative, he must fight or be wretched. He soon learns to whip a top, run after a hoop, and jump over a rope. These exercises promote health and spirits; strengthen his whole frame, and often rectify those enormous errors committed in the nursery (*that baneful prison with a fashionable name!*) the consequences of which are rather confirmed than relaxed by the future education of girls; committed to illiterate teachers, and as illiterate school-mistresses, ignorant of manners, books, and men.—With these tyrants, they are cooped up in a room, confined to needle-work, deprived of exercise, reproved without being faulty, and schooled in frivolity, until they are reduced to mere automatons in the most active and best part of their lives. . . . These are some of the many disadvantages we are doomed to suffer, while the boys are encouraged in activity, instructed in sciences and languages, and rendered familiar with the best authors, by which they may refine their taste, improve their judgement, and form a system of morals that may ensure their happiness ever after. . . .

Thus, it is the united folly of parents which has brought on so wide a distinction of the sexes; not the impartial wisdom of the creator, who must equally delight in seeing all his creatures wise and happy. . . .

Men contribute to their own wretchedness when they neglect the culture of our minds. They are our mental qualities that give their truest enjoyment; and men are seldom brutish to such a degree, as long to enjoy the company of women who can only gratify the lowest appetite. . . .

FRONTISPIECE.

Publish'd at Philad.ª *Dec.ʳ 1ˢᵗ 1792.*

The caption for this frontispiece to *Lady's Magazine* describes its figures: "The Genius of the Ladies Magazine [*center*], accompanied by the Genius of Emancipation [*right*], who carries in her hand a laurel crown, approaches Liberty [*left*], and kneeling, presents her with a copy of the Rights of Woman." The "Rights of Woman" may have referred to Mary Wollstonecraft's 1792 *Vindication of the Rights of Woman*, a radical defense of woman's equality, parts of which *Lady's Magazine* published.

Voltaire

Voltaire was the pen name of François-Marie Arouet, one of the leading writers and philosophers of the eighteenth century.

Voltaire said, the minds of women were capable of whatever was performed by those of the men; and refused the invitation of the King of Prussia for the company of Madame de Chatelot, telling the king, that . . . he loved a lady better than a king. This lady knew by heart most of the beautiful passages in Horace, Virgil, and Lucretius, and all the philosophical works of Cicero; could write Latin elegantly, and speak all the languages of Europe: was perfectly conversant with the works of Locke, Newton, and Pope and was particularly fond of mathematics and metaphysics. . . . Does this not draw conviction, that we possess faculties which are by no means inferior to the greatest ornaments of the other sex; and that the highest felicity man can possess must arise from the society of well educated women.

But what must be the sentiments of such women, when they hear from the lips of an idiot husband, that men are created their lords and masters? When they find themselves united to those who know not their worth? And discover, that where they looked up for protection, they are quickly taught submission? When they find the fawning slave of yesterday the tyrant of to-day; and having resigned *themselves*, they are given to understand that they have neither liberty nor property—like the lion in the fable, all is his by right of lion—can the soul subside its feelings, and not revolt against the hidden baseness? Disappointment chills the heart, stagnates affection, and draws on that morbid indifference which we often observe in the married state. . . .

Thus, then, the superiority of man consists only in that strength which he pretends is needful for our protection; and his boasted protection resembles that of a ruffian, who should guard you from a pick-pocket, only that himself might do you a more selfish and more irreparable injury. Let them withdraw their injuries, and we shall easily spare their protection; but did our education disencumber them from our dependence, they could not as readily dispense with the assistance of our solicitudes.

The Attack on Slavery

The fiercest social conflict in the wake of the Revolution was over the fate of slavery. Inspired by revolutionary ideology and a growing conviction among Quakers and evangelical Christians that slavery was a sin, large numbers of African Americans and whites worked to destroy slavery. White opposition to slavery was most intense in the northern states, which had over fifty-five thousand slaves at the time of the Revolution. Between 1780 and 1800, every northern state except Delaware abolished slavery within its borders. Most did so gradually, leaving thousands of people enslaved well into the nineteenth century. Despite its gradual nature, emancipation in the northern states helped set the North on a divergent course from the South, where slavery was expanding. Pennsylvania's emancipation law, passed in 1780, shows the new thinking on slavery and race that was being adopted by many revolutionaries.

WHEN we contemplate our abhorrence of that condition, to which the arms and tyranny of Great Britain were exerted to reduce us, when we look back on the variety of dangers to which we have been exposed, and how miraculously our wants in many instances have been supplied, and our deliverances wrought, . . . we are unavoidably led to a serious and grateful sense of the manifold blessings, which we have undeservedly received from the hand of that Being from whom every good and perfect gift cometh. Impressed with these ideas, we conceive that it is our duty, and we rejoice that it is in our power, to extend a portion of that freedom to others, which hath been extended to us. . . . It is not for us to inquire why, in the creation of mankind, the inhabitants of the several parts of the earth were distinguished by a difference in feature or complexion. It is sufficient to know, that all are the work of an Almighty Hand. We find, in the distribution of the human species, that the most fertile as well as the most barren parts of the earth are inhabited by men of complexions different from ours; . . . from whence we may reasonably, as well as religiously, infer, that He, who placed them in their various situations, hath extended equally His care and protection to all, and that it becometh us not to counteract his mercies. . . .

AND WHEREAS the condition of those persons who have heretofore been denominated Negro and Mulatto slaves, has been attended with circumstances which not only deprive them of the common blessings that they were by nature entitled to, but has cast them into the deepest afflictions. . . .

All persons . . ., who shall be born within this state, shall not be deemed . . . servants for life or slaves; and all servitude for life, or slavery of children, in consequence of the slavery of their mothers . . . shall be, and hereby is, utterly taken away, extinguished and forever abolished.

Provided always, . . . That every negro and mulatto child, born within this state after the passing of this Act as aforesaid (who would, in case this Act had not been made, have been born a servant for years, or life as a slave) . . . shall be . . . the servant of such person or his or her assigns, who would in such case have been entitled to

Although the caption on this medallion vigorously asserts the enchained slave's common humanity, he is depicted not as an equal but as a subordinate calling out for the benevolent aid of a superior. The image of the kneeling, begging slave with the slogan "Am I Not a Man and a Brother?" was first adopted in 1787 as the seal of the London-based Society for Effecting the Abolition of the Slave Trade. The English porcelain manufacturer Josiah Wedgwood, a society member, had hundreds of thousands of these jasperware medallions made. A year later, the medallions became an item of popular fashion in Philadelphia and were made into snuffboxes, bracelets, and hair clips.

In middle-class clothes, Richard Allen, founder of the African Methodist Episcopal Church and a key leader in the Philadelphia black community, strikes a dignified pose for his portrait. African Americans did not accept white abolitionists' view of them as helpless, servile objects of benevolence.

the service of such child, until such child shall attain unto the age of twenty-eight years. . . .

Once freed, northern African Americans strove to end slavery and racial discrimination in both the North and the South. Theirs was a campaign of publicity and moral appeal; the typical weapons were the speech, the petition, and the pamphlet. In 1794, Absalom Jones and Richard Allen, former slaves who rose to positions of leadership in the Philadelphia black community, published a pamphlet entitled *An Address to Those Who Keep Slaves and Uphold the Practice*.

It [is] unreasonable, that a superior good conduct is looked for, from our race, by those who stigmatize us as men, whose baseness is incurable, and may therefore be held in a state of servitude, that a merciful man would not deem a beast to; yet you try what you can to prevent our rising from the state of barbarism, you represent us to be in, but we can tell you . . . that a black man . . . can think, reflect, and feel injuries. . . . We believe if you would try the experiment of taking a few black children, and cultivate their minds with the same care, and let them have the same prospect in view, as to living in the world, as you would wish for your own children, you would find . . . they were not inferior in mental endowments.

We do not wish to make you angry, but excite your attention to consider, how hateful slavery is in the sight of that God, who hath destroyed kings and princes, for their oppression of the poor slaves; Pharaoh and his princes . . . were destroyed by the protector and avenger of slaves. Would you not suppose the Israelites to be utterly unfit for freedom, and that it was impossible for them to attain to any degree of excellence? Their history shews how slavery had debased their spirits. Men must be willfully blind . . . that cannot see the contrary effects of liberty and slavery upon the mind of man; we freely confess the vile habits often acquired in a state of servitude, are not easily thrown off; the example of the Israelite shews, who with all that Moses could do to reclaim them from it, still continued in their former habits more or less; and why will you look for better from us? . . . It is in our posterity enjoying the same privileges with your own, that you ought to look for better things. . . .

If you love your children, if you love your country, if you love the God of love, clear your hands from slaves, burden not your children or country with them. . . .

The situation of southern African Americans was far different from that of northern blacks. Whereas northern laws put slavery on a slow but

sure road to extinction, by the mid-1790s slavery in the South was growing rapidly. Still, white southerners were deeply divided over the issue of slavery. Many individual slaveholders were convinced that slavery was a violation of natural rights, a sin, or both. Many of these masters freed their slaves. One such master was John Randolph of Virginia, a relative of Thomas Jefferson. Randolph died in 1797; his will freed his slaves and explained his reasons for doing so.

An 1829 lithograph, *A Sunday Morning View of the African Episcopal Church of St. Thomas in Philadelphia*, depicts the central community institution among northern African Americans: the church. Faced with discrimination, white paternalism, and economic dependence on whites, African Americans built community institutions that provided them with autonomy from whites and allowed them to forge a collective life as a people.

To make retribution, as far as I am able, to an unfortunate race of bondmen, over whom my ancestors have usurped and exercised the most lawless and monstrous tyranny, and in whom my countrymen (by their iniquitous laws, in contradiction of their own declaration of rights, and in violation of every sacred law of nature . . .) have vested me with absolute property; to express my abhorrence of the theory as well as the infamous practice of usurping the rights of our fellow creatures, equally entitled with ourselves to the enjoyment of liberty and happiness; . . . to impress my children with just horror at a crime so enormous and indelible; to conjure them, in the last words of a fond father, never to participate in it in any the remotest degree, however sanctioned by laws . . . or supported by false reasoning . . . for the aforesaid purposes and, with an indignation, too great for utterance, at the tyrants of the earth, from the throned despot of a whole nation to the most despicable . . . petty tormentors of single wretched slaves, I do hereby declare that it is my will and desire, nay most anxious wish that my negroes, all of them, be liberated, and I do declare them by this writing free and emancipated to all intents and purposes whatsoever.

THE TIMES; & POLITICAL PORTRAIT

The Cannibals are landing

Volunteers

Stop de wheels of

de gouvernement

Triumph Government: perish all its enemies.—
Traitors be warned: justice though slow, is sure.

CHAPTER 2

Creating a Political Order

This Federalist cartoon from 1795 offers a partisan interpretation of the party conflict that began during the 1790s. George Washington drives a chariot symbolizing the federal government, while Thomas Jefferson and his allies try to stop its wheels. Citizen Genet, a representative of the French government, helps Jefferson. In the background, American Indians, pirates, and foreign savages arrive on shore and threaten violence to American citizens.

Alexander Hamilton had never felt so humiliated. Or angry. Or fearful for his country. Like all good revolutionaries, he knew that a free government could survive only if all citizens put aside personal ambition and united to pursue the good of the country. He knew that there was only one public good—one course of action on which all reasonable and patriotic men could agree. Ongoing political conflict was a sign that at least one side in the conflict was pursuing selfish aims. Political factions or parties were always controlled by ambitious scoundrels who would sacrifice their country's interests and liberties to obtain power. Hamilton also believed that educated, worldly, wealthy, well-connected gentlemen were in the best position to know what the good of the country was. Poor and middling men, he felt, had a duty to defer to the opinions of their superiors.

A mere seven years after the adoption of the federal Constitution, it was all coming apart. For three years, opposition to George Washington's administration had grown. The strongest opposition was to the economic policies of Hamilton, who was Washington's secretary of the Treasury. By 1795, opponents were calling themselves Republicans, while the supporters of Hamilton and Washington called themselves Federalists. In that year, when Washington's emissary John Jay negotiated a treaty with England that many believed betrayed the interests of the United States and revolutionary France, Republicans called meetings in several cities to oppose the treaty. Hamilton was outraged. When did the rabble of a town obtain the right to tell the president what to do? When a meeting was announced in New York for Saturday, July 18, 1795, Hamilton and a group of his supporters marched down to put a stop to the subversion. When the time for the meeting arrived, Hamilton mounted a set of stairs and began to speak against the gathering. But instead of quieting down and going home, the men in the crowd interrupted him with "hissings, coughings and hootings," according to a newspaper report. When Hamilton tried to offer a resolution adjourning the meeting, the crowd roared out: "We'll hear no more of it!" "Tear it up!" Some boys even began to throw rocks at him, injuring one of his supporters. Stung by the insults, Hamilton stomped out of the meeting, followed by his coterie. On their way home, Hamilton and his supporters met with two groups of opponents, who continued to insult him. So deep was his humiliation, Hamilton offered "to fight the Whole Detestable faction one by one."

Hamilton's misery was a symptom of dramatic changes in American political life during the 1790s. One was the beginning of party politics. Jefferson and Madison feared parties as much as Hamilton did, but both sides felt compelled to unite and organize to defeat their enemies. Each side bitterly opposed the principles and the policies of its opponent, believing that its enemy would destroy republican government, introducing either monarchy or the ideas and political methods of the French Revolution to the United States. The other major change was popular political mobilization. In their desperation to defeat their opponents, both Hamilton's and Jefferson's allies drew ordinary voters (almost all of whom were propertied white men) into politics in new ways. The result was a transformation of American politics.

To participants on both sides, the political conflicts of the 1790s were inseparable from foreign policy. Republicans celebrated France as a sister republic whose ideals and fate were intertwined with those of the United States, and they despised monarchical England, which was at war with France. Federalists admired the political stability and commercial greatness of England, while they recoiled with horror at the radicalism, atheism, and instability of revolutionary France. Federalists believed that Republicans sought to bring French-style revolution to the United States, while Republicans were convinced that their opponents sought to impose an English-style monarchy or aristocracy on the new republic. These loyalties, hatreds, and fears lent a genuine sense of crisis to the political conflicts of the 1790s.

The Federalists' Political Vision

From the start, Alexander Hamilton was at the center of political controversy in the United States. It was his idea to hold a convention to draft a new federal constitution, and he was a leader in that convention and

View of the TRIUMPHAL ARCH, and the manner of receiving General Washington at Trenton, on his Route to New-York, April 21st 1789.

George Washington (the horseman at right) rides toward a triumphal arch erected in his honor as president-elect, while the women and girls of Trenton, New Jersey, scatter flowers in his path and sing an ode to him, a common ceremony during his tour along the East Coast on his way to his first inauguration. With events like this one, portrayed in the May 1789 issue of *Columbian Magazine*, the Federalists sought to turn Washington's popularity into a source of national unity and political deference. The ceremonies enacted a central Federalist belief: that all Americans ought to obey the federal government and its officers.

in the public campaign to get the Constitution adopted. When the first federal government was formed, President Washington appointed Hamilton secretary of the Treasury, and Hamilton quickly outlined a series of policies that would define both the Washington administration and its supporters. One of the fundamental beliefs of the Federalists concerned the questions of who should rule and of the proper relationship between rulers and ordinary citizens. In number 15 of *The Federalist*, a series of essays written in 1788 to win support for the Constitution, Hamilton laid out Federalist beliefs on that matter.

The idea of an actual representation of all classes of the people by persons of each class is altogether visionary. Unless it were expressly provided in the Constitution that each different occupation should send one or more members the thing would never take place in practice. Mechanics and manufacturers will always be inclined . . . to give their votes to merchants in preference to persons of their own professions or trades. Those discerning citizens are well aware that the mechanic and manufacturing arts furnish the materials of mercantile enterprise and industry. . . . They know that the merchant is their natural patron and friend; and they are aware that however great the confidence they may justly feel in their own good sense, their interests can be more effectually promoted by the merchant than by themselves. They are sensible that their habits in life have not been such as to give them those acquired endowments, without which in a deliberative assembly the greatest natural abilities are for the most part useless; and that the influence and weight and superior acquirements of the merchants render them more equal to a contest

Visionary

To eighteenth-century Americans, "visionary" meant unrealistic and utopian.

Mechanics and manufacturers

Mechanics and manufacturers were artisans—people who produced goods with their hands; for example, bricklayers, butchers, or tailors. A few artisans became wealthy, but most were of middling wealth. Although many merchants were middling men as well, the merchants to whom Hamilton refers were wealthy, educated men. Along with members of the learned professions, they were the main element of the urban economic and political elite.

with any spirit which might happen to infuse itself into the public councils unfriendly to the manufacturing and trading interests. . . . Artisans and manufacturers will commonly be disposed to bestow their votes upon merchants and those whom they recommend. We must therefore consider merchants as the natural representatives of all these classes of the community. . . .

The representative body . . . will be composed of land-holders, merchants, and men of the learned professions. But where is the danger that the interests and feelings of the different classes of citizens will not be understood or attended to by these three descriptions of men? Will not the land-holder know and feel whatever will promote or injure the interests of landed property? And will he not from his own interest in that species of property be sufficiently prone to resist every attempt to prejudice or incumber it? Will not the merchant understand and be disposed to cultivate as far as may be proper the interests of the mechanic and manufacturing arts to which his commerce is so nearly allied? Will not the man of the learned profession, who will feel a neutrality to the rivalships between the different branches of industry, be likely to prove an impartial arbiter between them, ready to promote either, so far as it shall appear to him conducive to the general interests of the society?

If we take into account the momentary humors or dispositions which may happen to prevail in particular parts of the society, and to which a wise administration will never be inattentive, is the man whose situation leads to extensive inquiry and information less likely to be a competent judge of their nature, extent and foundation than one whose observation does not travel beyond the circle of his neighbors and acquaintances? Is it not natural that a man who is a candidate for the favour of the people and who is dependent on the suffrages of his fellow citizens for the continuance of his public honors should take care to inform himself of their dispositions and inclinations and should be willing to allow them their proper degree of influence upon his conduct? This dependence, and the necessity of being bound himself, and his posterity, by the laws to which he gives his assent, are the true, and they are the strong chords of sympathy between the representatives and the constituent.

Once the new government was established, Hamilton quickly outlined a controversial set of economic policies. With English economic policy as his model, he sought to make the United States into a commercial power, using the power of the federal government to promote manufacturing and commercial growth. Seeking to ally English and American

financiers with the new American government, he proposed that the federal government take over the states' Revolutionary War debts and pay them in full. In this report to Congress in December 1790, he also called for Congress to establish a national bank, a private, for-profit institution that would handle the federal government's money and provide the capital needed for rapid commercial development.

The Secretary of the Treasury . . . respectfully reports:

That, from a conviction . . . that a National Bank is an Institution of primary importance to the prosperous administration of the Finances, and would be of the greatest utility in the operations connected with the support of the Public Credit, his attention has been drawn to devising the plan of such an institution. . . .

It is a fact, well understood, that public Banks have found admission and patronage among the principal and most enlightened commercial nations. They have successively obtained in Italy, Germany, Holland, England, and France, as well as the United States. . . .

Trade and industry, wherever they have been tried, have been indebted to them for important aid. And Government has been repeatedly under the greatest obligations to them, in dangerous and distressing emergencies. . . .

The following are among the principal advantages of a Bank.

First. The augmentation of the active or productive capital of a country. . . .

Secondly. Greater facility to the Government in obtaining pecuniary aids, especially in sudden emergencies. . . .

Thirdly. The facilitating of the payment of taxes. This advantage is produced in two ways. Those who are in a situation to have access to the Bank can have the assistance of loans to answer with punctuality the public calls upon them. . . . The other way, in which the effect . . . is produced. . . , is the increasing of the quantity of circulating medium and the quickening of circulation.

Just as the English government placed the king's likeness on coins, Alexander Hamilton proposed putting the president's bust on the money of the new republic. In this way, he hoped to encourage citizens to identify with the United States and to obey the federal government. Most congressmen, however, thought this 1792 prototype of a cent coin smacked of monarchical traditions, and defeated Hamilton's proposal.

An Elite Opposition Emerges

Hamilton's economic program involved a dramatic assertion of the power of the federal government. In 1791, Thomas Jefferson, Washington's secretary of state, began to oppose Hamilton's economic program as an unconstitutional expansion of federal power. In a letter to Washington, he outlined his constitutional objections to Hamilton's plan for a national bank. Jefferson's method of interpreting the Constitution, called "strict construction," became a hallmark of the opposition party that grew up around him.

I consider the foundation of the Constitution as laid on this ground: That "all powers not delegated to the United States by the Constitution, nor prohibited by it to the States, are reserved to the States or to the people." To take a single step beyond the boundaries thus specifically drawn around the powers of Congress, is to take possession of a boundless field of power, no longer susceptible of any definition.

440   *Plan for the Improvement of the Art of Paper War.*
whilſt a paſſionate man, engaged in a warm controverſy, would thunder vengeance in

French Canon

It follows of courſe, that writers of great iraſcibility ſhould be charged higher for a work of the ſame length, than meek authors; on account of the extraordinary ſpace their performances muſt neceſſarily occupy; for theſe gigantic, wrathful types, like ranters on the ſtage, muſt have ſufficient elbow-room.

For example: Suppoſe a newſpaper quarrel to happen between * M and L.   M begins the attack pretty ſmartly in

Long Primer.

L replies in
Pica Roman.
M advances to
Great Primer.
L retorts in
Double Pica.

And ſo the conteſt ſwells to

Raſcal,
Villain

* Leſt ſome ill-diſpoſed perſon ſhould miſapply theſe initials, I think proper to declare, that M ſignifies Merchant, and L, Lawyer.

Plan for the Improvement of the Art of Paper War. 441

Cow-
ard,

in five line Pica; which, indeed, is as far as the art of printing, or a modern quarrel can well go.

A philoſophical reaſon might be given to prove that large types will more forcibly affect the optic nerve than thoſe of a ſmaller ſize, and are therefore naturally expreſſive of energy and vigour. But I leave this diſcuſſion for the amuſement of the gentlemen lately elected into our philoſophical ſociety. It is ſufficient for me, if my ſyſtem ſhould be found to be juſtified by experience and fact, to which I appeal.

I recollect a caſe in point. Some few years before the war, the people of a weſtern county, known by the name of Paxton Boys, aſſembled, on account of ſome diſcontent, in great numbers, and came down with hoſtile intentions againſt the peace of government, and with a particular view to ſome leading men in the city. Sir John St. Clair, who aſſumed military command for defence of the city, met one of the obnoxious perſons in the ſtreet, and told him that he had ſeen the maniſeſto of the inſurgents, and that his name was particulariſed in letters as long as his fingers. The gentleman immediately packed up his moſt valuable effects, and ſent them with his family into Jerſey for ſecurity. Had ſir John only ſaid that he had ſeen his name in the manifeſto, it is probable that he would not have been ſo ſeriouſly alarmed: but the unuſual ſize of the letters was to him a plain indication, that the inſurgents were determined to carry their revenge to a proportionable extremity.

I could confirm my ſyſtem by innumerable inſtances in fact and practice. The title-page of every book is a proof in point. It announces the ſubject treated of, in conſpicuous characters; as if the author ſtood at the door of his edifice, calling
H

5

Coward,

Larger and larger typefaces, "indeed . . . as far as the art of printing or a modern quarrel can conveniently go," poke fun at the political competition between gentlemen, who waged battles in print known as "paper war." The satirical *Plan for the Improvement of the Art of Paper War* (1792) shows that such conflicts typically began over matters of policy but almost always devolved into attacks on one's enemy's reputation and a spirited defense of one's own.

The incorporation of a bank, and the powers assumed by this bill, have not, in my opinion, been delegated to the United States, by the Constitution.

I. They are not among the powers specially enumerated: for these are: 1st. A power to lay taxes for the purpose of paying the debts in the United States; but no debt is paid by this bill, nor any tax laid. . . .

2d. "To borrow money." But this bill neither borrows money nor ensures the borrowing it. . . .

3. To "regulate commerce with foreign nations, and among the States, and with the Indian tribes." To erect a bank, and to regulate commerce, are very different acts. . . . The bill does not propose the measure as a regulation of trade, but as "productive of considerable advantages to trade." . . .

II. Nor are they within either of the general phrases, which are the two following:—

1. To lay taxes to provide for the general welfare of the United States, that is to say, "to lay taxes for *the purpose* of providing for the general welfare." . . . They are not to lay taxes *ad libitum for any purpose they please*; but only *to pay the debts or provide for the welfare of the Union*. In like manner, they are not *to do anything they please* to provide for the general welfare, but only to *lay taxes* for that purpose. To consider the latter phrase, not as describing the purpose of the first, but as giving a distinct and independent power to do any act they please, which might be good for the Union . . . would reduce

the whole instrument to a single phrase, that of instituting a Congress with power to do whatever would be for the good of the United States; and, as they would be the sole judges of good or evil, it would be also a power to do whatever evil they please. . . .

2. The second general phrase is, "to make all laws *necessary* and proper for carrying into execution the enumerated powers." But they can all be carried into execution without a bank. A bank therefore is not *necessary*, and consequently not authorized by this phrase.

It has been urged that a bank will give great facility or convenience in the collection of taxes. Suppose this were true: yet the Constitution allows only the means which are "*necessary*," not those which are merely "convenient" for effecting the enumerated powers. If such a latitude of construction be allowed to this phrase as to give any non-enumerated power, it will go to every one, for there is not one which ingenuity may not torture into a *convenience* in some instance *or other* to *some one* of so long a list of enumerated powers. It would swallow up all the delegated powers, and reduce the whole to one power. . . .

Where Jefferson sought to restrain the power of the federal government, Hamilton sought to expand it. In replying to Jefferson's objection to a national bank, Hamilton offered a different method of interpreting the Constitution that became a hallmark of the Federalist Party.

. . . It appears to the Secretary of the Treasury, that this *general principle* is *inherent* in the very *definition* of *Government* and *essential* to every step of the progress to be made by that of the United States, namely—that every power vested in a Government is in its nature *sovereign*, and includes by *force* of the *term*, a right to employ all the *means* requisite, and fairly *applicable*, to the attainment of the *ends* of such power. . . .

There are *implied*, as well as *express powers*, and . . . the *former* are as effectually delegated [by the federal Constitution] as the latter. . . .

A power of erecting a corporation may as well be *implied* as any other thing; it may as well be employed as an *instrument* or

An anonymous cartoonist from 1802 mocks the duelist DeWitt Clinton (*far right*) for declaring the argument settled after five shots, while his opponent, John Swartout (*far left*), calls for more. (As was usually the case, both duelists survived.) Political duels typically took place soon after an election, with the leader of the losing faction seeking to regain honor and public approval by challenging the victor to combat. The allies publicized the duels after the fact, seeking to portray their leader as brave and their enemy as dishonorable.

means of carrying into execution any of the specified powers, as any other instrument or mean whatever. The only question must be . . . whether the mean to be employed, or in this instance the corporation to be erected, has a natural relation to any of the acknowledged objects or lawful ends of the government. Thus a corporation may not be erected by congress, for superintending the police of the city of Philadelphia because they are not authorized to *regulate* the *police* of that city; but one may be erected in relation to the collection of taxes, or to the trade with foreign countries, or to the trade between the States, or with the Indian Tribes, because it is the province of the federal government to *regulate those objects* and because it is incident to a general *sovereign* or *legislative power* to *regulate* a thing, to employ all the means which related to its regulation to the *best* and *greatest advantage*.

Alexander Hamilton's policies soon won opponents in both Congress and Washington's cabinet. By early 1792, Thomas Jefferson and James Madison, Hamilton's ally in creating a new federal constitution and now a congressman from Virginia, had begun to organize opposition to those policies among members of Congress. In that year, they convinced Philip Freneau, a classmate of Madison's at Princeton and editor of the antiadministration *Daily Advertiser* in New York City, to establish the *National Gazette*, a newspaper dedicated to voicing opposition to Hamilton's policies. Perhaps the most influential contributor to the *Gazette* wrote under the pen name "Brutus." His letters on Hamilton's plan for a national debt and bank laid out some of the central ideas of the growing opposition.

A system of finance has issued from the Treasury of the United States, and has given rise to scenes of speculation calculated to aggrandize the few and the wealthy, by oppressing the great body of the people, to transfer the best resources of the country for ever into the hands of speculators, and to fix a burthen on the people of the United States and their posterity, which time, instead of diminishing, will serve to strengthen and increase. . . .

This system . . . has given an additional weight to the general government, particularly the treasury department, never contemplated by its framers, by throwing the enormous sum of fifty million dollars, into the hands of the wealthy, and has attached them to all its measures, by motives of private interest. . . .

It has combined this great monied interest and has made it formidable by means of a bank monopoly. . . .

Mr. Madison cooperating with Mr. Jefferson is at the head of a faction decidedly hostile to me and my administration, and actuated by views in my judgment subversive to the principles of good government and dangerous to the union, peace and happiness of the Country. . . .

Mr. Jefferson with very little reserve manifests his dislike of the funding system generally; calling in question the expediency of funding a debt at all. . . .

In almost all the questions great & small which have arisen, since the first session of Congress, Mr. Jefferson and Mr. Madison have been found among those who were disposed to narrow the Federal authority. . . .

In respect to our foreign politics the views of these Gentlemen are in my judgment equally unsound & dangerous. *They have a womanish attachment to France and a womanish resentment against Great Britain.* They would draw us into the closest embrace of the former & involve us in all the consequences of her politics, & would risk the peace of the country in their endeavours to keep us at the greatest possible distance from the latter. . . .

—Alexander Hamilton to his political ally
Edward Carrington, May 26, 1792

By means of unlimited impost and excise laws, . . . it has anticipated the best resources of the country, and swallowed them all up in future payments. . . .

Because the certificates [of Revolutionary War debt] are generally got into the hands of wealthy foreign and domestic speculators, it has transferred the public wealth into their possession, and has given them a fee simple in the resources of the country; while the industrious mechanic, the laborious farmer, and generally the poorer class of people . . . are all made tributary . . . to these highly favored classes. . . .

Every measure coming from the Secretary of the treasury . . . has a tendency to combine the monied interest by fiscal arrangements, or to increase the energy of government by new assumptions of power. . . . This . . . is an evil which will be still increasing, . . . as new taxes are introduced, and new powers are assumed, because hosts of public officers, particularly collectors and excisemen, will arise. . . . Thus, besides the support of a combined and wealthy body of public creditors will be added a host of revenue officers . . . who will all be combined under the funding system and its offsprings to increase the influence of the treasury department and the energy of the government; they will all look up to the Secretary of the treasury as their champion and founder, and while he is originating measures by which they exist and thrive, will with their pens, their tongues, and their votes, zealously give him all their support.

From these considerations it appears, that a powerful faction has been already raised up under the funding system; whose interests and views . . . are in direct opposition to the interest and happiness of the people. . . . A well arranged and systematic plan is formed, to increase the energy and power of the general government, to the destruction of the little importance left to the state governments; and . . . to the extinction of those republican principles . . . which have been so lately, so arduously, and so gloriously achieved. . . .

A Popular Opposition Emerges

At first, the brewing conflict between Hamilton's supporters and the allies of Jefferson and Madison was limited to a few dozen political leaders in the national capital and their closest allies in the states. By 1793, however, many ordinary citizens had come to agree with Jefferson that Hamilton's policies threatened to turn the United States into an oligarchy or

impost and excise
An impost was a tax on goods imported from other countries, while an excise was a tax on domestic production.

Fee simple
"Fee simple" means unencumbered legal ownership.

a monarchy. These citizens were not led by elite politicians. Without any leadership from Madison, Jefferson, or their elite allies, they organized themselves into small political associations that they called Democratic Republican Societies. Wealthy men were members, but so were middling and even lower-class men; in many societies, these poorer men were a large majority. In all, forty-two societies were formed during the early 1790s. In an address published in 1793 through the *National Gazette*, a Democratic Republican Society organized among German American citizens in Philadelphia explained its purposes and political principles.

Friends and Fellow Citizens,

　　In a republican government it is a duty incumbent on every citizen to afford his assistance, either by taking part in its immediate administration, or by his advice and watchfulness, that its principles may remain incorrupt; for the spirit of liberty, like every other virtue of the mind, is to be kept alive by constant action—It unfortunately happens that objects of general concern seldom meet with the individual attention which they merit, and that individual exertion seldom produces

The Federalists depicted the Democratic Republican Societies as a selfish, unruly mob that threatened the stability of government. This 1793 Federalist cartoon portrays the society as a gluttonous, greedy, and drunken crew, whose "Creed" (*far left*) includes such statements as "All power in one body and that body ourselves" and "Laws are unwholesome restraints on natural rights."

a general effect; it is therefore . . . essential . . . that political societies should be established in a free government, that a joint operation may be produced, which shall give that attention and exertion so necessary to the preservation of civil liberty. . . . There is a disposition in the human mind to tyrannize when cloathed with power, men therefore who are entrusted with it, should be watched with the eye of an eagle to prevent those abuses which never fail to arise from a want of vigilance—Jealousy is a security, nay it is a virtue in a republic, for it begets watchfulness; it is a necessary attendant upon a warm attachment to our country.

The society wish to call the attention of their countrymen to affairs of state; they wish to inspire them with jealousy to guard them against every encroachment on the equality of freemen. . . .

One of the ways in which the societies educated their members and publicized their views was through holding civic festivals— celebrations of important civic dates like the Fourth of July. In 1794, the Democratic Republican Societies of Philadelphia held a celebration of the victories of the French revolutionary armies. The choice of occasion, the symbolism of the celebration, and the toasts, published in the *American Minerva* of New York, sought to educate members and the public in the societies' political principles.

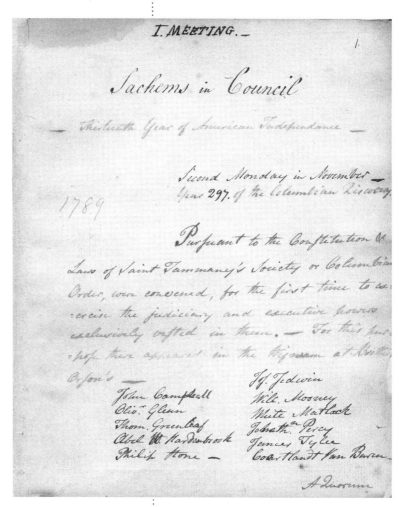

St. Tammany's Society began as a fraternal organization with an elaborate ritual, in which each member took on a fictitious identity as a "sachem," the term for an Algonquian leader. The Indian theme, recorded in their journal, was meant to signify authentic Americanness, natural liberty, and manliness. By the mid-1790s, the Tammany Society was clearly a Republican organization, one of several voluntary political associations that sprang up in the postrevolutionary era.

On Thursday last, May 1st the Democratic and German Republican Societies of this city, together with a number of their fellow-citizens, assembled at the place of Citizen Israel, about three miles from town, to celebrate the late successes of their French brethren. . . .

[A]bout 800 citizens among the Governor and several officers of the State and Federal government attended, assembled to celebrate those events which have eminently conduced to consolidate French liberty and guarantee our independence. The Minister and other officers of the French republic favored the citizens with their company.

The Flags of the sister republics [the United States and France] marked and ornamented the seat of festivity. At two the company partook of a plain yet plentiful repast, after which the following toasts were drank accompanied by universal marks of approbation.

I. The Republic of France one and indivisible—May her triumphs multiply until every day in the year be rendered a Festival in the calendar of Liberty, and a fast in the calendar of [royal] Courts.

II. The People of the United States—May each revolving year increase their detestation of every species of tyranny and their vigilance to secure the glorious inheritance acquired by their Revolution.

III. The Alliance between the sister republics of the United States and France—May their Union be as incorporate as light and heat and their friendship as lasting as time. . . .

VI. The Great Family of Mankind—May the distinction of nation and of language be lost in the association of freedom and friendship, till the inhabitants of the various sections of the globe shall be distinguished only by their virtues and their Talents.

VII. The Constitution of the United States—May its form and spirit be the invariable guide of all who administer it—may its authority never be prostituted for the purposes of party nor its departments illegally blended for the purpose of intrigue.

At the time of the festival, the allies of Jefferson and Madison were in the minority of the U.S. Senate and the majority of the House of Representatives.

VIII. The Men of the People—the Minority of the Senate and the Majority of the House of Representatives of the United States.—May they on future as on past occasions, have wisdom to discover and fortitude to resist every attack upon the constitution and the rights of their country, while they enjoy for their services the patriot's true reward, the love and confidence of their fellow citizens.

IX. A Revolutionary Tribunal in Great Britain—May it give lessons of liberty to her King, examples of Justice to her Ministry, and honesty to her corrupt legislature.

X. The Armies of the French Republic—May they be invincible and unshaken till by their glorious efforts Liberty and Peace, exalted in the same Triumphal Car, shall be drawn to the temple of Janus by the humbled tyrants who have dared to molest them.

XI. The Extinction of Monarchy—May the next generation know kings only by the page of history, and wonder that such monsters were ever permitted to exist.

XII. Reason—May it successfully counteract the baneful effects of executive influence, expose the insidious arts of judicial sophistry, and preserve inviolate the purity of legislation.

XIII. Knowledge—May every citizen be so learned as to know his rights, and so brave as to assert them.

XIV. The fair daughters of America & France—May they ever possess virtue to attract merit and sense to reward it.

XV. The Democratic and Republican societies of the United States—May they preserve and disseminate their principles, undaunted by the frowns of power—uncontaminated by the luxury of aristocracy, till the Rights of Man shall become the supreme law of every land, and their separate fraternities be absorbed, in one great democratic society comprehending the Human Race.

The Democratic Republicans' political ideal of an activist citizenry meeting to criticize the actions of its elected leaders frightened and dismayed Federalists. The Democratic Republican Societies had disappeared by 1795, victim to Federalist efforts to discredit them. But in that year the allies of Jefferson and Madison adopted their methods, calling meetings in every major city to oppose a treaty negotiated with England by George Washington's envoy John Jay. Federalists denounced the meetings as a usurpation of the authority of federal officials. The *American Minerva*, a Federalist newspaper in New York City, outlined the qualifications it saw as necessary to pass judgement on the treaty.

In order to decide on the Treaty, the following qualifications are requisite.

I. To read the Treaty and understand it.

II. To understand the Law of Nations.

III. To read and understand all our other subsisting Treaties with other nations.

IV. To know the state of the commerce, not only of the United States, but of most of the trading nations of Europe.

Without these qualifications, no man is capable of determining the real merits or demerits of the Treaty; and without these requisites any general decision will probably be materially erroneous.

In a second editorial, the *Minerva* offered another argument against the propriety of public meetings passing judgement on policy—one that quickly became a belief shared by all Federalists.

Law of Nations

The "Law of Nations" was not a body of written laws. Rather, it referred to an Enlightenment belief that a set of natural laws governed the relationship of individual nations to one another and to individuals and groups that did not fall under their sovereignty. Several eighteenth- and nineteenth-century writers sought to enumerate these laws but often disagreed as to what they were. The United States and European nations frequently invoked (and argued about) the law of nations in dealing with pirates and conflicts with other nations.

In 1810, Pennsylvania Republicans put on a mock funeral procession for the black cockade (an emblem symbolizing Federalist loyalty and an identification with England), which ended in a "Hurrah for the Red and Blue" cockade (a Republican emblem). Many ordinary citizens became involved in politics through such parades and other civic rituals.

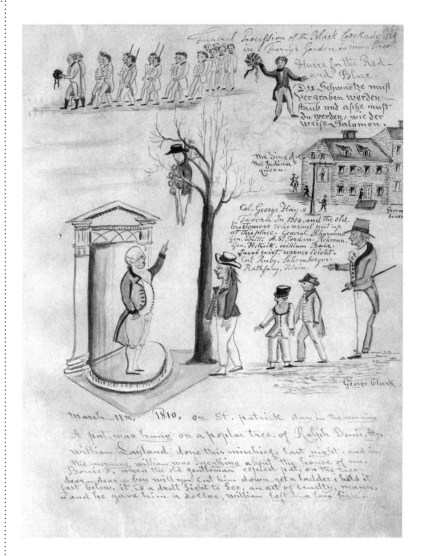

Where Federalists condemned ordinary citizens' entry into policy debates, Republicans celebrated it. A correspondent to the Philadelphia Aurora General Advertiser, *a leading Republican newspaper, depicted efforts to silence public protests of the Jay Treaty as a monarchist ploy.*

Notwithstanding the many little attempts and intrigues to condemn the voice of the people . . . by a few old tories and British agents . . . it is clear that seven eights [sic] of the people, who have been moved at the same moment . . . to condemn the treaty; are more competent to form just ideas and right conclusions as to its commercial and political interests of this country, than a "small party" of pardoned refugees and despicable British agents who advocate it. . . . The people know and feel their own strength and importance, they will never suffer an ambassador or any number of senators to sell their hard earned rights and liberties to a corrupt British ministry; and if the president of the United States signs and publishes a proclamation . . . to inforce the treaty, it is to be feared he would sign and publish his own political condemnation.

The constituted authorities of the country are the *only* organs of the national Will.—What is done by them is an act of the *nation* as a body politic.

The citizens of New-York, Boston, Philadelphia, &c. are *not* the nation.—Their voice is the voice of individuals only.

Every attempt of towns or small bodies of men to influence the representatives of the nation, is an attempt to make a *part* govern the *whole*.

The representative of a nation must act for the good of the whole. If he acts without external influence, he alone is responsible for his conduct. If he is to wait for the opinions of a nation collected in small bodies he never can act at all—if he is influenced by a small portion of the nation, he suffers a part to dictate to the whole, and his responsibility is diminished.

If the people have not confidence in their Representative, government will have neither uniformity nor stability. France is the most deplorable example of external influence offered to the National Representative.

The Clash of Parties

By 1796, the Republicans were clearly an opposition party. In that year, they ran candidates against the Federalists in most congressional districts and nominated Thomas Jefferson to run against John Adams for the presidency. To Federalists, an organized opposition and popular political mobilization threatened the same sort of chaos they perceived as occurring in France. In his farewell address, which he delivered when he announced his retirement from politics in 1796, George Washington articulated the dangers that most Federalists saw in the existence of an opposition party and public criticism of the government, as well as in the Republicans' opposition to expanding the power of the federal government and sympathy for the French revolutionary cause.

This government . . . has a just claim to your confidence and your support. Respect for its authority, compliance with its laws, acquiescence in its measures, are duties enjoined by the fundamental maxims of true Liberty. . . . The very idea of the power and the right of the people to establish Government, presupposes the duty of every individual to obey the established Government.

All obstructions to the execution of the Laws, all combinations and associations, under whatever plausible character, with real design to direct, control, counteract, or awe the regular deliberation and action of the constituted authorities, are destructive of this fundamental principle, and of fatal tendency. They tend to organize faction, to give it an artificial and extraordinary force—to put in the place of the delegated will of the nation, the will of a party, often a small but artful and enterprising minority of the community; and, according to the alternate triumphs of different parties, to make the public administration the mirror of the ill-concerted and incongruous projects of faction, rather than the organs of consistent and wholesome plans digested by common councils, and modified by mutual interests. . . .

Combinations and associations . . . are likely in the course of time and things, to become potent engines, by which cunning, ambitious and unprincipled men will be enabled to subvert the power of the people, and to usurp for themselves the reins of Government;

In its early years, the French Revolution seemed much like the American Revolution. The main aim of most revolutionaries before 1791 was to establish a constitutional monarchy and to abolish feudal privilege—aims that even the most conservative Americans applauded. In 1793, however, the Revolution's main legislative body, the Convention, voted to execute King Louis XVI. Soon thereafter, radical Jacobins, backed by the poor and middling ranks of Parisian society, took over the Convention and the other main revolutionary body, the Committee of Public Safety. Once in power, the Jacobins passed a new constitution that included universal male suffrage, exhibited deep hostility to the Catholic Church, and unleashed the "Reign of Terror," in which tens of thousands of people accused of being enemies of the Revolution were executed. Factional conflicts and bloody military struggles between counterrevolutionaries and the revolutionary armies followed. French politics remained bloody and unstable throughout the 1790s.

See Porcupine, in Colours just Portray'd, | Veil'd in darkness, acts the assassins part,
Urg'd by old Nick, to drive his dirty trade, | And triumphs much to stab you to the heart.

In this Republican cartoon from the 1790s, the English émigré and Federalist pamphleteer who wrote as "Peter Porcupine" chews up the writings of revolutionary pamphleteer Tom Paine, saying, "I Hate this Country, and will sow the seeds of discord in it." The lion, symbol of monarchist England, looks on and says, "Go on dear Peter, my friend & I will reward you." The devil adds, "More scandal, let us destroy this Idol liberty." Lady Liberty sits in mourning, leaning on a monument to American independence and a portrait of Benjamin Franklin, America's revolutionary envoy to France. A torn "Treaty with France, 1778" and other scraps of paper detailing British attacks on American ships lie at her feet.

destroying afterwards the very engines which have lifted them to unjust dominion.

Towards the preservation of your Government, and the permanency of your present happy state, it is requisite . . . that you resist with care the spirit of innovation upon its principles. . . . One method of assault may be to effect in the forms of the constitution alterations which will impair the energy of the system, and thus to undermine what cannot be directly overthrown. . . . For the efficient management of your common interest, in a country so extensive as ours, a government of as much vigor as is consistent with the perfect security of liberty, is indispensable. Liberty itself will find in such a government . . . its surest guardian. It is indeed little else than a name, where the government is too feeble to withstand the enterprises of faction, to confine each member of the society within the limits prescribed by the laws, and so maintain all in the secure and tranquil enjoyment of the rights of person and property. . . .

Let me . . . warn you in the most solemn manner against the baneful effects of the spirit of party. . . .

The alternate domination of one faction over another, sharpened by the spirit of revenge, natural to party dissension, . . . is itself a frightful despotism.—But this leads at length to a more formal and permanent despotism.—The disorders and miseries, which result, gradually incline the minds of men to seek security and repose in the absolute power of an individual: and sooner or later the chief of some prevailing faction more able or more fortunate than his competitors, turns this disposition to the purposes of his own elevation, on the ruins of Public Liberty. . . .

It serves always to distract the Public Councils and enfeeble the Public Administration. It agitates the community with ill-founded jealousies and false alarms; kindles the animosity of one part against another, foments occasionally riot and insurrection. It opens the door to foreign influence and corruption. . . .

Nothing is more essential than that permanent, inveterate antipathies against particular nations, and passionate attachments for others, should be excluded. . . . Antipathy in one nation against another disposes each more readily to offer insult and injury, . . . and to be haughty and intractable, when accidental or trifling occasions of dispute occur. Hence frequent collisions, obstinate, envenomed and bloody contests. The nation, prompted by ill will and resentment, sometimes impels to war the government, contrary to the best calculations of policy. . . .

So likewise, a passionate attachment of one nation for another . . . betrays the former into a participation in the quarrels and wars of the latter, without adequate inducement or justification. It leads also to concessions to the favorite nation of privileges denied to others, which is apt doubly to injure the nation making the concessions. . . . And it gives to ambitious, corrupted or deluded citizens facility to betray or sacrifice the interests of their own country, without odium, sometimes even with popularity. . . .

As avenues to foreign influence . . . , such attachments are particularly alarming. . . . How many opportunities do they afford to tamper with domestic factions, to practice the arts of seduction, to mislead public opinion, to influence or awe the Public Councils!

Such an attachment of a small or weak, towards a great and powerful nation, dooms the former to be the satellite of the latter. . . .

Against the insidious wiles of foreign influence . . . the jealousy of a free people ought to be *constantly* awake. . . .

In February 1798, the escalating conflict between Federalists and Republicans erupted into violence on the floor of Congress. *Congressional Pugilists*, an anonymous engraving from that year, depicts the fight between the Republican Matthew Lyon of Vermont (wielding the fire tongs on the left) and Roger Griswold of Connecticut (brandishing the cane on the right).

He in a trice struck Lyon thrice   Who seiz'd the tongs to ease his wrongs,   Congress Hall,
Upon his head, enrag'd sir.   And Griswold thus engag'd sir.   in Philadᵃ Feb. 15, 1798.

Most Federalists shared George Washington's fear of dissent, opposition parties, and foreign influence. To them, the Republican Party represented all of these dangers. In June and July 1798, with Federalists in firm control of the federal government and preparing for a possible war with France, Congress passed the Alien and Sedition Acts. The

third of three laws, the Sedition Act sought to punish attacks on the Federalist administration.

An Act in addition to the act, entitled "An act for the punishment of certain crimes against the United States."

Section 1. *Be it enacted . . .* That if any persons shall unlawfully combine or conspire together, with intent to oppose any measure or measures of the government of the United States, which are or shall be directed by proper authority, or to impede the operation of any law of the United States, or to intimidate or prevent any person holding a place or office in or under the government of the United States, from undertaking, performing or executing his trust or duty; and if any person or persons, with intent as aforesaid, shall counsel, advise, or attempt to procure any insurrection, riot, unlawful assembly, or combination, . . . he or they shall be deemed guilty of a high misdemeanor, and on conviction . . . shall be punished by a fine not exceeding five thousand dollars, and by imprisonment during a term not less than six months nor exceeding five years. . . .

Sec. 2. That if any person shall write, print, utter, or publish . . . any false, scandalous, and malicious writing or writings against the government of the United States, or either house of the Congress of the United States, or the President of the United States, with intent to defame the said government, or either house of the said Congress, or the said President, or to bring them, or either of them, into contempt or disrepute . . . or to aid, encourage, or abet any hostile designs of any foreign nation against the United States, their people or government, then such person . . . shall be

THE PROVIDENTIAL DETECTION

A Federalist etching published during the 1800 presidential election between Thomas Jefferson and John Adams depicts Jefferson as making burnt offerings of Republican, radical, and atheist writings on the "Altar to Gallic Despotism"—that is, to French tyranny. The American eagle stops him from making a final sacrifice: the American Constitution.

punished by a fine not exceeding two thousand dollars, and by imprisonment not exceeding five years.

Republicans were quick to protest the Alien and Sedition Acts. The state legislatures of Kentucky and Virginia, where the Republicans were particularly strong, took the lead. Both states adopted resolutions that denounced the acts as unconstitutional and sought to assert the authority of the states to check the power of the federal government. The following is from the Virginia Resolves, the more moderate of the two.

This Assembly . . . views the powers of the Federal Government as resulting from the compact to which the states are parties, as limited by the plain sense and intention of the instrument constituting that compact; as no further valid than they are authorized by the grants enumerated in that compact; and that, in case of a deliberate, palpable, and dangerous exercise of other powers not granted by the said compact, the states, who are parties thereto, have the right and are duty bound to interpose for arresting the progress of the evil, and for maintaining within their respective limits the authorities, rights, and liberties appertaining to them.

That the General Assembly doth also express its deep regret, that a spirit has in sundry instances been manifested by the Federal Government to enlarge its powers by forced constructions of the constitutional charter which defines them; and that indications have appeared of a design to expound certain general phrases . . . so as to destroy the meaning and effect of the particular enumeration which necessarily explains and limits the general phrases; and so as to consolidate the states, by degrees, into one sovereignty, the obvious tendency and inevitable consequence of which would be to transform the present republican system of the United States into an absolute or, at best, a mixed monarchy.

The *Aurora General Advertiser* of Philadelphia was the most influential and controversial Republican newspaper of the 1790s and early nineteenth century. Newspapers like the *Aurora* played a central role in party activists' efforts to mobilize ordinary voters. Between 1790 and 1810, the number of newspapers in the United States grew from just over one hundred to almost four hundred. The majority of them were loyal to the Republicans or Federalists. Newspapers served as the propaganda arm of each party, a breeding ground for partisan activists, and a key gathering place for local party leaders.

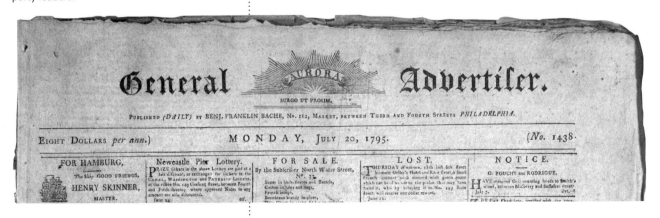

AT a numerous Meeting of Committees and Electors, from ten Towns in the County of Washington, at Hartford, on the 22d of April, 1800,

Alexander Webster, Esq. Chairman,
Zebulon R. Shipherd, Clerk,

The following Nominations were with great unanimity agreed on:

GENERAL JOHN WILLIAMS, *for Member of Congress.*

STEPHEN LUSH,
JAMES GORDON, } SENATORS.

SETH ALDEN,
GARRET G. LANSING,
TIMOTHY LEONARD,
DAVID HOPKINS,
WILLIAM M'AWLEY,
PLINY ADAMS, } ASSEMBLYMEN.

To the Electors of the Eastern District.

Fellow Citizens,

AT a period like this, so interesting to the political welfare of the United States, and the general happiness of the People, we conceive that no apology can be necessary, to justify us in addressing you, on the subject of the approaching Election. Conscious that we have no other object in view, than the common good of our Country, the freedom and prosperity of its Citizens, we venture to hope that the end we propose on this occasion, will meet the approbation and support of the Patriot and the honest Man. It is much to be lamented that, party strife has succeeded, in its designs, to create a difference in political sentiments, among the great body of the People, who have but one interest to defend, the independence and respectability of their Government, and their individual equal rights; which, by our best of Constitutions, and wholesome Laws, are well secured to us. It is not surprising that the ingenuity of artful and designing men, should invent arguments to induce the unthinking and unsuspicious, to look, with an unfavorable eye, at the management of public affairs; for, besides the necessary imperfection of all human things, which renders our best efforts liable to captious objections, (though made chiefly by those who are disposed to see objects on their work side) experience tells us that it is much easier to find fault, than to point out the manner of correcting the evil; and if it should be found that the thing objected to is under a consideration of all circumstances, as good as might reasonably be expected, it becomes every man who reasons justly, to give it his encouragement. Hence, we conclude, that the malicious declamations so frequently heard, against the administration of Government, are dictated by a perverse propensity, to make unnecessary objections, or from downright selfish motives—strong examples might be given of both.

From an unfeigned and disinterested belief then, that our Constitution is founded on the principles of liberty and equal rights; and that the administration of it has been wise and productive of many salutary effects to the Community—as much so as the state of things and expediency would allow of—We have considered it proper to promote the election of men, whose integrity, abilities and attachment to the true interests of the Country, we have the strongest reason to confide in; and who have evinced their disposition to support such a system and spirit of administration, as are alone correspondent to the principles of that Constitution, and can only furnish a well grounded security to national independence, and private liberty and property.

We would, for this purpose, recommend to you, as Candidates for the Senate, JAMES GORDON AND STEPHEN LUSH, men who we presume answer the description just mentioned. We are the more encouraged to urge your suffrages in their favor, as they have been nominated and recommended by various respectable meetings and committees, in many parts of the District.

A person to represent the state in the House of Representatives in Congress, from the District comprehending the Counties of Washington, Saratoga, Clinton and Essex, is also to be elected; and this highly interests the attention of his constituents. The duties expected from the man who will be called, by his Fellow Citizens, to execute this trust, are arduous, and of the greatest consequence, and prudence dictates, that one who has given proofs of his capacity to sustain this task, is the character on whom the Electors should unite their suffrages. JOHN WILLIAMS has already, by respectable associations in the District, been nominated and recommended as a proper candidate for this situation; and we fully concur in the Nomination—conceiving from the repeated testimonies in his favor, furnished by the frequent suffrages of the people, to represent them, both in the State and General Government; and the usefulness of his services and exertions, in these respective places, that he is a person conspicuously elligible to be supported. Confiding in his abilities to do justice to his trust, relying on his disposition to exert them for the public benefit; and assured of his attachment to the Constitution and Laws, we solicit the support of our Fellow Electors in the District in his favor. We further beg permission, respectfully, to recommend to the support and suffrages of our Fellow-Electors, of the County of Washington, the Candidates for the Assembly above named. In selecting these Gentlemen, we have had nothing in view but a desire to present to our Fellow-Citizens, a list of persons against whose characters the most daring partizan and unprincipled slanderer, will not be bold enough to breathe a whisper. They are men unanxious for office, of plain and honest lives and manners; such as claim to be venerated, and should form the distinguishing marks of good Citizens, and genuine Federal Republicans. Most ardently wishing that all party animosities may be henceforth discarded; that unanimity may prevail among us, and that we may be awake to the insidious and sinister schemes of artful and ambitious men, (however plausible formed) and who impudently call themselves the friends of the People, while they are secretly undermining their most precious Rights and Liberties; preparing them for all the horrors of War and Bloodshed, that many Nations at present experience by similar means; and conducting us, by rapid step, to that tremendous system of delusive Liberty and Equality, which may be dispensed to us, in due time, by some American Robespierre or Buonaparte.

Rensselaer Schuyler,	Daniel Mason,	William Dellingham,	Wadsworth Bull,	Jonathan Gable,
Garret Peebles,	Matthias Ogden,	James M'Crea,	Jonathan Wood,	Aaron Norton,
Daniel Curtis,	Jonathan Mosiere,	James Flack,	John Perigo,	Elijah Sacket,
David Mason,	Luther Newcomb,	Ashabel Hodge,	Theophilus Tracy, jun.	George Gilson,
Zina Hitchcock,	Asa Eitch,	Alexander Gillis,	Levi Maxwell,	Eli Eastman,
Anthony I. Blanchard,	Abraham Allen,	Garret Quackenbush,	Aaron Inglesbee,	Wait Doolittle,
David Cartwell,	Daniel Earl,	Phineas Hitchcock,	Eleazer Dewey,	Daniel Comstock,
Sylvester Rowley,	Elijah White,	Robert Loop,	John White,	Zachariah Lee,
John P. Becker,	Lewis Berry,	Daniel Brown,	Amby Higly,	Zebulon R. Shipherd,
Andrew Prouckit,	Samuel Beeman,	Jeremiah Spicer,	Thomas Worden,	Israel Eli,
Alexander Webster,	Ebenezer Dewel,	Collins Hitchcock,	Coalman Barrel,	Parbin Cantrell.

This 1800 Federalist broadside announces the candidates nominated by the Federalist convention in Washington County, New York, and presents the convention's address to the voters. It illuminates one of several new methods for mobilizing voters: the nominating convention, in which ordinary citizens (or delegates elected by previous meetings of citizens) nominate candidates for office. In addition to mobilizing voters, conventions named an official slate of candidates for each party, preventing candidates from the same party from competing for the same office.

That the General Assembly doth particularly PROTEST against the palpable and alarming infractions of the Constitution in the two late cases of the "Alien and Sedition Acts," passed at the last session of Congress; the first of which exercises a power nowhere delegated to the Federal Government, and which, by uniting legislative and judicial powers to those of the executive, subverts the general principles of free government, as well as the particular organization and positive provisions of the Federal Constitution; and the other of which acts exercises, in like manner, a power not delegated by the Constitution, but, on the contrary, expressly and positively forbidden by one of the amendments thereto,—a power which, more than any other, ought to produce universal alarm, because it is levelled against the right of freely examining public characters and measures, and of free communication among the people thereon, which has ever been justly deemed the only effectual guardian of every other right. . . .

This state having, by its Convention which ratified the Federal Constitution, expressly declared that . . . "the liberty of conscience and of the press cannot be cancelled, abridged, restrained or modified by any authority of the United States," and . . . having . . . recommended an amendment for that purpose, which amendment was in due time annexed to the Constitution,—it would mark a reproachful inconsistency and criminal degeneracy, if an indifference were now shown to the palpable violation of one of the rights thus declared and secured, and to the establishment of a precedent which may be fatal to the other. . . .

[T]he General Assembly doth solemnly appeal to the . . . other states, in confidence that they will concur with this Commonwealth in declaring . . . that the acts aforesaid are unconstitutional; and that the necessary and proper measures will be taken by each for co-operating with this state, in maintaining unimpaired the authorities, rights, and liberties reserved to the states respectively, or to the people.

President Jefferson

The party battles of the 1790s and 1800s inspired several electoral innovations. Normally, voters wrote the names of the candidates for whom they wished to vote on a piece of paper and put it in the ballot box. But in this 1800 circular, the Virginia state Republican committee directs county committees to print ballots with the names of Republican candidates for electors for president and vice president. This made voting easier and less prone to error and encouraged citizens to vote the straight Republican ticket. The document also indicates that Virginia Republicans were relatively institutionalized, with electoral committees operating at the state and county levels. This level of party organization became more common during Jefferson's presidency.

850

RICHMOND, *August* 9th, 1800.

SIR,

WE have taken the liberty to advise you, to have the Tickets for Electors of President and Vice-President of the United States written; and have thought proper to recommend to you the following form. We think it advisable that the Committees in the different Counties should procure to be written, a sufficient number of Tickets to be distributed among the Freeholders. In the formation of the Ticket, particular attention should be paid, in discriminating between the Republican Candidate William H. Cabell, and the Federal Candidate William Cabell.

WE are happy to inform you, that we have received possitive assurances from Colonel Ellzey, that he will with pleasure serve as an Elector, if he should be honored by the suffrages of a majority of his fellow citizens.

We are Sir, very respectfully,
Your fellow citizens,
P. N. NICHOLAS, CHAIRMAN.
MERIWETHER JONES,
SAMUEL PLEASANTS, *Jun.*   } COMMITTEE.
JOSEPH SELDEN,
GERVAS STORRS,
JOHN H. FOUSHEE, SECRETARY.

Form of the Republican Ticket.

The following persons are selected by the Voter, whose name is written on the back of this Ticket, for Electors of President and Vice-President.

George Wythe,	of the City of Richmond
William Newsum,	of Princess Anne.
Edmond Pendleton, sen.	of Caroline.
William H. Cabell,	of Amhurst.
James Madison, jun.	of Orange.
John Page,	of Gloucester.
Thomas Newton, jun.	of Norfolk Borough.
Carter B. Harrison,	of Prince George.
General Joseph Jones,	of Dinwiddie.
William B. Giles,	of Amelia.
Creed Taylor,	of Cumberland.
Thomas Read, sen.	of Charlotte.
George Penn,	of Patrick.
Walter Jones,	of Northumberland.
Richard Brent,	of Prince William.
William Ellzey,	of Loudoun.
Andrew Moore,	of Rockbridge.
General John Brown,	of Hardy.
General John Preston,	of Montgomery.
Hugh Holmes,	of Frederick.
Archibald Stuart,	of Augusta.

The election of 1800, following on the heels of the Alien and Sedition Acts and the Virginia and Kentucky Resolves, was bitterly fought. The Federalist attempt to outlaw dissent proved unpopular and helped swing the election to the Republicans. Thomas Jefferson was elected president, and his party won control of both houses of Congress. Thus commenced twenty-eight years of Republican rule; the Federalists would never again win control of the federal government. In his inaugural address, delivered on March 4, 1801, in the new capital of Washington, D.C., Jefferson sought to reconcile the embittered Federalists to Republican rule and outlined the principles that would guide that rule.

For that was as real a revolution in the principles of our government as that of 76 was in it's form; not effected indeed by the sword, as that, but by the rational and peaceable instrument of reform, the suffrage of the people.

—Thomas Jefferson in a letter describing the election of 1800, September 6, 1819

During the contest of opinion through which we have passed, the animation of discussion and of exertions has sometimes worn an aspect which might impose on strangers unused to think freely and to speak and to write what they think; but this being now decided by the voice of the nation, announced according to the rules of the constitution, all will, of course, arrange themselves under the will of the law, and unite in common efforts for the common good. All, too, will bear in mind this sacred principle, that though the will of the majority is in all cases to prevail, that will to be rightful, must be reasonable; that the minority possess their equal rights. . . . Let us, then, fellow citizens, unite with one heart and one mind. Let us restore to social intercourse that harmony and affection without which liberty and even life itself are but dreary things. . . . Every difference of opinion is not a difference of principle. We have called by different names brethren of the same principle. We are all republicans—we are all federalists. If there be any among us who would wish to dissolve this Union or to change its republican form, let them stand undisturbed as monuments of the safety with which error of opinion may be tolerated where reason is left free to combat it. I know, indeed, that some honest men fear that a republican government cannot be strong; that this government is not strong enough. But would the honest patriot . . . abandon a government which has so far kept us free and firm, on the theoretic and visionary fear that this government, the world's best hope, may by possibility want energy to preserve itself? I trust not. I believe this, on the contrary, the strongest government on earth. I believe it is the only one where every man, at the call of the laws, would fly to the standard of the law, and would meet invasions of the public order as his own personal concern. Sometimes it is said that man cannot be trusted with the government of himself. Can he, then, be trusted with the government of others? Or have we found angels in the forms of kings to govern him? Let history answer this question. . . .

With all these blessings, what more is necessary to make us a happy and prosperous people? Still one thing more, fellow citizens—a wise and frugal government, which shall restrain men from injuring one another, which shall leave them otherwise free to regulate their own pursuits of industry and improvement, and shall not take from the mouth of labor the bread it has earned. . . .

It is proper that you should understand what I deem the essential principles of our government, and consequently those which ought to shape its administration. . . . Equal and exact justice to all men, of whatever state or persuasion, religious or political; peace, commerce, and honest friendship, with all nations—entangling alliances with none; the support of the state governments in all their rights, as the most competent administrations for our domestic concerns and the surest bulwarks against anti-republican tendencies; the preservation of the general government in its whole constitutional vigor, as the sheet anchor of our peace at home and safety abroad; a jealous care of the right of election by the people . . . ; absolute acquiescence in the decisions of the majority—the vital principle of republics, from which there is no appeal but to force, the vital principle and immediate parent of despotism; a well-disciplined militia—our best reliance in peace and for the first moments of war, till regulars may relieve them; the supremacy of the civil over the military authority; economy in the public expense, that labor may be lightly burdened; the honest payment of our debts and sacred preservation of the public faith; encouragement of agriculture, and of commerce as its handmaid; the diffusion of information and the arraignment of all abuses at the bar of public reason; freedom of religion; freedom of the press; freedom of person under the protection of the *habeas corpus*; and trial by juries impartially selected—these principles form the bright constellation that has gone before us, and guided our steps through an age of revolution and reformation. . . . They should be the creed of our political faith. . . .

William Leney's *Infant Liberty Nursed by Mother Mob* offers a Federalist view of American politics at the end of Jefferson's second term. By the time of this engraving, Federalists were well out of power and embittered by an increasingly democratic political culture. Mother Mob's breasts are clearly deleterious to young Liberty: one is labeled "Whiskey," the other "Rum."

CHAPTER 3

Expanding the National Territory

The artist depicts treaty negotiations after the stunning defeat of the Western Confederacy at the Battle of Fallen Timbers as a meeting of radically different cultures. While U.S. representatives wear gentlemen's coats, waistcoats, pants, and wigs, Confederacy leaders wear tunics, feather headdresses, and large earrings and other jewelry. The Confederation granted most of what is now Ohio to the United States. The Indian leaders were at a disadvantage: the treaty was written in English, which they could not read. Instead, they had to depend on translators and intermediaries whose loyalties could not always be trusted. Pressuring native leaders to cede more land was a major component of U.S. Indian policy.

As a boy, Asa Sheldon had poor prospects for success. His father, he recalled in his autobiography, owned "but a few acres of land" and made his living lining the walls of cellars and wells with stones. It was dirty, back-breaking work, and it kept him away from his family for most of each week. Nor did it pay very well. Jeremiah and his wife, Elizabeth, had trouble supporting their eight children, and there was no hope that they could provide Asa or any of his three brothers with the land to become independent farmers. So in 1797, when Asa was nine, his father apprenticed him to David Parker, a farmer in their hometown of Lynnfield, Massachusetts. A bitter, controlling man, Parker occasionally beat Asa and pocketed the money he earned in his off hours. After a few years, Asa ran away and began working a long string of waged jobs, some of them for kind employers, many of them for bosses who were cruel or tight-fisted or relentlessly demanding. With each new job, Asa moved to a new town. By the time he was twenty, he had worked in every corner of eastern Massachusetts.

Asa's experience with wage labor was a humiliating one. Although he was white, his mother described him as "bond slave" to Mr. Parker, and he agreed; more than sixty years later, he still remembered Mr. Parker's and other employers' unkindness with bitterness. His experience reinforced what every American farmer knew: to be truly free, a man had to have property so he could work for himself.

Asa's experience was becoming a common one in the eastern states during the late eighteenth and early nineteenth centuries. The reason was simple: there were more people than there was available land. *Since colonial settlement, farmers had raised families as large as Asa's, or even larger. During the first few generations of settlement, land was plentiful and cheap, so with hard work, careful planning, and some luck, the son of a farmer could acquire the land he needed to farm for himself. But after a few generations, the local supply of unoccupied land ran out. Land became expensive and out of the reach of many families. A growing number of men made their living by wage labor or renting a farm, joining the ranks of the not-quite-free. More than anything else, propertyless people wanted to earn the money to get enough property to become "independent"—that is, to earn a moderate prosperity working for themselves. Like Asa Sheldon, they moved from place to place in hopes of realizing this dream. Most, like Asa, stayed relatively close to home. But a large minority went further afield, and this choice set in motion some of the most dramatic changes of the era. Some went to the cities and factory towns of the Northeast, becoming workers and entrepreneurs—the personnel of an industrial revolution. Others sought land where it was cheap: in the lands of the West that were being seized from Indians.*

Although African Americans also dreamed of propertied independence, westward expansion was a white person's enterprise, undertaken at the expense of Indians and black Americans. White expansion stripped Indians of land, placed a hostile, powerful people in their midst, upset their subsistence strategies, and threatened their sovereignty over their own territory. Western lands promised not only propertied independence for white farmers but also new territories for slave-based agriculture. Migrants from the East included large numbers of slave owners, who needed cheap, fertile lands to cash in on a new, spectacularly profitable crop: short-staple cotton. They brought with them tens, perhaps hundreds of thousands of enslaved people who had no say in whether or not to migrate. From the start, the expansion of the United States perpetuated and exacerbated the growing division between independent proprietorship and slavery.

In the sixty years that followed the Revolution, hundreds of thousands of land-hungry farmers, planters, and enslaved people moved west. To ensure the supply of land for these migrants, the federal government annexed over six and a half million acres, nearly tripling the new nation's size. The white population living west of the Allegheny Mountains grew fiftyfold, from 165,000 in 1790 to over six million in 1840. This seizure of territory and movement of people sparked fierce conflicts between Indians and U.S. citizens, squatters and great landowners, settlers and their government. It transformed the United States, forcing Indians from their lands, expanding the territory under the control of white Americans, increasing the num-

ber and political power of both independent proprietors and slave owners, and turning the young republic into an empire spanning most of a continent.

Acquiring the Land

Republican administrations sought to cater to farmers' land hunger by opening up western lands to settlement. This meant first acquiring land from the European empires who claimed it. The United States took over European claims to most lands east of the Mississippi with the Revolution. It greatly extended its reach in 1803 with the Louisiana Purchase, in which it bought France's claim to most of the territory between the Mississippi Valley and the Rocky Mountains. After the treaty with France was signed but before it was ratified by Congress, President Thomas Jefferson explained the purchase to a political ally and expressed even more ambitious plans for future expansion.

The boundaries . . . are the highlands on the western side of the Mississippi enclosing all its waters, the Missouri . . . , and terminating in the line drawn from the northwestern point of the Lake of the Woods to the nearest source of the Mississippi, as lately settled between Great Britain and the United States. We have some claims, to extend on the seacoast westwardly to the Rio Norte or Bravo, and better, to go eastwardly to the Rio Perdido, between Mobile and Pensacola, the ancient boundary of Louisiana. These claims will be a subject of negotiation with Spain, and if, as soon as she is at war, we push them strongly with one hand, holding out a price in the other, we shall certainly obtain the Floridas, and all in good time. . . .

Objections are raising to the eastward against the vast extent of our boundaries, and propositions are made to exchange Louisiana, or a part of it, for the Floridas. But . . . we shall get the Floridas without, and I would not give one inch of the waters of the Mississippi to any nation, because I see in a light very important to our peace the exclusive right to its navigation, and the admission of no nation into it, but . . . with our consent and under our police. These Federalists see in this acquisition the formation of a new confederacy. . . . These combinations depend on so many circumstances which we cannot foresee, that I place little reliance on them. . . . The future inhabitants of the Atlantic and Mississippi States will be our sons. . . . We think we see their happiness in their union, and we wish it. Events may prove it otherwise; and if they see their interest in separation, why should we take side with our Atlantic rather than our Mississippi descendants? . . . God bless them both, and keep them in union, if it be for their good, but separate them, if it be better. The inhabited part of Louisiana, from Point Coupèe to the sea, will of course be immediately a territorial government, and soon a state. But above that, the best use we can make of the country for some time, will be to give establishments in it to the Indians on the east side of the Mississippi, in exchange for their present country, and open land offices in the last. . . . When we shall be full on this side, we may lay off a range of States on the western bank . . . and so, range after range, advancing compactly as we multiply.

Once an area had been acquired from a European power, the United States had to gain title to it from the Indians who lived there. Between 1789 and 1840, the U.S. government wrested the lands that are now Ohio, Illinois, Indiana, Wisconsin, Arkansas, Missouri, Mississippi, and Florida from their Indian inhabitants, along with part of the land that lies within Pennsylvania, New York, Tennessee, Iowa, Kansas, Nebraska, Oklahoma, Georgia, Alabama, Michigan, Minnesota, Kentucky, and Texas. In a letter to William Henry Harrison, governor of the Michigan Territory, President Thomas Jefferson explained his policy toward Indians.

Our system is to live in perpetual peace with the Indians, to cultivate an affectionate attachment from them, by everything just and liberal which we can do for them within the bounds of reason, and by giving them effectual protection against wrongs from our own people. The decrease of game rendering their subsistence by hunting insufficient, we wish to draw them to agriculture, by spinning and weaving. . . . When they withdraw themselves to the culture of a small piece of land, they will perceive how useless to them are their extensive forests, and will be willing to pare them off from time to time in exchange for necessaries for their farms and families. To promote this disposition to exchange lands, which they have to spare and we want, for necessaries, which we have to spare and they want, we shall push our trading uses, and be glad to see the good and influential individuals among them run into debt, because . . . when these debts get beyond what the individuals can pay, they become willing to lop them off by a cession of lands. At our [U.S. government] trading houses, . . . we mean to sell so low as merely to repay use cost and charges. . . . In this way our settlements will gradually circumscribe and approach the Indians, and they will in time either incorporate with us as citizens of the United States, or remove beyond the Mississippi. . . . In the whole course of this, it is essential to cultivate their love. As to their fear,

This medal, which Meriwether Lewis and William Clark presented to the Nez Perce Indians in 1805, was typical of the medals presented by federal emissaries to native leaders. It offered a mixed message. On the one hand, the back promised "peace and friendship" between the two nations, with the shaking hands suggesting equality between the two. On the other, the bust of Jefferson hanging around the neck of an Indian leader suggested that the wearer was the dependent client of the powerful president.

we presume that our strength and their weakness is now so visible that we must see we have only to shut our hand to crush them, and that all our liberalities to them proceed from motives of pure humanity only. Should any tribe be fool-hardy enough to take up the hatchet . . . , the seizing the whole country of that tribe, and driving them across the Mississippi, as the only condition of peace, would be an example to others, and a furtherance of our final consolidation.

Indians, White Settlers, and the Federal Government

Jefferson's hope that Americans' acquisition of Indian lands would be peaceful was never realized. Wherever whites settled, conflict with neighboring Indians erupted. Few had more extensive experience with such conflict than Benjamin Hawkins. As the federal agent to the Creek nation, Hawkins sought to carry out federal Indian policies, prevent conflict between Creeks and settlers, and convey important developments among the Creeks to his superiors at the nation's capital. During the late 1790s, Hawkins recorded the following events in his diary and letters.

July 14, 1797: Some of the Upper Creeks have murdered John Gentry, in the neighbourhood of Cumberland; he was a worthy man, friendly to the Indians.

September 20, 1797: On the 12 of this month[,] two men who live in Hancock County crossed over the Oconnee on the Indian lands, went up the Little River about 10 Miles, fired upon and wounded a Cussetuh Chief who was hunting there.

November 13, 1797: Zachariah Cox and his associates seem obstinately bent on attempting to settle somewhere on the Indian lands by force. By my last advises from Tellico, I find that he intended to attempt to descend the river Tennessee by force; he had a large boat, 80 feet by 23, and armed with cannon. Col. Butler, who commands in that quarter, has had orders to prevent him.

December 23, 1797: A runner arrived this morning about 10 o'clock . . . to inform me . . . that last evening, just before moon down, his camp had been fired on by some men supposed to be Georgians; that one Indian was killed dead and two badly wounded, one of them Nehah Tustunnuggee, a Commissioner; that the white people had robbed the camp of some skins, kettles and three horses. . . .

Wherever there was extensive unfenced and uncultivated land, farmers treated it as "common land"—open to the use of all. This use of the land was indispensable to frontier settlers, who came to their new homes with little money or property. Where white settlers lived near Indians, free-roaming animals devastated Indian crops, as Indians, unlike white farmers, did not fence their cropland. Rebecca Burlend, an English-born settler in Illinois, describes her neighborhood's use of common lands in a book about her experience.

By the beginning of March our Indian corn [their main source of food] was done. . . . There was however by this time a little fresh grass in the woods, to which we were very glad to turn our little stock, consisting . . . of a cow and calf, and a mare near foaling. . . . All unenclosed lands, whether purchased of government or otherwise, are considered common pasturage; and as there are in Illinois thousands of acres in that state, any person can keep as many cattle during summer as he chooses. They are turned out at spring, and thus run where they please. . . . Where so many different herds of cattle run at large, there is a greater danger of their intermixing than of being lost. To prevent this, great care is taken by each grazier at the spring to mark his own. Some cut their ears in various ways. Others burn certain marks on their horns with a hot iron.

Pass

Under federal law, white Americans were required to obtain a pass from the Indian agent in order to travel through the territory of any Indian nation.

February 16, 1798: There are some families on the Indian lands west of the line; I believe not more than sixteen. . . . The settlers made their establishments under the laws of the state of Georgia and with the expectation and general belief that they would be on the East side of the line. They have conducted themselves well and appeared to be a poor, decent, orderly and industrious set of people. I told them they would not be permitted to make another crop on the Indian lands, and that they would do well to make arrangements to move by the spring. . . .

April 16, 1798: Some travelers from South Carolina, who came by Fort James and obtained passes from Ensign Thompson to go to Tensaw, have been plundered in the Cussetuh by some Indians from one of the upper towns. The motives they assign for this improper conduct are that the passes are not regular, and that they were advised to do it to put a stop to white people's traveling through their land until arrangements can be made to secure the Indians from the imposition of worthless characters. . . .

May 26, 1798: This day the Chiefs of the towns of all the upper, and a deputation from the lower Creeks and Seminoles convened at the public square. . . .

Efau Haujo . . . addressed first the Chiefs and then the superintendent.

"The first thing I will mention is relative to the cattle ranging on our lands. They cannot be restrained well; they do not understand stipulations relative to boundaries. . . . We wish you to discourage all you can the white people from driving their stock on our lands, or permitting them to come over, and we hope you will prevent it if possible. We wish not to encourage our young men to injure their neighbors; when the men come over on our lands, after cattle or horses[,] let them come without arms of any kinds . . . and if they meet an Indian, let them show signs of kindness, offer their hands, and if they can speak our language, tell what they have lost and the Indian will help them to recover it.

. . . It is time to look about us, our land is small, game is scarce, the white people are on our hunting grounds, particularly near Cumberland and its neighborhoods."

May 27 [1798]: Mr. Hawkins called on the Chiefs to attend . . . to horse stealing and encouraging negros to leave the service of their masters to come into the Creek land and there find protection from the Indians who claim them and found their claims on the getting possession of them first. . . .

June 5 [1798]: I find it extremely difficult to restrain the young men from stealing horses. Some unworthy citizens on the frontiers will purchase them and hitherto I have no aid from the magistrates to restrain them.

August 2 [1798]: The Indians are invited into the settlements to trade. . . . Here a serious injury arises, the Indians when they can, will get drunk,

Benjamin Hawkins, the agent of the federal government to the Creeks, introduces some Creek men to a plow, while the male Indian at right enjoys the material abundance promised by Euro-American agriculture. This 1805 painting celebrates a major component of federal Indian policy before 1829: the effort to "civilize" American Indians. The association of the plow and crops with men was a central element of the civilization program. In most Indian societies, women tended crops; the advocates of "civilization" insisted that men do the farming while women engage in housekeeping, childcare, and domestic manufacturing.

and are then rude to the Citizens. They take provisions and small articles of property whenever they can lay their hands upon it. The Citizens must be restrained from hunting on their lands and keeping their stock there. . . .

Indians throughout the area between the Alleghenies and the Mississippi contended with the problems that Hawkins describes: land invasions, conflict with white settlers, alcohol abuse. They also faced a growing shortage of game, which had long been an important part of Indian subsistence strategies. Many saw this as a moment of crisis and sought a sacred path out of it. Between the mid-eighteenth century and the War of 1812, dozens of prophets sprang up between the Allegheny Mountains and the Mississippi River. Seeking spiritual purity, reconciliation with the divine, and a revival of older Indian lifeways, prophets won tens of thousands of followers. One of the most influential such leaders was the Shawnee prophet Tenskwatawa. A contemporary white biographer of his brother, the military leader Tecumseh, describes the origins of that movement in 1805 on the lands of the Delaware Indians, which lay within the boundaries of the territory of Michigan.

In the early part of . . . 1805, . . . an old Shawanoe, named Penagashega, or the Change of Feathers, who had for some years been engaged in the respectable calling of a prophet, fell sick and died. Laulewasi-kaw . . . assumed his sacred office. He changed his name . . . to Tensk-wautauwau, meaning the Open Door, because he undertook to point out to the Indians the new modes of life which they should

Tenskwatawa, the Shawnee Prophet, preached a complete rejection of Euro-American lifeways and a return to native traditions. The portrait, painted long after his death by an American painter, emphasizes his rejection of Euro-American clothing and his emphasis on native ritual items.

pursue. In the month of November, . . . he assembled a considerable number of Shawanoes, Wyandots, Ottaways, and Senecas, at Wapakonatta, on the Auglaize river, when he unfolded to them the new character with which he was clothed. . . . In this assemblage he declaimed against witchcraft, which many of the Indians practiced and still more believed. He pronounced that those who continued bewitched, or exerted their arts on others, would never go to heaven nor see the Great Spirit. He next took up the subject of drunkenness, against which he harangued with great force. . . . He told them that since he had become a prophet, he went up into the clouds; that the first place he came to was the dwelling of the Devil, and that all who had died drunkards were there, with flames issuing out of their mouths. . . . Such was the effect of his preaching . . . that many of his followers became alarmed, and ceased to drink the "fire-water." . . . He likewise declaimed against the custom of Indian women intermarrying with white men, and denounced it as one of the causes of their unhappiness. Among other doctrines of his new code, he insisted on a community of property. . . . He declaimed with vehemence against all innovations in the original dress and habits of the Indians . . . , and promised to all his followers, who would believe his doctrines and practice their precepts, the comforts and happiness which their forefathers enjoyed before they were debased by their connection with the whites. . . .

The Prophet's movement quickly took on two ambitious new aims: uniting all Indian peoples into one people, and opposing white expansion. The Prophet's brother Tecumseh had already fought the United States to stop white expansion during the 1790s. On August 12, 1810, in council with Governor William Henry Harrison of Michigan, Tecumseh explained the beliefs and aims of his and his brother's movement.

Sir, you have liberty to return to your own country. The being within, communing with past ages, tells me, that once, nor until lately, there was no white man on this continent. That it then all belonged to red men, children of the same parents, placed on it by the Great Spirit that made them, to keep it, to traverse it, to enjoy its productions, and to fill it with the same race. Once a happy race. Since made miserable by the white people, who are never contented, but always encroaching. The way, and the only way to check and stop this evil, is, for all the red men to unite in claiming a common and equal right in the land, as it was at first, and should be yet; for it never was divided, but belongs to us all, for the use of each. That no part has a right to sell, even to each other, much less to strangers. . . . The white people have no right to take the land from the Indians, because they had it first; it is theirs.

Tecumseh's and the Prophet's movement was in part a campaign of political and moral reform within each Indian nation. But it was also a military campaign. Beginning in 1810, Tecumseh visited different nations from the Canadian border to the Southwest, seeking to convince them to join the fight against the Americans. When the United States went to war with England in 1812, Tecumseh and his followers sided with the British. The warrior accepted a commission as a general into the British army and solicited arms from the English. Many Indian people fought on the side of the British as well. In 1811, while visiting the nations of the South, Tecumseh held a council with Choctaw and Chickasaw leaders. His speech was recounted years later by Peter Pitchlynn, the son of an English trader and a mixed-blood Choctaw woman living among the Choctaws. Pitchlynn was five years old at the time of Tecumseh's visit. The son of a powerful man, he may have been at the council; more likely, he had heard accounts of it from Choctaw leaders who had attended.

The whites are already nearly a match for us all united, and too strong for any one tribe alone to resist; so that unless we support one another with our collective and united forces; unless every tribe unanimously combines to give check to the ambition and avarice of the whites, they will soon conquer us apart and disunited, and we will be driven away from our native country and scattered as autumnal leaves before the wind. . . .

Our broad domains are fast escaping from our grasp. Every year our white intruders become more greedy, exacting, oppressive, and overbearing. Every year contentions spring up between them and our people and when blood is shed we have to make atonement whether right or wrong, at the cost of the lives of our greatest chiefs, and the yielding up of large tracts of our lands. Before the palefaces came among us, we enjoyed the happiness of unbounded freedom, and were acquainted with neither riches, wants nor oppression. How is it now? Wants and oppression are our lot; for are we not controlled in everything, and dare we move without asking, by your leave? Are we not being stripped day by day of the little that remains of our ancient liberty? Do they not even kick and strike at us as they do their black-faces? How long will it be before they will tie us to a post and whip us, and make us work for them in their corn fields as they do them? Shall we wait for that moment or shall we die fighting before submitting to such ignominy?

Tecumseh supported his brother Tenskwatawa's demand for a native cultural revival and a return to ritual purity. This portrait from the late nineteenth century presents the military leader in the red hunting jacket, tunic, and feathered cap favored by many northeastern Indians.

Tecumseh's death (*center right*) in 1813 at the Battle of the Thames brought an end to the leader's effort to unite Indian peoples against white territorial expansion. The battle is depicted as one between civilization and savagery. The American troops are all dressed in respectable, middle-class clothing, while Tecumseh's troops wear red tunics and headdresses. Tecumseh wears a multicolored skirt. The man portrayed as Tecumseh's killer is Richard M. Johnson. Johnson won fame as Tecumseh's killer, which helped him build a distinguished political career after the war.

. . . Let us by unity of action destroy them all, which we now can do, or drive them back whence they came. War or extermination is now our only choice. . . . I am now at the head of many warriors backed by the strong arm of English soldiers. Choctaws and Chickasaws, you have too long borne with grievous usurpation inflicted by the arrogant Americans. Be no longer their dupes.

Another strategy for cultural renewal adopted by many Indians was to welcome American leaders' offer to teach them American-style "civilization." No nation adopted this approach more thoroughly than the Cherokees. John Ridge, a member of the Cherokee National Council, described Cherokee progress in "civilizing" itself to a white American patron in 1826, when the process had been under way for more than two decades. Since he was writing to a patron, Ridge may have had good reason to minimize the persistence of older lifeways and to play up cultural change among his people. Even so, the document reveals much about the ideals that elite Cherokees embraced and the goals they sought to achieve in embracing the "civilization" program.

The . . . population is dispersed over the face of the Country on separate farms; villages, or a community, having a common enclosure to protect their hutches, have disappeared long since. . . . They are farmers and herdsmen. . . . It is true that there are distinctions now existing & increasingly so in the value of property possessed by individuals, but this only answers a good purpose, as a stimulus to those in the rear to equal their neighbors. . . . Their principal dependence for subsistence is on the production of their own farms. . . . I take pleasure to state, tho' cautiously, that there is not to my knowledge a solitary Cherokee to be found that depends upon the chase for subsistence and every head of family has his house & farm. The hardest portion of manual labor is performed by the men. . . . They [the women] sew, they weave, they spin, they cook our meals and act well the duties assigned them by Nature as mothers as far as they are able & improved. The African slaves are generally mostly held by Half breeds and full Indians of distinguished talents. In this class . . . the farms are conducted in the same style with the southern white farmers. . . . Their houses are usually of hewed logs, with brick chimneys and shingled roofs, there are also a few excellent Brick houses & frames. . . .

Domestic manufactures is still confined to women. . . . These consist of . . . domestic cloths. . . . Cherokees on the Tennessee river have already commenced to trade in cotton & grow the article in large plantations and they have realized a handsome profit. . . .

. . . This kind of government existed [previously] in our Nation. Their chiefs were numerous and their responsibility was a trifling. Lands then could be obtained of them at a price most convenient to the U. States as their commissioners with the assistance of their agent could always procure a majority for a Cession, & when this was done, all yielded to secure their shares for the trifling equivalent. At length the eyes of our Nation were opened to see their folly. Their existence was in danger & the remedy was within ourselves & this could only be affected in the amendment of their Government. . . . These Chiefs organized themselves into a Standing body of Legislators who meet in October annually at New Town, their seat of Government.

They are composed of two departments, the National Committee & the Representative Council. . . . All laws of course are passed with the concurrence of these two departments & approved of by the head Chiefs. Their laws at present are written in the English Language. . . . There is a Court of Justice in every district. . . . There is also a Supreme court of the Nation held once annually at New Town when all appeals from the district Courts are finally decided. . . . We

Kahmungdaclegeh, the Cherokee leader who adopted the English name Major Ridge, is dressed in the formal garb of an early nineteenth-century middle-class Euro-American in his 1838 lithographic portrait. The Cherokee leader was one of the early advocates of the project to adopt Euro-American ways, and a wealthy cotton planter and slave owner. A fervent nationalist, he played a leading role in strengthening the Cherokee National Council and in outlawing the granting of land to the United States.

have not as yet many written laws, it being the policy of our Government to regulate itself to the capacity and state of improvement of our people. I will give you a sketch of a few of these laws.

1. Law to regulate our Citizens agreeable to the Intercourse laws of the U. States for the purpose of Securing peace on the frontiers.
2. A law prohibiting the introduction of Intoxicating liquors by the whites.
3. Regulating intermarriages with the whites, making it necessary for a white man to obtain licence & be married by a Gospel minister or some authorized person.
4. Against Renting land & introducing white people without a special written permission of the Legislative Council. Penalty: Expulsion of the white people so introduced as intruders, a fine of $500 on the aggressor and one hundred stripes [lashes with a whip] on the naked back.
5. Giving indefeasible title to Lands improved—houses &c.—to the Citizens with power to sell or transfer them among each other, but not to Citizens of the adjoining States. . . .
7. Law, prohibiting the sale of any more Lands to the United States except it be done by the concurrences of the Nat. Committee & Council; Penalty: disgrace and death to the offender. . . .

In regard to Intemperance, we are still as a nation grossly degraded. We are however on the improve. . . .

I suppose that there are one third of our Citizens, that can read & write in the English Language. George Guess a Cherokee who is unacquainted with the English has invented 86 characters, in which the Cherokees read and write in their own Language and regularly correspond with their Arkansas friends. This mode of writing is most extensively adopted by our people particularly by those who are ignorant of the English Language. A National Academy of a high order is to be soon established by law at our seat of Government. . . . It is also in contemplation to establish an English & Cherokee printing press & a paper edited in both languages at our seat of Government. . . .

Cherokee leaders hoped that by adopting "civilization" and building a modern, constitutional nation-state, they would keep their land and win

Americans' respect for their sovereignty. In this, they were sorely disappointed. In 1828, the state of Georgia declared itself sovereign over the Cherokee territory within its borders and made plans to distribute tribal lands to white Georgians. The Cherokee National Council and its allies among white evangelicals fought Georgia's move. In June 1830, the council appealed to the federal courts for an injunction against Georgia's laws, arguing that the Cherokees were a foreign nation, not subject to Georgia's jurisdiction. The U.S. Supreme Court denied the Cherokees' request on the grounds that the tribe was not a foreign state and therefore could not sue in U.S. courts under the Constitution. The majority decision, written by Chief Justice John Marshall, laid the foundation of all subsequent law regarding Indian sovereignty.

Is the Cherokee nation a foreign state in the sense of the constitution? . . . .

. . . In general, nations not owing a common allegiance are foreign to each other. . . . But the relations of the Indians to the United States is marked by peculiar and cardinal distinctions which exist no where else. . . . In all our intercourse with foreign nations, they are considered as within the jurisdictional limits of the United States, subject to many of those restraints which are imposed upon our own citizens. They acknowledge themselves in their treaties to be under the protection of the United States: they admit that the United States shall have the sole and exclusive right of regulating the trade with them, and managing all their affairs as they think proper. . . .

Though the Indians are acknowledged to have an unquestionable, and, heretofore, unquestioned right to the lands they occupy, until that right shall be extinguished by a voluntary cession to our government, yet it may well be doubted whether those tribes which reside within the acknowledged boundaries of the United States can, with strict accuracy, be denominated foreign nations. They may, more correctly, perhaps, be denominated domestic dependent nations. They occupy a territory to which we assert a title independent of their will, which must take effect in point of possession when their right of possession ceases. Meanwhile they are in a state of pupilage. Their relation to the United States resembles that of a ward to his guardian.

They look to our government for protection; rely on its kindness and its power; appeal to it for relief to their wants; and address the president as their great father. They and their country are considered by foreign nations, as well as by ourselves, as being

While the Cherokee suit claiming status as a foreign nation was being heard, another case was making its way to the Supreme Court. Seven missionaries refused to obtain the license required by Georgia for living in Cherokee territory and were sentenced to prison. They appealed their case, which was heard by the Supreme Court as Worcester v. Georgia *in 1831. In the majority opinion, Chief Justice John Marshall clarified the sovereign status of Indian tribes. Although they were not foreign states under the Constitution, Marshall wrote, they were nonetheless separate political communities, with sovereignty over their territory. Georgia's effort to extend its jurisdiction over Cherokee territory was unconstitutional.*

The Indian nations had always been considered as distinct, independent political communities, retaining their original natural rights, as the undisputed possessors of the soil, from time immemorial. . . .

The Cherokee nation, then, is a distinct community occupying its own territory, with boundaries accurately described, in which the laws of Georgia can have no force, and which the citizens of Georgia have no right to enter, but with the assent of the Cherokees themselves. . . . The whole intercourse between the United States and this nation, is, by our constitution and laws, vested in the government of the United States.

Sequoyah, inventor of the Cherokee writing system, wears a hybrid of traditional Cherokee clothing (the turban, pipe, and outer jacket) and middle-class Euro-American dress (the inner jacket, collared shirt, and scarf). A medal bearing the bust of the president of the United States hangs around his neck, but he is pointing to his contribution to Cherokee nationalism: the syllabary that allowed the Cherokee language to be written.

so completely under the sovereignty and dominion of the United States, that any attempt to acquire their lands, or to form a political connexion with them, would be considered by all as an invasion of our territory, and an act of hostility. . . .

. . . After mature deliberation, the majority is of opinion that an Indian tribe or nation within the United States is not a foreign state in the sense of the constitution, and cannot maintain an action in the courts of the United States.

When the Supreme Court's decision in *Worcester v. Georgia* was handed down, President Andrew Jackson refused to enforce it. Instead, he endorsed Georgia's seizure of Cherokee lands. Jackson offered a different solution to the crisis: the removal of all Native Americans from the eastern United States to new lands west of the Mississippi River. At his request, Congress set aside lands in what would later become the states of Kansas and Oklahoma for Indians who were to be removed from the east. In his first message to Congress, on December 8, 1829, Jackson introduced and defended his new policy, which would reserve all the lands east of the Mississippi for white settlers and their African American slaves.

I suggest for your consideration the propriety of setting apart an ample district west of the Mississippi, and without the limits of any State or Territory now formed, to be guaranteed to the Indian tribes as long as they shall occupy it, each tribe having a distinct control over the portion designated for its use. There they may be secured in the enjoyment of governments of their own choice, subject to no other control from the United States than such as may be necessary to preserve peace on the frontier and between the several tribes. There the benevolent may endeavor to teach them the arts of civilization, and, by promoting union and harmony among them, to raise up an interesting commonwealth, destined to perpetuate the race and to attest to the humanity and justice of this Government.

This emigration should be voluntary, for it would be as cruel as unjust to compel the aborigines to abandon the graves of their fathers and seek a home in a distant land. But they should be distinctly informed that if they remain within the limits of the States they must be subject to their [the states'] laws. In return for their obedience as individuals they will without doubt be protected in the enjoyment of those possessions which they have improved by their industry. But it seems to me visionary to suppose that in this state of things claims can be allowed on tracts of country on which they have neither dwelt nor made improvements, merely because they have seen them from the mountains or passed them in the chase. Submitting to the laws of the States, and receiving, like other citizens, protection in their persons and property, they will ere long become merged in the mass of our population.

One year later, in his Second Annual Message to Congress, Jackson reported on the progress of his policy.

It gives me great pleasure to announce to Congress that the benevolent policy of the Government, steadily pursued for nearly thirty years, in relation to the removal of Indians beyond the white settlements is approaching to a happy consummation. Two important tribes [the Choctaw and Chickasaw] have accepted the provision made for their removal at the last session of Congress, and it is believed that their example will induce the remaining tribes also to seek the same obvious advantages.

The consequences of a speedy removal will be important to the United States, to the individual States, and to the Indians themselves. . . . It puts an end to all possible danger of collision between the authorities of the General and State Governments on account of the Indians. It will place a dense and civilized population in large tracts of country now occupied by a few savage hunters. By opening the whole territory between Tennessee on the north and Louisiana on the south to the settlement of the whites it will incalculably strengthen the southwestern frontier and render the adjacent States strong enough to repel future invasions without remote aid. It will relieve the whole State of Mississippi and the western part of Alabama of Indian occupancy, and enable those States to advance rapidly in population, wealth, and power. It will separate the Indians from immediate contact with settlements of whites; free them from the power of the States; enable them to pursue happiness in their own way under their own rude institutions; will retard the progress of decay, which is lessening their numbers, and perhaps cause them gradually, under the protection of the Government and through the influence of good counsels, to cast off their savage habits and become an interesting, civilized, and Christian community. . . .

Humanity has often wept over the fate of the aborigines of this country, and Philanthropy has been long busily employed in devising means to avert it, but its progress has never for a moment been arrested, and one by one have many powerful tribes disappeared from the earth. To follow to the tomb the last of his race and to tread on the graves of extinct nations excites melancholy reflections. But true philanthropy reconciles the mind to these vicissitudes as it does to the

William Cooper was born a poor wheelwright, but by gaining possession of the 39,000-acre Otsego Patent in 1786, he became a rich man. In this portrait, painted by the leading American artist of the 1790s, Cooper presents his new identity as a gentleman. The document in his hand is a map of Cooperstown—the village on his estate that he named after himself.

extinction of one generation to make room for another. . . . Philanthropy could not wish to see this continent restored to the condition in which it was found by our forefathers. What good man would prefer a country covered with forests and ranged by a few thousand savages to our extensive Republic, studded with cities, towns, and prosperous farms, embellished with all the improvements which art can devise or industry execute, occupied by more than 12,000,000 happy people, and filled with all the blessings of liberty, civilization, and religion?

The present policy of the Government is but a continuation of the same progressive change by a milder process. The tribes which occupied the countries now constituting the Eastern States were annihilated or have melted away to make room for the whites. The waves of population and civilization are rolling to the westward, and we now propose to acquire the countries occupied by the red men of the South and West by a fair exchange, and, at the expense of the United States, to send them to a land where their existence may be prolonged and perhaps made perpetual. . . .

Indian removal was not voluntary. When the Cherokee National Council, the main body of its national government, refused to move, Jackson's representatives negotiated a treaty with a handful of dissident chiefs, despite the Cherokee constitution's clear language that only the National Council could sell or give away land. All but two thousand Cherokees rejected the treaty and refused to leave their homes. In 1838, the U.S. Army expelled fifteen thousand Cherokees from their homes and marched them to Oklahoma. Thus began the infamous Trail of Tears, in which four thousand Cherokees—a quarter of the nation—died. The letters of Evan Jones, a Baptist missionary among the Cherokees, describe how the army dispossessed them.

The Cherokees are nearly all prisoners. They have been dragged from their houses, and encamped in the forts and military posts all over the nation. In Georgia, especially, multitudes were allowed no time to take any thing with them, except the clothes they had on. Well-furnished houses were left a prey to plunderers, who, like hungry wolves, follow in the train of the captors. These wretches rifle the houses, and strip the helpless, unoffending owners of all they have on earth. Females, who have been habituated to comforts and comparative affluence, are driven on foot before the bayonets of brutal men. Their feelings are mortified by vulgar and profane vociferations. . . . The property of many has been taken, and sold before their eyes for almost nothing—the sellers and buyers, in many cases, being combined to cheat the poor Indians. . . . Many of the Cherokees, who, a

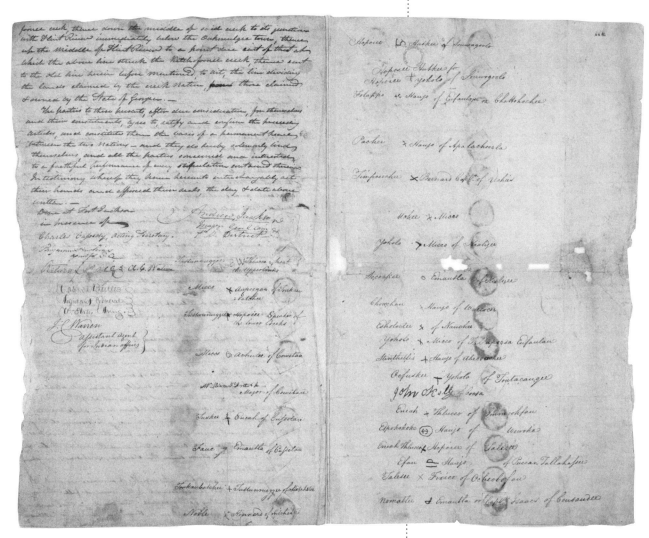

few days ago, were in comfortable circumstances, are now victims of abject poverty.

Squatters and the Federal Government

Once land was acquired from European powers and Indian nations, it still had to be distributed to settlers. In the Ordinance of 1785, the U.S. Continental Congress provided that half of federal lands would be sold in townships of six square miles and the other half auctioned off in sections of 640 acres each. This put federal lands out of the reach of ordinary settlers. Most federal lands, as well as most land sold by the states, were purchased by large-scale speculators who hoped to make profits by re-selling the land in smaller lots to settlers. Most settlers had neither the

In the Treaty of Fort Jackson, pictured here, the Creek nation ceded 14 million acres to the United States in 1815. Although most Creek villages had sided with the United States during the War of 1812, Andrew Jackson, the negotiator for the United States, treated the Creeks as a conquered enemy and demanded the land as payment for the costs of the war. Jackson and other negotiators won similar concessions throughout the trans-Allegheny West. While the American negotiators affixed their signatures to the document, Indian representatives added their marks, as most could not read—a fact that gave enormous advantages in negotiations to the Americans.

money nor the desire to pay what speculators charged, however. They got their land by squatting—settling on lands without buying them, paying rent, or asking the permission of the legal owner. In a letter to the United States secretary of state, Governor Arthur St. Clair of the Northwest Territory wrote of an encounter with squatters on federal lands near the lands of the Miami Indians.

What the Intentions of the Government, are with regard to the Sale of the Lands in this Country I am entirely ignorant, but it is my duty to inform you Sir, that in my opinion, if they are not disposed of soon, such numbers of People will take possession of them, as may not easily be removed should that be thought necessary—before I set out for the westward numbers of People from Kentucky had entered on the Lands of the U.S. to the westward of the Miami, and were making what are called improvements, I warned them to desist, without much effect, and it was all I could do, unless Actions had been brought against them as Trespassers which I had no Orders to do. The number however of these improvements had increased surprisingly before my return, so much so that, along the River, and a considerable distance inland is covered with Hutts, and I am told the Case is the same in the Country above, quite up to the Penn line.

Although they expected to pay for their land eventually, squatters opposed speculators' control of the land, believing that the soil should go to the people who tilled it. A petition from inhabitants of the Northwest Territory complained that federal law prevented them from buying government land, and asked Congress to change that law. Responding to petitions like these, in 1800 Congress reduced the minimum number of acres that a person could buy to 320 and allowed buyers to spread their payments out over four years. Later revisions lowered the minimum purchase to 80 acres.

Your petitioners claiming no landed property in the different parts of the United States from which they removed and unable to purchase land at the enormous prices it sold for in those parts with the little money they had earned by their honest Industry . . .

  Under these circumstances and prompted by a desire natural to the human mind of Obtaining barely a competency in life[,] they have left their friends and dearest connections [and] have taken their lives as in their hands and faced danger and all the hardships attendant on the first settlers of an uncultivated frontier forest. . . . Your Honourable body passed a law on the 18th day of May 1796 providing for the sale of the lands of the United States North West of the Ohio River— by this law we find a reserve is made of a certain part of those lands[;] another part is to be disposed of in tracts containing 5760 Acres and

Improvements

Improvements were the changes made on land by human labor: plots cleared of trees and ploughed, fences, buildings, orchards.

The Favored Few

The land system of the colonies and states (and, before 1800, of the federal government) was designed to create and maintain a landed gentry. Lands were usually granted in large parcels to favored individuals, who then sold or rented their lands to settlers. If things went well (and they usually did not), this system provided the proprietors with a generous living. Political pressure from settlers compelled Congress to lower the cost and the minimum parcel size of federal lands after 1800, making it more accessible to poor and middling migrants.

Competency

A competency was a modest prosperity founded on property ownership.

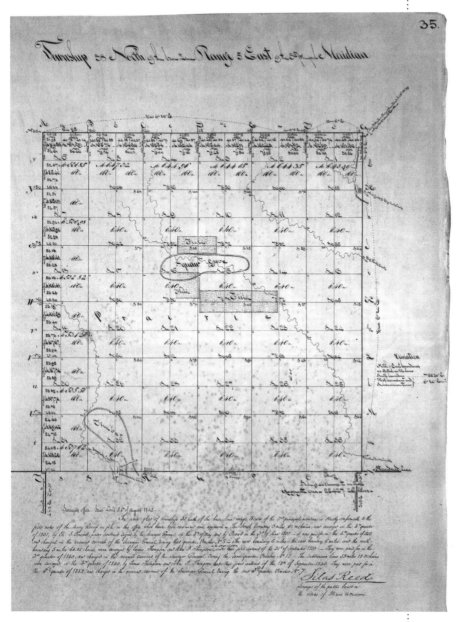

35.

The Federal Survey

The system for surveying and selling federal land created by the Ordinance of 1785 was a masterpiece of Enlightenment social and political planning. The public lands, eventually spanning most of the continent, were divided into a series of equal, square townships of six square miles, with every other township divided into thirty-six lots of 640 acres, each numbered exactly like the others. This division of the land was rational from the point of view of the administrators of the land system and distant buyers, as it made the land *legible* from a distance. A federal land agent in Washington, D.C., or an eastern speculator could easily buy, sell, and keep track of a lot or township. The system also had the advantage of precision: its measurements avoided the ambiguous boundaries and frequent disputes over them that plagued the eastern states. But from the point of view of a practical settler, the system could be deeply irrational, as the abstract, uniform division of the land ignored the realities of geography. The federal survey of Squaw Grove, Illinois, left some lots with no access to rivers or streams, while others were left underwater. Some lots had timber, which every farm needed, while others had little or none.

the remaining part in tracts of 640 acres. . . . On a consideration of this law we humbly conceive the smallest tracts too large for us to purchase . . . and we farther consider that one half the lands are to be disposed of in tracts containing 5760[.] [W]e consider ourselves in a truly deplorable situation and should an Indian War take place (which may God forbid) we leave your Honourable Body to Judge of our situation— Sixty miles from any settlement of consequence in the midst of an Indian Country and the most exposed part thereof—Disappointed in getting lands on easy and equitable terms in hopes of which we adventured <u>our lives</u> and the lives of <u>our families</u>.—. . .

Your petitioners therefore humbly hope and pray that your Honourable Body will . . . pass a law Authorizing the Surveyor General to lay of[f] a tract of land on the Sioto River Thirty miles square. . . . The one half into tracts . . . containing 160 acres and the other half into tracts of 640 acres. Your petitioners further Humbly pray that the said Tracts of land may be sold to none but those who will become actual settlers thereon or have them settled in a limited time which they may not exceed twelve months from the time of such purchase be made. . . . Your petitioners humbly beg leave to mention that was your Honourable Body to grant this their petition . . . the interest of their common country would be promoted and that in case an Indian war should take place they would be so strengthened as to be able to defend themselves and prevent the effusion of <u>Blood</u> of their wives children and friends.

Life in the Western Farm Settlements

Families moved to the frontier to gain what they called a "competence"—not great wealth, but a comfortable prosperity that rested on independent property. Most arrived at their new homes with little property, and the early years of settlement were an unrelenting struggle to create property through sheer hard work. Even for the more prosperous and better prepared settlers, this process was fraught with hardship and danger. Rebecca Burlend, an Englishwoman who moved with her husband and children to Illinois in 1831, was among the successful migrants, for her and her family's labor paid off, gaining them substantial property. In 1848, she published a book narrating her life on the frontier. After buying an eighty-acre farm with a two-room log house and twelve acres cleared of trees, the family set to work.

We had indeed a house . . . but we had no furniture except two large boxes, two beds, and a few pots and cooking utensils. . . . Our nearest neighbor lived about half-a-mile from us, and we were at least two miles and a-half from any place at which flour was sold; thither, however, my husband went, and as our money was growing scarce, he bought a bushel of ground Indian corn, which was only one-third the price of wheaten flour. . . . We had now some meal, but no yeast, nor an oven; we were therefore obliged to make sad paste, and bake in our frying pan in some hot ashes. . . .

Thus we lived for the first few weeks. . . . Hasty pudding, sad bread, and a little venison . . . were our ordinary food. . . .

Sad paste
Sad paste and sad bread were heavy, hard pancakes and bread made without yeast or other leavening. Hasty pudding was a gruel made by boiling grain meal in water or milk.

My husband . . . [made] for himself and me each a stool, and a low bench for our children, or more properly a log of wood, squared and laid across the hearth for a seat. He . . . also . . . [made] a table . . . having met with a section of the tree about two feet long, he rolled it into the house, and set it upon its end; . . . we . . . nailed a few boards upon it, making them fit as well as we could. . . .

We had not much intercourse with the rest of the world. For a while no one seemed to notice us, except Mr. B., our neighbor Mr. Paddock, and one Mr. Burns, who lived about two miles off. . . . One thing was very afflictive, our being deprived of Christian Sabbath ordinances. . . . At this time we were five miles from any place where public worship was regularly conducted. . . .

Am I then asked if we thus far were satisfied with the step we had taken, my answer is, we regretted it very much. We had indeed plenty of corn-bread and milk, but neither beer nor tea; coffee was our chief beverage, which we used very sparingly, for want of money. All the water we wanted we had to thaw, and during the nights, on account of the severe frosts, we were very cold indeed. . . . Our bed-clothes we had taken with us from England, and we were unable to procure any more, as they were dear, and our means almost exhausted. We had indeed some good land, but it was nearly all uncultivated, and we had nothing to sell except our cattle, which we wanted. Our only ground of hope was in our industry and perseverance. My husband worked very hard; the little time we had to spare, after feeding the cattle and procuring fuel, was spent in splitting trees to make rails. . . .

It was now the middle of March, when Indian corn, the most useful produce of that country, must be sown, or the season would be past. We had land and seed, but no plough, nor any team [of draft animals]. . . . What could we do? If we did not sow we could not reap; we should have nothing to feed our cattle with the ensuing winter. *Labor omnia vincit* ["Labor conquers all"] was our motto. We set to work with our hoes; I, husband, and son, the latter under ten years of age, and day after day, for three successive weeks, did we toil with unwearied diligence till we had sown and covered nearly four acres. . . .

As soon as we had sown our Indian corn, and planted a few potatoes, we began to prepare for taking in more land. . . . Accordingly my husband worked hard every day with his grubbing hoe and

The settler's cabin, the fence, the cleared land—everything in the 1808 drawing *First Cottage of Angelica* (a town in western New York)—was the property of the owner, created by applying labor to natural resources. Whether or not the family held title to the land, they could sell the property they created.

ATTENTION! ANTI-RENTERS!

AWAKE!   AROUSE!

A Meeting of the friends of Equal Rights will be held on *Second Tuesday - February at Ent Bane*

in the Town of *Bane* at / O'clock.

Let the opponents of Patroonry rally in their strength. A great crisis is approaching.   Now is the time to strike.   The minions of Patroonry are at work. No time is to be lost. Awake! Arouse! and

Strike 'till the last armed foe expires,
Strike for your altars and your fires—
Strike for the green graves of your sires,
God and your happy homes!

☞ The Meeting will be addressed by PETER FINKLE and other Speakers.

This mid-1840s broadside exhorts renters on one of the great estates of New York to fight for ownership of the land they occupy. In upstate New York, some 260,000 tenant farmers worked on a score of great estates. Beginning in 1839, tenants built the anti-rent movement, which aimed at destroying great estates and granting ownership of the land to the people who lived on them. At its peak, the movement claimed between twenty-five and sixty thousand supporters. Settlers' and farm tenants' movements for land were widespread between the Revolution and the Civil War.

axe, tearing up the roots of underwood and cutting down some of the largest trees. . . . Thus, by continued exertions, we had cleared three or four acres by the end of May, and made a fence half round the piece we intended to enclose as our next field, consisting of eight acres. . . .

Towards the end of June our three acres of wheat began to look ripe, and we consequently had to consider how we should reap it; we had no sickles, nor were any to be had under a dollar each; we therefore . . . resolved to go to our friend Mr. B., who lent us two, for which we were thankful enough, although they were poor ones. As we were returning home, my husband had the misfortune to stumble over a log of wood, and having a sickle in his hand, he pitched upon the edge of it with his knee, and cut it severely. . . . The following day it began to swell very much, and to be exceedingly painful at a distance from the cut. The pain took away his appetite for food, and symptoms of inflammation and fever became rapidly apparent. My situation requires no comment: . . . I was likely to lose my dearest earthly friend, and with him all visible means of supporting myself, or maintaining my family. I was almost driven to frenzy. Despair began to lay hold of me. . . . My eldest child alone manifested any signs of sympathy: the poor boy went up to his father's bed, and with affectionate and child-like simplicity said, "Don't die, father, don't die." . . . I fomented the swelling with increased diligence, till at length he began to perspire. . . . A change for the better had evidently taken place, and by degrees all the bad symptoms disappeared. . . .

Our wheat was quite ripe . . . and if not cut soon, would be lost. We had no means of hiring reapers, and my husband could not stir out. I was therefore obliged to begin myself; I took my eldest child into the field to assist me, and left the next in age to attend to their father and take care of the youngest, which was still unweaned.

I worked as hard as my strength would allow; the weather was intolerably hot, so that I was almost melted. In little more than a week, however, we had it all cut down. . . .

The produce of the three acres might be about eighty bushels, one fourth of which was . . . unsaleable. . . . Mr. Varley [the nearest merchant] offered half a dollar per bushel. . . . We borrowed a waggon and a yoke of oxen of one of our neighbors, and carried to the store fifty bushels. The first thing we did was to settle our meal account [the family had earlier bought a little cornmeal on credit]; we next bought two pairs of shoes for self and husband. . . . The truth is, we had intended to have a little more clothing, but finding the prices so extravagant, we felt compelled to abandon that intention. . . . Our next purchase was a plough, bought in hopes that we should, at some time, have cattle to draw it, as we were tired of the hoeing system. We also bought two tin milk bowls . . . a few pounds of coffee, and a little meal. . . . On balancing our account. . . , we found that we had to take about five dollars, which we received in paper money. . . .

The first Sunday in November was the anniversary of our landing in America. . . . The tattered appearance of our children's clothes, compared with what they had worn in England, made an impression on our minds. . . . We were again on the eve of a hard winter with less warm clothing to meet it, than we had the preceding winter. . . .

There was however one cheering consideration: in all respects except clothing, we were better situated than we had been the foregoing season. We had four acres more of wheat sown this year than the year before; we were now in possession of a plough; our cattle had likewise increased in value; the cow had calved again, and the former calf had grown a fine-looking heifer, we therefore saw, after all, we were gaining ground. . . .

I ought here to state that both I and husband had the ague very bad this month; happily not both at the same time. . . .

At the end of June [of our second year], we began to cut our wheat, retaining the old sickles which we had borrowed the year before. . . .

We may indeed date the commencement of a moderately comfortable existence from this occurrence. The wheat was very fine indeed. . . ; we had about two hundred and twenty bushels, forty of which were unsaleable. . . .

We purchased several articles of wearing with our wheat, paid off a small account . . . , and obtained gearing for a yoke of oxen, proposing to plough our land this fall with young oxen bought of

Ague
The ague was malaria or similar diseases marked by severe fever and chills.

Vanderoozen [Garret Van Dusen, a neighboring farmer and stock dealer], besides supplying our immediate wants in clothing, which we did only sparingly, we were enabled to leave in the hands of Mr. Varley, forty dollars, for which he agreed to pay us interest. . . .

Burlend ended her book with a description of her family's situation in 1848, seventeen years after they first arrived.

The house we at present occupy has recently been erected, and though in externals there is nothing to boast of, it is much superior to the one we occupied during former years. The situation is more airy and open. Our furniture is also more in accordance with modern times. . . . It is however not so much either in the house or its furniture that our success manifests itself; . . . there are after all few cottagers in England that would not be on an equality with us, with this exception, theirs are generally rented, while ours is our own freehold. . . .

We have known no lack of good food, such as beef, pork, butter, fowls, eggs, milk, flour, and fruits, all of which we have, as Yorkshire farmers say, within ourselves. . . . At this time we had at least twenty head of horned cattle, of which we kill or sell off some at every autumn; we have seven horses, . . . besides pigs, sheep, and poultry, the number of which I am not able to state as they keep continually breeding, and are never to be seen altogether. Our land, which is of excellent quality and very productive, . . . we have by purchases made at sundry times three hundred and sixty acres, more than half of which is cultivated.

Cottagers and Freehold

In England, cottagers were rural laborers, who rented cottages with a little land to farm for their food. A freehold was privately owned land.

A QUILTING PARTY IN WESTERN VIRGINIA.

This 1854 engraving of a quilting bee in western Virginia captures an important part of frontier life: collective work. Women work together to make one or more quilts while men, children, and other adult women visit, eat, and drink. Farmers and artisans frequently mixed work with visiting and playing. Farm men and women often worked with members of other families, either by hiring young people or by sharing work with other adults. Usually women worked separately from men, but on certain occasions women and men came together for work and conviviality.

Not wishing to manage the whole ourselves, we have two small farms let off, for which we receive as rent a dollar an acre. . . .

We have seen a neighborhood rise around us; and in some situations, where at our first coming, everything appeared in its native wildness, small villages have now begun to rise. . . . By the increase of population, we can now easily obtain anything we require, either as food, physic, or clothing, and were we disposed to give up labour, we could live very comfortably on the fruits of our former toil. . . . If our success has been ultimately greater than at one time we anticipated, or even than that of many of our neighbors, as indeed it has, it must be borne in mind that our industry and perseverance have been unremitting. . . .

Expanding Slavery

The dispossession of Indians made possible the expansion of slavery as well as of family farming. This expansion was fueled by a booming world demand for cotton and sugar, which sent prices upward and promised prosperity, even riches, for planters. Most of the growth in cotton production was in the West, where upwardly mobile men and the children of planters took advantage of cheap, fertile lands recently wrenched from Indian tribes. Where the move west promised profits to planters, it meant severe hardship to slaves. The English geographer George Featherstonhaugh traveled through the western territories during the early 1830s. In a book about his travels in the United States, he described an encounter, in 1834, with a party of slaves and slave drivers.

Just as we reached New River, in the early grey of the morning, we came up with . . . a camp of negro slave-drivers, just packing up to start; they had about three hundred slaves with them, who had bivouacked the preceding night *in chains* in the woods; these they were conducting to Natchez, upon the Mississippi River, to work upon the plantations in Louisiana. . . . They had a caravan of nine wagons and single-horse carriages, for the purpose of conducting the white people, and any of the blacks that should fall lame. . . . The female slaves were, some of them, sitting on logs of wood, whilst others were standing, and a great many little black children were warming themselves at the fires of the bivouac. In front of them all, and prepared for the march, stood, in double files, about two hundred male slaves, *manacled and chained to each other.* . . .

Some of the principal white slave-drivers, who were tolerably well dressed, and had broad-brimmed white hats on, *with black crepe around them,* were standing near, laughing and smoking cigars. . . .

Slave coffles were a frequent sight in the antebellum South, as masters and slave traders moved enslaved people from the eastern states, where plantation agriculture was in decline, to the new settlements of the trans-Allegheny Southwest, where cotton culture was booming.

It was an interesting, but a melancholy spectacle, to see them effect the passage of the river. . . . There was much method and vigilance observed, for this was one of the situations where the gangs—always watchful to obtain their liberty—often show a disposition to mutiny, knowing that if one or two of them could wrench their manacles off, they could soon free the rest, and either disperse themselves or overpower and slay their sordid keepers, and fly to the Free States. The slave-drivers, aware of this disposition in the unfortunate negroes, endeavour to mitigate their discontent by feeding them well on the march, and by encouraging them to sing "Old Virginia never tire," to the banjo. . . .

[I]n the Southern Slave-States all men have an interest in protecting this infernal trade of slave-driving, which, to the negro, is a greater curse than slavery itself, . . . too often tearing, without an instant's notice, the husband from the wife, and the children from the parents; sending the one to the sugar plantations of Louisiana, another to the cotton-lands of Arkansas, and the rest to Texas. . . .

This land traffic has grown out of the wide-spreading population of the United States, the annexation of Louisiana, and the increased cultivation of cotton and sugar. The fertile lowlands of that territory can only be worked by blacks, and are almost of illimitable extent. Hence negroes have risen greatly in price, from 500 to 1000 dollars. . . .

The soil of Virginia has gradually become exhausted with repeated crops of tobacco and Indian corn; and when to this is added the constant subdivision of property which has overtaken every family since the abolition of entails it follows of course that many of the small proprietors, in their efforts to keep up appearances, have become embarrassed in their circumstances, and, when they are pinched, are compelled to sell a negro or two. The wealthier proprietors also have frequently fractious and bad slaves, which, when they cannot be reclaimed, are either put into jail, or into those depots which exist in all the large towns for the reception of slaves who are sold, until they can be removed. All this is very well known to the slave-driver, one of whose associates goes annually to the Southwestern States, to make his contracts with those planters there who are in want of slaves for the next season. These fellows then scour the country to make purchases. Those who are bought out of jail are always put in fetters, as well as any of those whom they may suspect of an intention to escape. The women and grown-up girls are usually sold into the cotton-growing States, the men and the boys to the rice and sugar plantations. Persons with large capital are actively concerned in this trade, some of whom have amassed considerable fortunes. But occasionally these dealers in men are made to pay fearfully the penalty of their nefarious occupation. I was told only two or three months before I passed this way a "gang" had surprised their conductors when off their guard, and had killed some of them with axes.

Contrary to their popular image as a chivalrous aristocracy, those slave owners who moved west ran their farms and plantations on a capitalist basis, striving to reap profits from cash crops in order to expand their enterprises. In a published account of his travels through the southern states in the early 1830s, the Irish actor Tyrone Power commented on the motivations and mind-sets of migrating masters.

These engravings from Timothy Flint's 1833 biography of Daniel Boone present Boone as a violent, self-sufficient man, simultaneously at home in and doing battle with a hostile environment. Frontier life played a central role in American mythology and national identity during the early nineteenth century, as Americans immortalized the aggressive, adventurous, and naturalistic masculinity of characters like Boone and Davy Crockett. Though these men were real, novelists, biographers, and playwrights created mythical adventures for them, winning wide audiences for their exploits.

Canebrake

A canebrake was a dense growth of the wild giant cane that was common in the southern United States.

The great cause of emigration from the Atlantic States is to be looked for in the temptation offered the planter by a soil of vastly superior fertility. In South Carolina and in most parts of Georgia, it will appear that a good average crop will give one bale or bag of cotton, weighing 310 lbs. for each working-hand employed on the plantation; now, in Alabama, four or five bales, each weighing 430 lbs. is a fair average for an able-bodied slave engaged in the cultivation. . . . We generally associate with the Southern planter ideas of indolence, inertness of disposition, and a love of luxury and idle expense: nothing, however can be less characteristic of these frontier tamers of the swamp and of the forest: they are hardy, indefatigable, and enterprising to a degree; despising and contemning luxury and refinement, courting labour, and even making a pride of the privations which they, without any necessity, continue to endure with their families. . . . They live in humble dwellings of wood, wear the coarsest habits, and live on the plainest fare. It is their pride to have planted an additional acre of canebrake, to have won a few feet from the river, or cleared a thousand trees from the forest; [or] to have added a couple of slaves to their family. . . .

Beyond the Mississippi

With the exception of Iowa, settlement under the American flag stopped at the Mississippi until 1840, but Americans ventured beyond that boundary. When they did so, they entered into areas controlled by other nations: the Spanish, the Mexicans, the Russians, and, above all, Native Americans. One group that penetrated into the western expanses of the continent was the Corps of Discovery led by Meriwether Lewis and William Clark. The corps' mission was to explore the interior of the North American continent, mapping its geography and describing its flora, fauna, and human societies; to find a water route from St. Louis to the Pacific Ocean; and to assert American hegemony over the western parts of the continent, which was challenged by the presence of the Spanish, English, Russians, and French. Establishing American hegemony was an impossible task for the small corps, which was ignorant of geography and local politics and diplomacy and dependent on the people they encountered for food, horses, and information. The supply of trade goods Lewis and Clark brought with them helped create friendly relations with local peoples, but hardly ensured native acceptance of American dominion. Lewis describes an early interaction with the Shoshoni Indians in his journal for August 17, 1805.

[A]bout 4 P.M. we called them together and through the medium of Labuish, Charbono, and Sah-cah-gar-weah, we communicated to them fully the objects which had brought us into this distant part of the country, in which we took care to make them a conspicuous object of our own good wishes and the care of our government. We made them sensible of their dependence on the will of our government for every species of merchandize as well for their defense & comfort; and apprized them of the strength of our government and it's friendly dispositions towards them. We also gave them as a reason why we wished to penetrate the country as far as the ocean to the west of them was to . . . find out a more direct way to bring merchandize to them. That as no trade could be carried on with them before our return to our homes that it was mutually advantageous to them as well as to ourselves that they should render us such aids as they had it in their power to furnish . . . that such were their horses to transport our baggage without which we could not subsist, and that a pilot to conduct us through the mountains was also necessary if we could not descend the river by water. But that we did not ask either their horses or their services without giving a satisfactory compensation in return. . . . They appeared well pleased with what had been said. The chief thanked us for friendship towards himself and nation & declared his wish to serve us in every rispect. That he was sorry to find that it must yet be some time before they could be furnished with firearms but said they could live as they had done heretofore untill we brought them as we had promised. . . . [W]e next enquired who were the chiefs among them. Cameahwait

Lyed corn

Lyed corn was hominy—field corn soaked in lye in order to remove the hulls.

pointed out two others whom he said were Chiefs. We gave him a medal of the small size with the likeness of Mr. Jefferson the President of the U' States in relief on one side and clasp hands with a pipe and tomahawk on the other, to the other Chiefs we gave each a small medal which were struck in the Presidency of George Washing Esqr we also gave small medals of the last discription to two young men whom the 1st Chief informed us wer good young men and much rispected among them. We gave the 1st Chief an uniform coat shirt a pair of scarlet legings a carrot of tobacco and some small articles, to each of the others we gave a shi[r]t legging[s] handkerchief a knife some tobacco and a few small articles. [W]e also distributed a good quantity paint mockerson [moccasins] awles knives beads looking-glasses &c among the other Indians and gave them a plentifull meal of lyed corn which was the first they had ever eaten in their lives. They were much pleased with it. Every article about us appeared to excite astonishment in ther minds; the appearance of the men, their arms, the canoes, our manner of working them, the b[l]ack man york and the sagacity of my dog were equally objects of admiration. . . . [O]ur hunters killed 4 deer and an Antelope this evening of which we also gave the Indians a good proportion. The cerimony of our council and smoking the pipe was in conformity of the custom of this nation perfo[r]med bearfoot. On those occasions points of etiquet are quite as much attended to by the Indians as among scivilized nations.

During the 1820s and 1830s, some Americans chose to leave the United States for the department of Texas in the Mexican state of Coahuila y Tejas. The Spanish and Mexican governments were unable to subdue the Comanche Indians in that region and sought to encourage immigration as a way to consolidate their control over it. They did so through the empresario system, in which the government granted large tracts of land to men who arranged for large groups of immigrants to settle. The system worked well; by 1834, thirty thousand people from the United States lived in Texas, compared to eight thousand Mexican-born citizens. In this 1825 contract, the Mexican government authorized Stephen F. Austin, who already had established a settlement in Texas, to settle another five hundred immigrant families in his colony.

Art. 1. The Govt. admits the proposition presented by citizen Stephen F. Austin . . . relative to the Colonization of three hundred foreign families, so far as may be conformable with the colonization law, passed by the honorable legislature of this State. . . .

Art. 3. In conformity with the said colonization law . . . the empresario citizen Stephen F. Austin, shall introduce the three hundred families which he proposes, within the term of six years, counting from the day on which the said empresario signs this contract, under the penalty of losing the rights and privileges granted to him by the 8th Article of said Law.

Art. 4. The families which are to compose this colony, besides being industrious as offered in the representation, must also be catholics, and of good moral habits. . . .

Art. 5. It shall be an obligation upon him, not to admit criminals, vagabonds, or men of bad conduct, and he shall cause all those of this description, who are found within his limits to leave it, and should it be necessary, he shall put them out by force of arms.

Art. 6. For this purpose, the colonists shall be formed into a body of national militia, of which he shall be the chief, until otherwise directed.

Art. 7. As soon as he shall have introduced at least one hundred families, he shall notify the government thereof, in order that a commissioner may be sent on with competent instructions, to put the new colonists in possession of their lands, and to establish the new towns agreeably to law.

Art. 8. The official communications with the government, and with the authorities of the state, instruments, and other public acts, must be written in the Spanish language, and when the new towns are formed he shall promote the establishment of schools in the Spanish language, in such towns.

Art. 9. It shall be his duty to promote the building of churches in said towns, and the providing of them with ornaments, sacred vases, and other furniture, destined for divine worship, and to solicit in due time, the necessary number of priests, for the administration of spiritual affairs.

In addition to the conditions outlined in the contract, all immigrants were required to take an oath of loyalty—before 1821 to the king of Spain, afterwards to the Republic of Mexico. But the northern settlers' obedience was questionable from the start. They rarely converted to Catholicism, which was required by their contract and by law. Slavery was illegal, but many migrants brought slaves with them and practiced slave-based agriculture. In 1830, the Mexican government prohibited further immigration to Texas from the United States, raised tariffs on American-made goods, repealed a ten-year exemption for immigrants from Mexican taxes, and insisted that farmers stop raising cotton in favor of grain and beef. It directed the northerners to obey Mexico's abolition of slavery, threatening military intervention if they failed to do so. Texans ignored the new laws. In 1834, President Antonio Lopez de Santa Ana dissolved the state legislature and disbanded the militia. He did the same to other states, where he faced a similar level of resistance to federal authority, and he abrogated the federal constitution of 1824. Texans resisted Santa Ana's centralization of power, and on March 2, 1836, a convention of delegates from several towns declared Texas's independence. In their declaration, the delegates sought to justify their act of separation. Texans quickly won their independence of Mexico, and the Republic of Texas was annexed to the United States in 1845. In this way, American territorial growth—and the extension of slavery—extended beyond the Louisiana Territory, opening a new phase in American expansion.

The Mexican government . . . invited and induced the Anglo-American population of Texas to colonize its wilderness under the pledged faith of a written constitution, that they should continue to enjoy that constitutional liberty and republican government to which they had been habituated in the land of their birth. . . .

In this expectation they have been cruelly disappointed, inasmuch as the Mexican nation has acquiesced in the late changes made in the government by General Antonio Lopez de Santa Anna, who having overturned the constitution of his country, now offers us the cruel alternative, either to abandon our homes, acquired by so many privations, or submit to the most intolerable of all tyranny, the combined despotism of the sword and the priesthood.

It has sacrificed our welfare to the state of Coahuila, by which our interests have been continually depressed through a jealous and partial course of legislation, carried on at a far distant seat of government, by a hostile majority, in an unknown tongue, and this too, notwithstanding we have petitioned in the humblest terms for the establishment of a separate state government. . . .

It incarcerated in a dungeon, for a long time, one of our citizens, for no other cause but a zealous endeavor to procure the acceptance of our constitution, and the establishment of a state government. . . .

It has suffered the military commandants, stationed among us, to exercise arbitrary acts of oppression and tyranny. . . .

It has dissolved, by force of arms, the state Congress of Coahuila and Texas, and obliged our representatives to fly for their lives from the seat of government, thus depriving us of the fundamental political right of representation. . . .

It denies us the right of worshipping the Almighty according to the dictates of our own conscience, by the support of a national religion, calculated to promote the temporal interest of its human functionaries, rather than the glory of the true and living God.

It has demanded us to deliver up our arms, which are essential to our defence, the rightful property of freemen, and formidable only to tyrannical governments. . . .

We, therefore, the delegates with plenary powers of the people of Texas, in solemn convention assembled, appealing to a candid world for the necessities of our condition, do hereby resolve and declare, that our political connection with the Mexican nation has forever ended, and that the people of Texas do now constitute a free, Sovereign, and independent republic. . . .

CHAPTER 4

The Transformation of the North

In *Yankee Peddler*, painted in 1852, a traveling peddler displays a coffee grinder to a farm woman while two younger women (presumably her daughters) examine a premade garment. The peddler's cart is filled with a clock, farm implements, and other goods. Such goods had been familiar to North Americans since before the Revolution, but they became increasingly available during the early nineteenth century, as English and American factories and workshops churned out goods for an ever-growing consumer market. The most numerous consumers were farmers, whose growing commercial production provided them with more money, part of which they spent on new goods.

To Harriet Hanson, factory work looked pretty good. Her father died in 1831, when she was seven, leaving her family in poverty. Soon afterward, the family moved to the factory town of Lowell, Massachusetts, where her aunt ran a boardinghouse. When Harriet reached the age of ten, she went to work in the textile mills, where she spent her days removing bobbins from spinning machines. "How proud I was," she wrote later, "when my turn came to stand up on the bobbin-box and write my name in the paymaster's book." Her family needed the money she earned, even with her brothers working and her mother helping run the boarding house. Earning cash gave Harriet a new sense of herself, allowing her to feel like an independent person and a contributor to her family's well-being.

Harriet hated the long hours she had to work in the factory. Labor began at five in the morning and ended at seven in the evening. In her autobiography, Harriet wrote that "it has taken nearly a lifetime for me to make up the sleep lost at that early age." But in other respects, she found the life of a factory worker a pleasant one. By combining her earnings with those of her brothers and her mother, the family lived comfortably. She found factory work easy to manage. And she loved the companionship of her fellow workers. "We had very happy hours with the older girls, many of whom treated us like babies, or talked in a motherly way. . . . And in the long winter evenings, we . . . gathered in groups and told each other stories, and sung the old-time songs our mothers had sung."

The master shoemaker faces forward in his Lynn, Massachusetts, shop. The scale of production in the late eighteenth and early nineteenth century was small: a few men (and often the master's wife or a boy or two) made custom shoes for particular customers, using hand tools. The notice of a town meeting on the wall makes clear that this workshop was part of a broader political community. The balding (and presumably older) journeyman indicates that, because of declining opportunity or other reasons, not all journeymen became masters.

Harriet was one of thousands of Americans who moved to the industrial towns of the Northeast in the early nineteenth century. Between 1815 and 1850, the economy of the northeastern United States underwent a revolution. Governments and corporations built hundreds of thousands of miles of roads, canals, and railroads, making it possible for goods and people to move cheaply over long distances. Farmers began producing more and more goods for distant markets. And manufacturing exploded as factories sprang up alongside the region's streams and rivers and as craft production expanded. In some ways, Harriet Hanson's experience typified the ways in which these changes transformed people's lives. Like many northeasterners, she entered industrial work out of economic necessity. For her as for others, doing so required leaving home. Like many others, she entered the industrial economy by taking on a status that had been relatively unusual before 1800—that of a wage earner.

In many ways, however, there was no typical experience of the Industrial Revolution. Everyone's way of working, living, and thinking changed, but **how** they changed depended on one's gender, age, race, marital status, and the conditions in one's industry. New England farm girls like Harriet had enjoyed few opportunities for earning money and had known little personal autonomy, and in the early years at Lowell they were paid and treated reasonably well. Many but not all of them saw industrial work as a kind of liberation. A majority of workers, male and female, saw industrial wage labor as a form of slavery. Members of a growing class of manufacturers, merchants, and professionals felt the impact of industrialization in yet another way. These different experiences of the new industrial economy led to new solidarities and new kinds of social conflict. Many workers came to see themselves as having different interests from their employers and began to join together in trade unions, working-class parties, and other organizations to fight for an end to "wage slavery." Whatever their specific experience of industrialization, all who took part in it developed new ways of working, living, and seeing themselves and the world around them.

Before the Industrial Revolution

In its early years, the United States was a nation of farmers. Seventy-two percent of Americans farmed for a living in 1820, a proportion that declined to sixty-four percent by 1850. American farmers were the envy of rural people throughout the world, for the majority of families owned the land they farmed and were free from a landlord's domination. Rural producers worked hard, but they controlled when and how they worked. More precisely, adult farmers decided when and how to do the work; children were expected to obey. Wage laborers and specialized craftsmen were scarce, so rural people relied on the work of family members for most of their labor needs. The result was extremely hard but varied and independent work. Husbandmen sought to produce goods for the market, but most sold only a small portion of their produce—about 20 percent of it. The rest they consumed at home. The diary of William Coventry, a farmer in Claverack, New York, offers a sense of the economic activities of a farmer in a long-settled area in the East.

> Thursday January the 4. . . . I was making Board fence at the Barn all day. . . .
>
> Tuesday January the 9. . . . I was cutting fire wood all day. . . .
>
> Friday January the 12. . . . I was to thrashing and Cleaning wheat all day. . . .
>
> Monday January the 15. . . . I was making shoes all day. . . .
>
> Tuesday Feby the 20. . . . I took a load of hay to Hudson. Sold hay at 4/ per hundred. . . .

Old mrs. Hansman Killing a Hog and a beef for me. Dr. John Rouse in 1802 her general practice

In 1786, William Coventry, a farmer in Columbia County, New York, wrote in his diary about his hopes for his children. His wishes reveal a number of attitudes and beliefs that he shared with other preindustrial farmers: a defense of his power as the patriarch of his family, an emphasis on hard work and frugality, and a combination of family cooperation and individual self-reliance.

My desire is this if I should die before my children . . . that whatever I leave to each of them be the same more or less. If when I come to die . . . [I] leave ten times as much to one of my children as all the rest. . . , that the rest Must Not Grumble or be discontented for it is My Will it Should be So. Not but I would have them agree & help one another in everything they can. . . . I would have every one of them Do for themselves & Not for to Depend on any of the others for a living. . . . I hope that None of them After they Get Married will keep more of a family than What's Needful, for Keeping more Cats than what does Catch Mice ruins many a family. My father has been ruined by Keeping a Lazy Idle Crew about him. . . . I wish if any of my Children ever happens to be farmers that they never Will hire a man or woman for more than one Month at a time and never hire done what they can do themselves. . . .

The lady of the house butchers a hog while her sons prepare to carry away the meat. For the Hansmans, a German American family in Pennsylvania, farm work was a family enterprise. Although all farmers distinguished between men's and women's work, what was defined as men's work and women's work varied from place to place and ethnic group to ethnic group. Most Yankee and Scotch-Irish farmers would have defined butchering as a man's work.

Ride dung

To "ride dung" was to carry manure from farm animals out into one's fields in order to fertilize them.

Peeling bark

Peeling bark was peeling bark from hemlock trees, which was needed by tanners (leather manufacturers) for the tannin it contained.

Shoe a sleigh

To shoe a sleigh was to shape and attach the metal runners on it.

Raising

A "raising" was an event in which neighbors worked together to erect a building.

Wednesday March the 7. . . . I was Cutting saw Logs all day. . . .

Wednesday March the 14. . . . I was riding saw Logs to Alsops Mill all day. . . .

Wednesday March the 21. . . . I was laying fence in the morning. Working in the barn all the rest of the day. . . .

Saturday March the 24. . . . I was pruning apple trees in the forenoon. . . .

Wednesday March the 28. . . . I was riding dung all day.

Saturday March the 31. . . . I was at the blacksmith shop all day.

Saturday April the 14. . . . I was shooting pigeons in the forenoon. Shot eighteen at one shot. Planting cherry trees in the after[noon]. . . .

Friday April the 27. . . . I was ploughing all day.

Friday May the 4 . . . I was after shad the Chief of the day. . . . Got fifty shad.

Saturday May the 5. . . . I was planting potatoes the Chief of the day.

Thursday May the 10. . . . I was peeling bark all Day. . . .

Tuesday May the 22 . . . I was planting corn all day. . . .

Saturday June the 16 . . . I was hoeing potatoes all day. . . .

Monday June the 18 . . . I was hoeing corn all day . . .

Wednesday June the 20 . . . I was making a plough all day. . . .

Saturday June the 30. . . . I was shoeing a sleigh all day. . . .

Monday July the 2d . . . I was ploughing corn in the forenoon. To the raising of Mr. Peter Van Rensselaer's sawmill in the after.

Thursday July the 12. . . . I was raking hay all day. . . .

Friday July the 13. . . . I was riding hay all day. . . .

Wednesday August the 8. . . . I was looking timber for ladders for a wagon all day. . . .

Thursday August the 9. . . . I was hewing timber all day. . . .

Saturday August the 11. . . . I was making Ladders for a wagon all day. . . .

Friday October the 26 . . . I was in Hudson buying rye the Chief of the day. . . .

Wednesday November the 31 . . . I was sowing rye all day. . . .

Tuesday November the 13. . . . I was to Hudson with hay all day. . . . Hay sold at 4 per hun[dred]

Saturday November the 17. . . . To Hudson in the after[noon] with swine [to sell].

Friday November the 23. . . . I was working at a hog pen all
day. . . .

Saturday December the 8. . . . I was making a horses neck yoke
all day. . . .

Monday December the 10. . . . I was working at harness all
day. . . .

Like rural men, farm women before the Industrial Revolution were jills-of-all-trades, combining a wide variety of activities to meet their families' material needs. Although they were subject to their husbands' authority, wives usually enjoyed autonomy in their work lives, deciding when and how to do their work, commanding the labor of daughters, and trading on their own account. Although all farmers were dependent on the help of neighbors, women were even more enmeshed in collective labor than men. The diary of Martha Ballard, a farm woman, midwife, and medical practitioner on the northeastern coast of Maine during the late eighteenth century, reveals the contours of women's work and exchange in the preindustrial countryside. Ballard did not mention the tasks that occupied most of farm women's time: cooking and cleaning. Part of the reason was that her grown daughters performed many of those tasks. Most likely, however, Ballard did much of that work herself but found it so unremarkable that she did not mention it.

August

1   . . . mr Ballard Doing Business at the hook. My Girls washt
foren [forenoon] & went to Quillt for mrs Pollard. . . .

2   *Birth Black hitties son.* . . . I put my Patient to Bed with a
Son at 1, morn & returnd home about Sunries; took a nap.
Mrs Livermr Sent for me to help her Dress a blister on
Patty's neck. Mrs Benjamin here to have a goun [gown]
made. Mrs Porter, Pitts & Dagt Pollard here. . . .

5   . . . mr Ballard went aftern[oon] to Do Surveying for mr
Vauhn. I went as far as mr Sheperds, Bot [bought] 2 lb
sugar @ /10, 1 Chip hat @ /9. . . .

7   . . . I pulld flax. mr Ballard & Ephm [her son Ephraim]
went to the meddow, Dolly weaving, Sally washd. Dolly
Conductd Patty part of the way home.

8   . . . I have been So unwell that I have kept my bed the most
of the Day. Cyrus working for mr Capin, the Girls weaving. . . .

14   . . . *gatherd ripe Beans.*

15   . . . I have been at home, was Doing a little in my gardin,
gatherd Parsnip Seed.

This wooden statue depicts one of preindustrial farm women's biggest jobs—spinning and weaving. The task often kept mothers and daughters up into the early morning hours. Their work was part of an effort by most families to preserve resources by providing for as many of their own material needs as possible through their own labor and exchange with neighbors. Farm women spun yarn out of wool or flax, weaved the yarn into cloth, and sewed the cloth into clothing. In the 1810s and 1820s, women also weaved cloth for merchants, who gave them cash or store credit in exchange—an early stage of industrialization in the industry.

16   . . . at home pulling flax.
23   . . . I helpt gather beans. mrs Pitts here, Dolly went home with her. Sally wove 4 yds [yards].
29   . . . Dolly went to her Brors [brother's], his oldest Son is very unwell. I have been at home, gatherd ripe Beet Seeds & one Cucumbr.

Economic Innovators

In earlier eras, middling people like William Coventry and Martha Ballard tended to be conservative in their economic decisions. They sought a moderate prosperity and generally pursued it in a time-honored fashion. But something changed in the early nineteenth century. In the East, a growing population and a resulting land shortage forced both landowners and the landless to seek out new ways of making money. Governments sought to promote economic growth by chartering banks and other corporations, enacting a protective tariff, and building roads and canals. These policies helped expand the supply of money and credit, encouraged entrepreneurs to engage in new and risky enterprises, and allowed goods and people to travel long distances cheaply. Some men and women seized on these opportunities, seeking out new kinds of economic activities and changing the face of farming, manufacturing, and trade.

One of these innovators was George Holcolm, who cultivated a 154-acre farm in Stephentown, New York. Holcolm's farm diary for 1840 reveals how much northeastern farming had changed since the days of William Coventry. In his use of wage labor and tenants, his production for market, and his rich and varied consumption, Holcolm typified the new practices of many prosperous northeastern farmers.

Jan. 8 . . . I went on to Troy and delivered the two hundred pounds of cheese to Bigelow Pierce and Nicks and took up my note. I then let them have fourty one pounds more of cheese at nine cts per pound and paid them one dol and fifty six cts in cash and took a round copper boiler that holds three pails of water, price three dol 25 cts and a tin baker or roaster, price two dol and I paid forty four cts a pair of brass snuffers and tray and I paid 28 cts for one ½ yard green ribbon. . . .

Jan. 9. . . This morning sold a cheese to the tavern keeper at nine cts, twenty three pounds . . . and I sold a late made cheese at six cts per thirty five pounds and on the way yesterday at the stage tavern at Sand Lake I sold a cheese that I had cut at nine cts, it came

Note
A "note" was an IOU; Holcolm was paying off a debt.

New means of transportation revolutionized the northern economy and society during the early nineteenth century. The most dramatic and successful new transportation route was the Erie Canal, which, when completed in 1825, joined Lake Erie to the Hudson River (and, via the Hudson, to the Atlantic Ocean). Canals, steamboats, and improved roads made the transportation of people and goods faster, easier, and cheaper. Where cheap transportation was available, farmers increased their production for distant markets, which fed a growing manufacturing and commercial workforce and bought increasing amounts of the goods that that workforce made and traded.

to two do[llars] and 94 cts and I paid one dol and fifty cts for twelve china plates . . . I bought two pounds old hyson tea two dollars and two ¼ pounds raisons eighteen cts . . . and I bought one yard and a quarter of silk velvet and paid three dollars. . . .

Feb. 10 Monday I tended to my chores and tended to Platt Wylies chores, I tended foddering his cattle for he is taken sick with the quinsy in his throat.

March 4 Wednesday I chopped and drew wood from the hill and Mr. Marells chopped for me towards his rent and today said Marrels bargained with me for the house and garden up to the road for one year from the first of April and agrees to pay me twelve dol if he has a cow, I do agree to pasture her on my Rodgers farm at 12 ½ cts per week. . . .

March 5 Thursday . . . I got my french bedstead to Alonzo Rodgers that he had made for me and he charged two dol for making. . . .

March 10 Tuesday this forenoon I chopped wood and made rods in my swamp, I this morning reckoned with James Chapman and found he owed me five days work on the rent. . . .

March 11 Wednesday today James Chapman drew logs and wood from my swamp towards his rent and Mr. Marrels chopped wood for me in said swamp towards his rent. . . .

April 18 Saturday I went to Pittsfield with my two horse team and my son Geo P went with me, I carried about fifteen dollars worth of cheese what I sold for cash I sold at eight cts per. . . . I sold half a barrel of apple sauce at 40 cts per gallon and two bushel and a peck of apples at one dollar per bushel and four cabbages at 25 cts and about twenty cts worth of walnuts. . . .

April 20 . . . today my boys plowed corn hills

April 23 Thursday . . . I took my two horse pleasure wagon and carried my two daughters to Elem Tildens Store and they traded as follows: 17 ½ yds calico at ¼ and 12 yds calico at nine

Quinsy
Quinsy was a sore, inflamed throat.

"Churning," an 1819 engraving from *The Progress of the Dairy: Descriptive of the Making of Butter and Cheese for the Information of Youth*, depicts women using two different methods for churning butter. A large proportion of commercial farm production in the Northeast consisted of butter and cheese—commodities produced by women from start to finish.

pence per 4 sk ⅛ footing 25 cts and 1 ½ yd calico 14 cts . . . and I had 84 ¾ pounds cheese credited at nine cts per. . . .

April 28 Tuesday today we worked on my Rodgers farm, my boys plowed and beat manure on the meadow and I mended fence. . . .

April 30 Thursday this morning Mr. Aaron Marrels butchered the second veal calf . . . and he took a piece of the veal to pay him and I took my single wagon and carried the veal to Lebanon and sold it at three cts and 3 ½ cts per pound.

May 8 Monday we drew manure and . . . planted corn and this afternoon I took my two horse wagon and drew twelve bushels of potatoes on my Rodgers farm for Elder Grant to plant to the halves, he finds half the seed and does all the work after I plow and harrow the ground and return me half the potatoes in my barn. . . .

May 30 Saturday . . . my daughters and their friend . . . bought them silk hats and a band box, I paid twelve dollars and 12 ½ yards mull for dresses and I paid six dol and two scarfs, one dol and six cts and other small articles such as laces to the amount of four dol and seven cts. . . .

June 10 Wednesday we hoed corn and finished weeding corn, today Asa Sheldon came and sheared my sheep and his boy Stephen helped him. . . .

June 13 Saturday I took my team and carried a load of potatoes of twenty one bushels over to the railroad . . . and sold them . . . I got seven dollars. . . .

August 5 Wednesday we hayed and today Asa Sheldon cradled . . . my oats that he had taken by the job and I paid him in potatoes. . . .

September 16 Wednesday we tended to chores and divided my flock of sheep, I drove 18 sheep on to my Rodgers farm for sale. . . . We went to Elder Grants and fetched his daughter home with us to spin for us. . . .

September 26 Saturday today I went to Pittsfield, I carried three barrels of cider and sold at two dol and fifty cents per barrel and five bushels of apples at fifty cents. . . .

September 27 Sunday . . . this evening I rode over to Elder Grants and fetched his daughter Lorenzy to work for us.

Manufacturers embraced innovation and entrepreneurship as enthusiastically as farmers. A capsule biography of William T. Merrifield, a building contractor and manufacturer in Worcester, Massachusetts, describes how he rose from a middling farm family to great wealth, changed the

To the halves

Doing something "to the halves" or "on shares" was to perform hired labor for a share of the crop.

Mull

Mull was a thin, soft muslin cloth.

Cradle

To cradle was to harvest grain with a cradle, a scythe with long blades attached that allowed the harvester to cut large amounts of grain with each sweep of the arm.

Men of the new middle class subscribed to a well-defined set of ethics. When Joseph Denny, who would later become an industrialist in Leicester, Massachusetts, was in his teens, he resolved never to take up alcohol, gambling, or swearing. According to an autobiographical sketch published in the late nineteenth century, he gave up boyhood games and amusements so that he might spend his evenings in "useful reading." And he set out principles of business ethics that would guide his life as an entrepreneur.

Resolved, That if frugality and application to business will ensure me a competency of wealth, I will never be poor. That, while I have my health, I will never spend faster than I earn, and on the contrary, while I have a sufficiency, I will never deny myself the conveniences of life for the purpose of hoarding up treasure. That, while I am prospered in business, I will never refuse charity, where I think it my duty to extend it. And should I ever accumulate property, may I have the satisfaction of reflecting that it was not obtained by oppressing the poor, unfair dealing or any other dishonorable means, and may a bountiful Providence prosper my undertakings.

process of lumber sawing and building, and helped transform the economy of his hometown. The biography is from a post–Civil War county history. Such biographies were written and paid for by either the person memorialized or his or her family.

William Trowbridge Merrifield . . . was born at Worcester, April 10, 1807. . . . He worked on his father's farm until the age of fifteen. . . . At the age of fifteen he began a six years' service as an apprentice in the carpenter trade. At the age of eighteen he was entrusted with the erection of several buildings, and soon after attaining his majority he erected a block of houses, a store and a mill. In 1830 he began his career as a builder, and soon became a prominent and leading contractor of that day. In 1832 he also included a general lumber business. In 1840, Mr. Merrifield put in operation one of the first, if not the first, steam-engines in Worcester, and added the manufacture of sash, doors, blinds and builders' finish, introducing into Worcester the first power planer. Two years later he erected at Princeton a steam saw-mill, and, so far as is known, this was the first engine set up in the woods for the manufacture of lumber. In 1848, Mr. Merrifield realized the advantages in making Worcester a leading mechanical centre, and with a large investment laid the corner-stone of her material growth and industrial progress. In those experimental days of industrial transition, the inventors and mechanics needed power and rooms, that they might perfect their various specialties. Mr. Merrifield furnished these at an all important era in the history of Worcester; he erected a series of buildings, exceeding one thousand two hundred feet in length, forty feet in width and four stories high, with over one and a half miles of main shafting, turned by a steam-engine of five hundred horse-power, and suitably dividing the buildings to meet the mechanical needs of Worcester at that day, and rented the same to fifty individuals and firms, many of whom now have world-wide reputations. New industries were immediately developed in these buildings, and Worcester, mechanically, was greatly expanded. From this point of beginning dates the energizing impetus which gave her the possibilities that made her what she is.

Religious Innovators

Americans engaged in a second kind of experimentation between the 1790s and the 1840s: in religion. During these decades, hundreds of thousands of unbelieving Americans became sincere Christians for the first time, and millions more exchanged a lukewarm Christianity for a fervent evangelicalism. The growth in religious commitment was partly the result of new, systematic methods of winning souls. Ministers downplayed teaching doctrine, appealing instead to their listeners' emotions. They created a high drama of salvation and damnation to heighten their emotional impact and made sophisticated use of community organizing, peer pressure, and the press to bring about the conversion of the ungodly. Nothing combined these methods more effectively than revivals—gigantic efforts to win large numbers of new converts. In a book documenting her travels in the United States during the early 1830s, Frances Trollope, an English visitor, described a revival she witnessed in Cincinnati.

We had not been many months in Cincinnati when our curiosity was excited by hearing "the revival" talked of by every one we met throughout the town. . . . The most enthusiastic of the clergy travel the country, and enter the cities and towns by scores, or by hundreds . . . and for a week or fortnight, or if the population be large, for a month; they preach and pray all day, and often for a considerable portion of the night, in the various churches and chapels of the place. This is called a Revival. . . .

These itinerant clergymen are of all persuasions, I believe, except the Episcopalian, Catholic, Unitarians, and Quaker . . . These itinerants are . . . lodged in the houses of their respective followers, and every evening that is not spent in the churches and meeting-houses, is devoted to what would be called parties by others, but which they designate as prayer-meetings. . . .

The guests . . . are called brothers and sisters, and the greetings are very affectionate. When the room is full, the company, of whom a vast majority are always women, are invited, intreated, and coaxed to confess before their brothers and sisters, all their thoughts, faults, and follies. . . . The more they confess, the more invariably are they encouraged and caressed. When this is over, they all kneel, and the Itinerant prays extempore. Then they eat and drink; and then they sing hymns, pray, exhort, sing, and pray again, till the excitement reaches a very high pitch indeed. These scenes are going on at some house or other every evening during the revival, nay, many at the same time. . . .

It was at the principal of the Presbyterian churches that I was twice witness to scenes that made me shudder; in describing one, I describe . . . every one; the same thing is constantly repeated. . . .

The church was well lighted, and crowded almost to suffocation. On entering, we found three priests standing side by side, in a sort of tribune, placed where the altar usually is, handsomely

Women outnumbered men in most revivals in the North. In 1831, a man in Rochester, New York, wrote to a local newspaper to complain about how a visit to his home by the revivalist minister Charles Grandison Finney, and his wife's subsequent conversion, unsettled relationships in his home.

He *stuffed* my wife with tracts, and alarmed her fears, and nothing short of meetings, night and day, could atone for the many fold sins my poor, simple spouse had committed, and at the same time, she made the miraculous discovery, that she had been "unevenly yoked [married]." From this unhappy period, peace, quiet, and happiness have fled from my dwelling, never, I fear, to return.

fitted up with crimson curtains, and elevated about as high as our pulpits. We took our places in a pew close to the rail which surrounded it.

The sermon had considerable eloquence, but of a frightful kind. The preacher described, with ghastly minuteness, the last feeble fainting moments of human life, and then the gradual progress of decay after death, which he followed through every process up to the last loathsome stage of decomposition. Suddenly he changed his tone, which had been that of sober accurate description, into the shrill voice of horror, he bent forward his head, as if to gaze on some object beneath the pulpit. . . . The preacher made known to us what he saw in the pit that seemed to open up before him. The device was certainly a happy one for giving effect to his description of hell. No image that fire, flame, brimstone, molten lead, or red hot pincers could supply, with flesh, nerves, and sinews quivering under them, was omitted. The perspiration ran in streams from the face of the preacher; his eyes rolled, his lips were

Potential converts came to a rural revival from miles around and stayed in tent encampments on the periphery of the meeting grounds (*background*). The seat up front was the "mourner's bench," where people who feared for their souls were given special attention by ministers. Women cry at the front, a man weeps at the back bench, and a minister supports a swooning woman at the front, while the people at center dance in rapture. The crowd is mostly female, and mostly young. By converting a disproportionate number of young people and women, revivals like this strained and transformed existing hierarchies of gender and generation.

covered with foam, and every feature had the deep expression of horror it would have borne, had he, in truth, been gazing at the scene he described. The acting was excellent. At length he gave a languishing look to his supporters on each side, as if to express his feeble state, and then sat down. . . .

The other two priests arose, and began to sing a hymn. It was some seconds before the congregation could join as usual; every up-turned face looked pale and horror-struck. When the singing ended, another took the centre place, and began in a sort of coaxing affectionate tone, to ask the congregation if what their dear brother had spoken had reached their hearts? Whether they would avoid the hell he had made them see? "Come, then!" he continued, stretching out his arms toward them, "come to us and tell us so, and we will make you see Jesus, the dear gentle Jesus, who shall save you from it. But you must come to him! You must not be ashamed to come to him! . . . We will clear the bench for anxious sinners to sit upon. Come then! come to the anxious bench, and we will show you Jesus! Come! Come! Come!" . . .

And now in every part of the church a movement was perceptible, slight at first, but by degrees becoming more decided. Young girls arose, and sat down, and rose again; and then the pews opened, and several came tottering out, their hands clasped, their heads hanging on their bosoms, and every limb trembling, and still the hymn went on; but as the poor creatures approached the rail their sobs and groans became audible. They seated themselves on the "anxious benches;" the hymn ceased, and two of the three priests walked down from the tribune, and going, one to the right, and the other to the left, began whispering to the poor tremblers seated there. . . . The sobs and groans increased to a frightful excess. Young creatures, with their features pale and distorted, fell on their knees on the pavement, and soon sunk forward on their faces; the most violent cries and shrieks followed, while from time to time a voice was heard in convulsive accents, exclaiming, "Oh Lord!" "Oh Lord Jesus!" "Help me, Jesus!" and the like. . . .

It is hardly necessary to say, that all who obeyed the call to place themselves on the "anxious benches" were women, and by far the greater number, very young women.

Conversion was a life-transforming event. It meant working to change both one's own life and the world in accordance with God's will. These changes helped prepare the way for the millennium—the return of Jesus to Earth and the commencement of his earthly rule. In 1831, after a

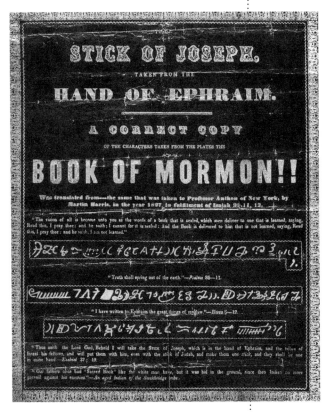

This broadside advertised a new sacred text in the 1830s: the Book of Mormon. The Mormons were the most successful of hundreds of new sects that sprang up during the Second Great Awakening. Their success depended in part on their savvy use of print technology to publicize their teachings.

massive revival, the Brick Presbyterian Church of Rochester, New York, rewrote its covenant to formalize its members' new commitments.

We do now, in the presence of the Eternal God, and these witnesses, covenant to be the Lord's. We promise to renounce all the ways of sin, and to make it the business of our life to do good and promote the declarative glory of our heavenly Father. We promise steadily and devoutly to attend upon the institutions and ordinances of Christ as administered in this Church, and to submit ourselves to its direction and discipline, until our present relation shall be regularly dissolved. We promise to be kind and affectionate to all the members of this church, to be tender of their character, and to endeavor to the utmost of our ability, to promote their growth in grace. We promise to make it the great business of our life to glorify God and build up the Redeemer's Kingdom in this fallen world, and constantly to endeavor to present our bodies a living sacrifice, holy and acceptable to Him.

Innovators in Family Life

While almost all classes of Americans participated in the religious innovations of the era, the emerging northeastern middle class introduced radical innovations in family life. Unlike farmers and many preindustrial artisans, the manufacturers and merchants who made up the new middle class did not work as families. Men's work took them away from home, while women's work remained centered in the household. Ministers, novelists, and authors of advice books celebrated this separation of women's and men's work. They developed new ideas of men's and women's separate "natures" and argued that men and women were destined to operate in separate "spheres" of life. These ideas spread rapidly through a flood of books, newspaper articles, and magazines. One such publication was Mrs. A. J. Graves's *Woman in America*, a book published in 1841.

Next to the obligations which woman owes directly to her God, are those arising from her relation to the family institution. That *home* is her appropriate and appointed sphere of action there cannot be a shadow of doubt; for the dictates of nature are plain and imperative on this subject, and the injunctions given in Scripture no less explicit. . . . "Let your women keep silence in the churches"—be "keepers at home"—taught to "guide the house." . . .

Whenever [woman] neglects these duties, or goes out of this sphere of action to mingle in any of the great public movements of this day, she is deserting the station which God and nature have assigned to her. She can operate far more efficiently in promoting the great interests of humanity by supervising her own household than in any other way. Home . . . is the cradle of the human race; and it is here the human character is fashioned either for good or evil. It is the "nursery of the future man and of the undying spirit"; and woman is the nurse and educator. Over infancy she has almost unlimited sway; and in maturer years she may powerfully counteract the evil influences of the world by the talisman of her strong, enduring love, by her devotedness to those intrusted to her charge, and by those lessons of virtue and of wisdom which are not of the world.

And is not this a sphere wide enough and exalted enough to satisfy her every wish? Whatever may be her gifts and acquirements, here is ample scope for their highest and noblest exercise. If her bosom burns with ardent piety, here she will find hearts to be kindled into devotion, and souls to be saved. Is she a patriot? It is here she can best serve her country, by training up good citizens, just, humane, and enlightened legislators. Has she a highly-cultivated

Sharon Female Seminary in Pennsylvania was one of many schools for women founded during the early republic. The schools were inspired in part by middle- and upper-class women's insistence on women's intellectual equality and especially by domestic writers' belief that rearing moral and patriotic children required women to be educated. They sought to prepare women for motherhood and for teaching, the one profession open to women.

intellect? Let her employ it, then, in leading those young, enquiring minds, which look up to her for guidance, along the pleasant paths of knowledge. . . . Oh! that the mind of woman were enlightened fully to discern the extent and the importance of her domestic duties—to appreciate her true position in society; for then she would be in no danger of wandering from her proper sphere, or of mistaking the design of her being.

That woman should regard home as her appropriate domain is not only the dictate of religion, but of enlightened human reason. Well-ordered families are the chief security for the permanent peace and prosperity of the state, and such families must be trained up by enlightened female influence acting within its legitimate sphere. . . . If man's duties lie abroad, woman's duties are within the quiet seclusion of home. If his greatness and power are most strikingly exhibited in associated action upon associated masses, her true greatness and her highest efficiency consist in individual efforts upon individual beings. The religion and politics of man have their highest sphere in the world without; but the religious zeal and the patriotism of woman are most beneficially and powerfully exerted upon the members of her household. It is in her home that her strength lies; it is here that the gentle influence, which is the secret of her might, is most successfully employed; and this she loses as soon as she descends from her calm height into the world's arena. . . .

We would fain hope . . . that the time is not distant when every American mother shall duly appreciate her domestic responsibilities; and when our homes shall be made attractive by the pure and satisfying enjoyments which religion, intellect, and the social affections have gathered around them. Then, when our husbands and our sons go forth into the busy and turbulent world, we may feel secure that they will walk unhurt amid its snares and temptations. Their hearts will be at home, where their treasure is; and they will rejoice to return to its sanctuary of rest, there to refresh their wearied spirits, and renew their strength for the toils and conflicts of life.

The ideology of domesticity was just that—an ideology. Few women outside the northern, white middle class embraced it, and many women in that group challenged it as well. Still more violated or stretched its ideals in practice. Even those who embraced domestic ideals were aware of the costs involved. In 1835, the writer and public intellectual Ralph Waldo Emerson married Lidian Jackson, a woman who was in every way his intellectual equal. Seven months later, when she was three months pregnant with their first child, Lidian wrote to her husband about her prospects as an intellectual.

The new importance assigned to mothers' cultivation of their children's minds and consciences put white, middle-class northeastern women under new sorts of strain. Abigail May Alcott wrote in an 1833 letter of the relentless demands of childrearing and her anxiety about her shortcomings as a mother.

I write but seldom to any one, excepting father; I frequently have an opportunity to send him a line and I always improve it . . . it costs me but little effort—but a full connected letter seems to me now a formidable undertaking—my eyes are very uncertain—and my time is abundantly occupied with my babies—It seems to me at times as if the weight of responsibility connected with these little immortal beings would prove too much for me—am I doing what is right? Am I doing enough? Am I not doing too much, is my earnest inquiry. I am almost at times discouraged if I find the result prove unfavorable.

Dr. Edward Jarvis [the local Unitarian minister] . . . asked of me to take a class of the eldest girls of the S. S. [Sunday School] which I gladly promised to do—and to be one of the "Reading committee" of the S. S. Library to which I shall have no objections if it will not take more time than I should spare from care of the family. The improvement of my own little share of intellect I long since—(that is ever since the loss of my worldly goods) quietly decided to postpone till my departure from the body. I seek only to improve my character—in doing which intellect will of course make some progress—but I shall never again as I formerly did make mental cultivation a chief aim. God help me to have no aim in future but to do his will in seeking the happiness of others—forgetting my own. He is helping me as far as a free agent can be helped. All that I suffer in body mind & heart—is kindly sent to make me practically willing to renounce self—But what an untoward pupil am I in the school of suffering—I have perverted the serene mercies of God. Pray that I may summon strength to arise from the dust—and gird myself with that armour of God which only I may overcome in this warfare.

Loss of worldly goods
Under the law in every state, when a woman married, all her wealth became her husband's property.

A New World of Wage Labor

Along with family life, members of the new middle class dramatically changed the world of work. Their efforts were helped by population growth. The same shortage of available farmland that led countless farmers' sons and daughters to move west inspired thousands more to seek out new jobs in the cities and factory towns of the Northeast. A large number became wage laborers—a status that many considered to be unfree. By 1850, half of the people in the Northeast counted by the census as economically active worked for wages. The growing ranks of propertyless laborers gave entrepreneurs an opportunity to change how work was done, particularly in manufacturing, where entrepreneurs redesigned the entire work process to cut production costs. In 1833, T. W. Dyott, the owner of a glass factory near Philadelphia, published a pamphlet in which he explained and defended the changes in work at his factory.

The importance of Domestic Manufactures . . . has been too universally acknowledged to require a train of reasoning to establish its truth. . . . Even those who oppose a System of *Tariff Protection*, concede to the fullest extent, the beneficial results of domestic industry to the independence and prosperity of our common country. . . .

[I]t is the exclusive property of irreclaimable savages, and intractable barbarians only, to remain in a state of vassalage and dependence on foreign countries, for a supply of those commodities . . . which enter into the consumption of civilized society. . . . As a people advance in Reason, they will necessarily improve in the *Arts*; as they increase in Industry, they will grow independent of others; and as they rise in the scale of Moral and Intellectual greatness, they will aspire to improve on the models presented for their study by other nations, intent only on achieving whatever can add to the utility, cheapness, or elegance of the product of labor. . . .

Pennsylvania . . . has long since abolished the slavery of her colored population; and will now listen . . . to the method by which the mental bondage of her white citizens and native sons, who produce her wealth, may be broken, and their Minds restored to intelligence; their hearts re-converted to Virtue, and their persons invested with the true dignity that belongs to freemen. . . .

The FEUDAL Institutions of Europe, by making all Laborers vassals, and all mechanics slaves, serfs or servants, naturally laid a sure foundation for the total *moral* ruin of the lower classes of society; making them *reckless* because they were without *hope*; and causing them to perish . . . dark as the tempest in mind, and wild as the hurricane in Morals. . . .

Under the old system of employing men in my Glass Factory, most of whom were from Europe,

During the late 1820s, Eli Whitney's workers made cheap, high-quality guns in this Connecticut factory and town. Like Whitney's enterprise, most antebellum factories were small and surrounded by farmland. They were uniformly built alongside streams, as they depended on water power. Like many factory owners, Whitney owned the entire town, including his workers' homes and the stores where they shopped.

tainted with intemperate and profane habits;—or Americans who had been saturated with these contagious vices—I found it utterly impossible to prosecute the business of the factory to a satisfactory or profitable result. Intemperance, swearing, and quarrelling, were the destructive obstacles to continued and persevering labor. . . .

In this emergency, I resolved to adopt a system on a plan entirely new, and congenial to the *principles* of our Government, which aims to make every man good and happy, by making him virtuous, religious, and industrious. Retaining a few of the best journeymen, who agreed to be bound by the new rules of temperance and decorum, which I had resolved to introduce into the establishment; I projected the plan of instructing boys in the art of *Glass Blowing*, taking them at so tender an age that their pliant natures could be moulded into habits of temperance, industry, docility, piety, and perfect moral decorum under a system of instruction within the walls of the *Factory*, fully adequate to develope all the moral and intellectual faculties, which make the happy man, the good citizen, and the valuable operative. . . .

In the various branches of this establishment nearly *Four Hundred* persons find constant and profitable employment. . . . Of these, one hundred and thirty are Apprentices. . . .

From fifteen to twenty females are also employed in cooking and tailoring; in the duties of the dairy and the business of the laundress.

The females occupy sleeping apartments in the dwelling-house of the Superintendent, Mr. Dyott, the brother of the proprietor; where every regard to morality, decorum and piety is strictly observed, and mildly enforced.

The unmarried men employed in the establishment, and who board with the proprietor, have their chambers apart from those of the apprentices, in a different building. . . . The married workmen occupy the square of two-storied dwellings. . . .

The proprietor . . . has organized a *School* in the establishment, under the superintendence of a competent teacher; with two assistants, in which the boys are instructed in Reading, Writing, and Arithmetic; and Grammar classes are formed for those who desire to progress further in their studies; but his principal object being to render them *useful* and moral beings; it became necessary to limit their acquirements to such knowledge as would make them good citizens, pious christians, happy men, and skillful as well as steady workmen.

A select LIBRARY is also provided for their use. . . .

The ringing of a bell announces to all the hours of rising, and of labor—the time of meals—of cessation from labor—the hour of schooling, and other periods assigned to distinct duties.

The first bell rings at daylight, when the apprentices and workmen arise—wash and cleanse themselves, and prepare for the duties of the day; care being taken that none of the boys neglect themselves in this particular requisite of health. After washing they are summoned to attend prayers in the school-room, when they repair to breakfast. They then prepare for work. The regular operation of blowing commences at 7 o'clock, and lasts till 12, the usual dinner hour; but in the interval a period is allowed for rest, during which a luncheon of crackers is furnished. The afternoon labor commences at 1 o'clock, and continues till 6; between which hours there is also a period for rest, when biscuit is again handed round as a refreshment. The day's labor having terminated, they [the apprentices] are required to wash and cleanse themselves, after which they eat supper, and are allowed a short time for play previous to attending the school, which opens and closes with prayer and singing. . . . At half past 8 o'clock the smaller boys retire to their sleeping chambers, the elder ones preferring to remain up till half past 9, occupying themselves in various diversions, improvements and studies, such as reading, drawing, flute-playing, and other rational means of pleasure, from which they are only interrupted by the last bell as it chimes the close of the day. At half-past nine the gates are closed, the watchman takes his stand and all retire to rest; undisturbed by brawl, riot or tumult, for no *spirits or alcohol* is admitted into the factory; and idleness is banished by labor during the day, and by education and religion during the night. . . .

Attached to the School House, I have caused to be constructed a CHAPEL, in which Divine Worship is performed three times on every Sabbath, and once in the course of the week, on every Wednesday evening.

Dyott supplemented his system of bells with a long list of rules.

1. Every person shall refrain from all manner of profane swearing, improper or abusive language, fighting, quarreling, and the use of spiritous liquors. This request is urged for their observance, with a particular view to their moral improvement. . . . Every person who shall be guilty of swearing, or making use of any vile language, or be found intoxicated, shall forfeit and pay for each and every such offence the sum of one dollar, to be deducted from his wages.

2. Any person who shall strike or improperly treat an apprentice, or disobey the orders of those who are put in charge to superintend the different branches of the establishment, for every such offence shall forfeit the sum of five dollars to be deducted from his wages. . . .

3. All kinds of spiritous liquors are forbid being brought into the factories, or on the premises. Any person who shall be found

infringing upon this rule, shall have the liquor taken from him, and forfeit the sum of five dollars, to be deducted from his wages. And it shall be optional with the proprietor, whether to discharge the said person from his employment, or continue his services after such an infringement. All sums of money which shall be collected from any of the preceding forfeitures, shall be appropriated and invested in the purchase of Books for the increase and enlargement of the DYOTTVILLE APPRENTICES' LIBRARY.

4. In cases of sickness, journeymen are required to send notice immediately to the superintendant, so that temporary substitutes may be selected to fill their station. Apprentices are requested to report themselves to the principal teacher.

5. Personal cleanliness being equally conducive to health and to cheerfulness, is especially recommended to the Apprentices. As every convenience for washing is provided for them, it is expected that no one will appear at meals, at school, or at church, without having performed the necessary ablution.

6. Every species of gambling is strictly prohibited. . . .

8. Every apprentice attached to the establishment is required . . . to attend the school, at the regular hours appointed for their instruction. It is also expected that they will be equally punctual in attendance at the Chapel on Sabbath days.

9. Persons employed at this establishment are solicited to attend public worship at the Church or Chapel erected at the factories, where service is performed three times on Sabbath days, and on Wednesday evenings. . . .

Most industrial work did not take place in factories. In the majority of industries, there were no labor-saving machines in the early nineteenth century. Instead, employers divided each job, which had once been done from start to finish by a single artisan, into several simple, repetitive tasks and hired unskilled workers at lower wages to do the work. In 1845, the *New York Tribune* published a series of reports on conditions in New York City's artisanal trades. These reports reveal the ways in which

PROGRESS OF COTTON Nº 6

SPINNING

This engraving of the spinning room of an English textile factory shows how most thread was made by the 1840s, in both England and the United States. Textiles were often made in highly mechanized, often huge factories. The child at lower left repairs threads when they break. In the largest of these factories, production workers were the same sort of people who had made thread by hand a generation earlier: the daughters of farmers. Men fixed the machines and supervised the female operatives. Factories like these made cloth cheap and plentiful, which freed farm women from the onerous work of spinning and weaving at home.

entrepreneurs had changed manufacturing and how those changes affected different groups of workers in very different ways.

The Tailors.

The employment of Journeymen Tailors is now principally confined to the making of custom Coats and the best custom Pantaloons. All Vests and common Pantaloons, and nearly all Southern and "slop-shop" work is done by women, who work for such prices as they can get. . . .

The present price for making Dress and Frock Coats is $6.25 [per garment]. . . . The Cutter of an establishment, (who receives in first-rate shops $1000 or even $1200 and $1500 per annum) has the privilege of giving out all the work, and generally has his favorites, perhaps a brother or cousin or particular friend, who gets the "cream of the shop," and is thus frequently enabled to make $30 or $40 per week. Besides this, the Journeymen have a practice of *giving out their work* to women or inferior workmen, and thus realizing a handsome income by their *farming* operations. The hands thus hired by the Journeymen do not generally get more than $3.50 or $4 per week, while the Journeyman receives his $6.25 for every Coat from the employer. . . . Sometimes, also, the principle is applied in another way: the Journeyman letting out his work by the piece to the lowest bidder, and thus making more or less profit on every garment given him by the Cutter—for which, of course, the proprietor of the shop is charged full prices.

Slop-shop work

Slop-shop work was the manufacture of cheap items (usually clothing and shoes) for slaves, sailors, and the urban poor.

Cutter

The Cutter in a clothing shop was the man who cut the cloth to a pattern—the first, and most skilled, part of the process of making clothes.

Young workers in industrialized workshops, whose wages allowed them to assert a great deal of independence from their parents, spent their earnings on a host of new consumer goods and commercial entertainments: contemporary fashions, cigars, cheap eateries, and a panoply of popular entertainments such as those advertised here. These young men and women created a distinct style of dress, hair, gesture, and speech that marked both their youth and their working-class status. Rapid urban growth, the emergence of an urban (and remarkably young) working class, and an ongoing consumer revolution gave rise to America's first youth culture.

The Seamstresses.

There are in this City . . . Ten Thousand women who exist on what they can earn by the needle.—The following are the prices for which a majority of these females are compelled to work. . . .

For making Common White and Checked Cotton Shirts, six cents each. These are cut in such a manner as to make ten seams in two pairs of sleeves. A common fast seamstress can make two of these shirts per day. Sometimes very swift hands, by working from sunrise to midnight, can make three. This is equal to seventy-five cents per week (allowing nothing for holidays, sickness, accidents, being out of work, &c.) for the first class and $1.12 ½ for the others. . . .

Duck Trowsers, Overalls, &c. eight and ten cents each. Drawers and Undershirts, . . . from six to eight cents. . . . One garment is a day's work for some—others can make two. . . .

These women generally "keep house"—that is, they rent a single room, or perhaps two small rooms, in the upper story of some poor, ill-constructed, unventilated house in a filthy street . . . where a sickening and deadly miasm pervades the atmosphere. . . . In these rooms all the processes of cooking, eating, sleeping, washing, working and *living* are indiscriminately performed.

For these rooms the tenants never pay less than three to four and a half dollars per month. . . . Of course every cent of the inmates' earnings is exhausted every week, and in many cases is not sufficient to buy any other food than a scanty supply of potatoes and indian meal and molasses for the family. When winter comes, therefore, they are destitute of the means not only of adding comfortable clothing to their wretched wardrobes, but of procuring an ounce of fuel. Their work, too, at this season is frequently cut off, and they are left no resource but the Almshouse or a paper-ticket for bread or coal. . . .

The Journeymen Printers.

Type-setting . . . is paid by the piece. . . . These rates enable a competent workman steadily employed, to realize nine, twelve and fifteen dollars per week, according as he labors on Book-work, an Evening or a Morning paper. . . .

Although there is very little, if any, regular apprenticing to the business now, every Printing Office has its quota of boys, ranging in number from one to twenty, or more. . . . These boys receive from

Almshouse
The Almshouse was an institution for incarcerating those too poor to support themselves; these institutions were notorious for their horrifying conditions.

Paper ticket
Paper tickets were given out to the poor by private charities. The recipients of the charity could exchange these tickets for specific goods like coal or food.

Two-thirder

A "two-thirder" or a "half-way man" was a worker who had not gone through a regular apprenticeship and did not have all the skills of a fully trained journeyman.

Sue

Eugène Sue was a French novelist and social critic. His popularity extended to England and the United States, and reached its peak during the 1840s.

$1.50 to $2.00 per week, for one or two years—when, if they have become at all skillful in the art of type-setting, they are permitted to work on their *own hook* as *two-thirders* . . . and thus oust from their legitimate places regular journeymen. If the boy has become remarkably quick and correct in composition, he can readily obtain a situation at from five to seven dollars a week—in every instance usurping the place of another, and not infrequently a man of family. . . . This class of interlopers is constantly accumulating from the surrounding country and by foreign influx. . . .

Others . . . have no permanent situations,—who live by *subing*, as it is termed, on the Daily Papers, and *rushing* out cheap publications, on the arrival of a steamer from Europe, when the public is on the *qui vive* for Dickens's or Sue's latest literary wonder. In flourishing times these men earn from seven to ten dollars per week.

Journeymen who have families live well or ill, according as they have or have not permanent situations. The condition of that man who is compelled to run from office to office, obtaining a week's work here and a few days' employment there, is not one to be coveted. On the other hand, those who have steady situations live comfortably, and in not a few instances in a certain style of gentility.

Origins of the American Labor Movement

Different groups of workers responded to the new industrial order in different ways. Although they remained one of the more privileged groups among industrial employees, journeymen artisans protested the new order the most. The old workshop order had provided them with a modest prosperity, a high degree of autonomy at work, and at least the hope of becoming masters. For them, industrial work brought a dramatic decline in labor conditions. Drawing on a long tradition of solidarity along trade lines, journeymen in every major city created trade unions during the late 1820s and the 1830s. The Mechanics' Union of Trade Associations, a citywide federation of trade unions in Philadelphia, explained its aims in its founding statement in 1827.

We, the Journeymen Mechanics of the City and County of Philadelphia, . . . appeal to the most intelligent of every community, and ask—Do not you, and all society, depend solely for subsistence on the products of human industry? Do not those who labor, while acquiring to themselves thereby only a scanty and penurious support, likewise maintain in affluence and luxury the rich who never labor? . . .

Is it just? Is it equitable that we should waste the energies of our minds and bodies, and be placed in a situation of such unceasing exertion and servility as must necessarily, in time, render the benefits of our liberal institutions to us inaccessible and useless, in order that the products of our labor may be accumulated by a few into vast pernicious masses, calculated to prepare the minds of the possessors for the exercise of lawless rule and despotism, to overawe the meagre multitude, and fright away that shadow of freedom which still lingers among us? Are we who confer almost every blessing on society, never to be treated as freemen and equals, and never be accounted worthy of an equivalent, in return for the products of our industry? . . .

All who toil have a natural and unalienable right to reap the fruits of their own industry; and that they who by labour (the only source) are the authors of every comfort, convenience and luxury, are in justice entitled to an equal participation, not only in the meanest and the coarsest, but likewise the richest and the choicest of them all. . . .

It is neither our intention nor desire to extort inequitable prices for our labour; all we may demand for this shall not exceed what can be clearly demonstrated to be a fair and full equivalent. . . .

The real object . . . of this association, is to avert, if possible, the desolating evils which must inevitably arise from a depreciation of the intrinsic value of human labor; to raise the mechanical and productive classes to that condition of true independence and equality which their practical skill and ingenuity, their immense utility to the nation and their growing intelligence are beginning . . . to demand: to promote, equally, the happiness, prosperity and welfare of the whole community—to aid in conferring a due and full proportion of that invaluable promoter of happiness, leisure, upon all its useful members; and to assist, in conjunction with such other institutions of this nature as shall hereafter be formed throughout the union, in establishing a just balance of power, both mental, moral, political and scientific, between all the various classes and individuals which constitute society at large.

In their conflicts with specific employers, trade unionists went well beyond "bread and butter" issues. When they went on strike in June 1834, the journeymen loaf-bread bakers of New York City wrote new rules for the city's bread bakeries and resolved to stay on strike against any employer who refused to adopt them.

RESOLVED, that the old system of working by the week be abolished, and that the Society deem it expedient that the following rules be

A Voice from the People!
—
Great Meeting in the Park!!

This 1837 newspaper illustration called a meeting to protest the jailing of striking tailors in New York. The image asserts the white and masculine identity of "the People." Journeymen's trade unions were exclusively male and white. They celebrated skill and resistance to tyranny, attributes they saw as exclusively male. By the late 1840s, many saw these qualities as belonging exclusively to whites as well. One of unions' central aims—keeping the unskilled out of the workshops—was, by definition, an effort to exclude women, children, immigrants, and people of color.

adopted, as the most equitable between the employer and employed, by which to regulate the Loaf Bread Business in this City hereafter. . . .

1st. RESOLVED, that we consider $1 per barrel a fair and reasonable equivalent for our labor.

2d. RESOLVED, that we consider 9 barrels per week for each hand, a fair average, and that no man or men be compelled to work at a lower rate.

3d. RESOLVED, that we consider it as conducive to the welfare of the Trade, that no employer retain more than one Apprentice at one time, and him under indenture for no less than five years; and said Apprentices' employer to be paid as he progresses.

4th. RESOLVED, that we deem it expedient, in accordance with the customs of man, sanctioned by the laws of God, that there be one day out of seven set apart as a day of peace and rest, on which every man may follow the dictates of his own conscience; and therefore

5th. RESOLVED, that no sponge be ready before 8 o'clock on the Sabbath evening. . . .

Few workers suffered lower wages and worse working conditions than women in the urban trades. In 1831, New York's female tailors formed their own union and struck their employers, demanding an increase in wages. They were part of a wave of women workers' activism during the 1830s. Female unionists faced a number of special obstacles: lower pay than men, a membership inexperienced in political activism, hostile public opinion, and the condescension of male unionists. In a speech to the striking women, the secretary of the New York tailors, Louise Mitchell, spoke to these problems while defending the strikers' cause.

Undoubtedly a great number (from their hitherto secluded lives) feel a reluctance to come forward, fearful of having their names made public. . . . I consider this a timidity unworthy of us; for in my estimation, the publicity of a respectable name can be no injury to the lady, or the cause she advocates; and is not this a cause worthy to be advocated by all who bear the name of woman? Are we not a species of the human race, and is not this a free country? Then why may not we enjoy that freedom? Because we have been taught to believe ourselves far less noble and far less wise than the other sex. They have taken advantage of this weakness, and, tyrant like, have stept from one ascendancy to another, till finally, and without resistance, they have us in their power; and severely they have abused that power; nay then have even trampled us under their feet (comparatively speaking), and we have made no resistance; our supposed

Sponge

"Sponge" was dough that had been raised by yeast or other leavening into a light mass, ready to bake.

helplessness has heretofore caused us to remain silent and submissive, but I hope and believe our eyes are now open to a scene of injury too glaring to be overlooked, and too painful to be submitted to. When we complain to our employers and others, of the inequality of our wages with that of the men's, the excuse is, they have families to support, from which females are exempt. Now this is either a sad mistake, or a willful oversight; for how many females are there who have families to support, and how many single men who have none, and who, having no other use for the fruits of their employers' generosity, they child like, waste it; while the industrious mother, having the care of helpless offspring, finds (with all the economy she is necessitated to practice) the scanty reward of her labors scarcely sufficient to support nature! . . . Let me urge the necessity of a joint interest in this our common cause, to enable us to go through with a mighty work began, namely, that of gaining our liberty; fore we are, literally, *slaves*. . . . Fear not public opinion; trust me, it will be in our favor; our proceedings will be garnished with a title no less formidable than that of female heroism—excited by oppression, and exerted in behalf of their just claim to a share of the boasted Independence.

Not all workers opposed the changes ushered in by industrial employers. Despite the fact that their wages were far lower than men's, many of the young, single farm women who flocked to the textile factories of New England saw numerous advantages to factory work. Mary Paul, the daughter of a Vermont farmer, worked in the textile factories of Lowell, Massachusetts, between 1845 and 1848. Her letters to her father tell of her experience in the factories.

Saturday Sept. 13, 1845
Dear Father
 . . . I want you to consent to let me go to Lowell if you can. I think it would be much better for me than to stay about here. I could earn more to begin with than I can any where about here. I am in need of clothes which I cannot get if I stay about here and for that reason I want to go to Lowell or some other place. . . . Mercy Jane Griffith is going to start in four or five weeks. Aunt Miller and Aunt Sarah think it would be a good chance for me to go if you would consent. . . .

Lowell Nov. 20th 1845
Dear Father
 . . . We arrived at Lowell. Went to a boarding house and staid until Monday night. On Saturday after I got here Luthera Griffith went round with me to find a place but we were unsuccessful. On Monday

Paid

Lowell operatives were paid monthly.

Doff

To doff was to remove spindles that had been filled with thread by a spinning machine and to replace them with empty spindles.

Frames

"Frames" were power-driven looms that wove thread into cloth.

we started again and were more successful. We found a place in a spinning room and the next morning I went to work. I like very well have 50 cts first payment increasing every payment as I get along in work have a first rate overseer and a very good boarding place. I work on the Lawrence Corporation. Mill is No 2 spinning room. . . .

Lowell Dec 21st 1845
Dear Father

. . . Last Tuesday we were paid. In all I had six dollars and sixty cents paid $4.68 for board. With the rest I got me a pair of rubbers and a pair of 50 cts shoes. Next payment I am to have a dollar a week beside my board. . . . I get along very well with my work. I can doff as fast as any girl in our room. I think I shall have frames before long. The usual time allowed for learning is six months but I think I shall have frames before I have been in three as I get along so fast. I think that the factory is the best place for me and if any girl wants employment I advise them to come to Lowell.

Lowell April 12th 1846
Dear Father

. . . I have a very good boarding place have enough to eat and that which is good enough. The girls are all kind and obliging. The girls that I room with are all from Vermont and good girls too. Now I will tell you about our rules at the boarding house. We have none in particular except that we have to go to bed about 10 o'clock. At half past 4 in the morning the bell rings for us to get up and at five for us to go into the mill. At seven we are called out to breakfast are allowed half an hour between bells and the same at noon till the first of May when we have three quarters [of an hour] till the first of September. We have dinner at half past 12 and supper at seven. . . .

The Beginnings of Mass Immigration

From the colonial era onward, immigration was a constant fact shaping American life. Immigration grew significantly during the early nineteenth century as migrants from the British Isles arrived, but the vast majority of wage earners remained native-born children of Americans. The proportion of American workers born abroad grew dramatically after 1846, as immigrants from Germany and Ireland (along with a smaller number from England, Scotland, and Scandinavia) flocked to the United States, as well as to Canada, Latin America, and the industrial cities of Europe. More than three hundred thousand Germans arrived in the United States between 1846 and 1850, fleeing growing landlessness, industrial depression, military service, religious persecution, and political repression. One of those migrants was Ernst Stille, the son of tenant farmers in northwestern Germany who left for the United States in 1846. Stille's letter, written in May 1847 to all his relatives and friends back home, revealed one effect of chain migration (migrants following relatives or friends from back home to the new country): the dense network of relatives and acquaintances that greeted immigrants fresh off the boat. Stille also offered an assessment of migrants' prospects in the United States.

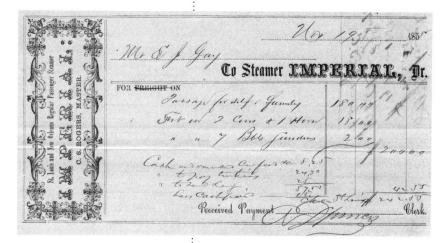

We all arrived here in America hale and hearty as we were when we met you, we went from Bremen to Neuorlians [New Orleans] in 2 months. . . . We went right into town and met a few friends: Homann who used to rent from Erpenbeck, W. Tostrik and many from Lienen. . . . When we went back to the ship in the evening where we had a place to stay for one more night, Wilhelmiene Henschen came with her husband Johan Munders because they'd heard that a ship had arrived from Germany and wanted to see if any friends were on it and were not a little pleased when they saw F. and Wilhelm Henschen. J. Munders lives from his teamster trade, he has 8 mules and since he needed 2 stableboys he took his two brothers-in-law on as drivers and gave them 12 dollars a month. He kept B. Brinkmann on as a servant for 5 dollars a month, and I worked for three weeks as a day laborer. . . . I set off on a trip to visit Uncle Wilhelm. The trip from Neuorliens to Cincinäti [Cincinnati] took 12 days and cost 22 talers. I stayed there 2 days and visited all the friends I could find, then I got back on the steamboat to Uncle Wilhelm's. . . . On the first of February I left Wilhelm and traveled back to Cincinäti when I got here there was little work and wage in the city . . . , but I was lucky enough to get a job with Fr. Lutterbeck from Ladbergen. I didn't earn more than 6 talers a month and my job was hauling bricks. At the beginning of April all the brickmakers started to work again, many Germans work this trade and earn a good wage and I set to work at this too and earn 1 dollar a day, of that I have to pay 7 dollars a month for board and washing, I work for Kuk from Brochterbeck,

Transportation expanded rapidly in the decades following the War of 1812, as entrepreneurs and state and local governments invested heavily in roads, canals, and steam-powered boats. The "transportation revolution" dramatically cheapened the costs of travel and of shipping goods, making possible widespread migration within the United States and between the United States and Europe. With this 1858 ticket, E. J. Gay bought passage for himself, his family, and some livestock on the steamboat *Imperial*, which ran between St. Louis and New Orleans.

Taler

"Taler" (also known as "thaler") referred to a silver coin, issued by German and Scandinavian states, that circulated throughout much of Europe from the fifteenth through the nineteenth centuries.

Johann Pritzlaff left the German state of Pomerania for the United States in 1839 with a group of fellow Old Lutherans to escape religious persecution. In 1842, he was working as a farm laborer in Milwaukee, Wisconsin Territory. In that year, he offered his assessment of the United States in a letter to his mother, brother, and sister.

For a man who works, it is much better here than over there; you can earn your daily bread better than in Germany, one doesn't live so restrictedly and in such servitude as you do under the great estate-owners, you don't have to put your hat under your arm or leave it at the door when you want to have the money you've earned. There is quite a fair amount of equality among men here in America. The high and wealthy aren't ashamed to associate with the poor and lowly. If one man works for another, he is not tied to any particular time, rather he leaves when he wants to; everyone is his own master. You can also travel freely and unhindered all through America without a passport or anything like that. . . .

As far as church matters go, I cannot write much that is good, for the Antichrist has also set up his see in America. But the best thing here is that everyone has the freedom to act according to his own belief. He who follows false teachings here does so of his own free will.

I have my board with Ernst Fiegenbaum from Ladbergen who works with me. . . . Now some of you might like to know how conditions are in general for the German immigrants here but I can't write too very much about that since it's so varied here. The only people who are really happy here are those who were used to hard work in Germany and with toil and great pains could hardly even earn their daily bread, when people like that come here, even if they don't have any money, they can manage, they rent a room and the husband goes to work, earns his dollar a day and so he can live well and happily with a wife and children. But a lot of people come over here who were well off in Germany but were enticed to leave their fatherland by boastful and imprudent letters from their friends or children and thought they could become rich in America, this deceives a lot of people . . . if they stay in the city they can only earn their bread at hard and unaccustomed labor, if they want to live in the country and don't have enough money to buy a piece of land that is cleared and has a house then they have to settle in the wild bush and have to work very hard to clear the trees . . . , but people who are healthy, strong and hard working do pretty well. Here in Cincinnäti I know a lot of people who have made it by working hard, like Ernst Lots for example he does very well he also owns a brickyard and earns good money. . . . F. Katkamp . . . sends along his best regards to you . . . he says that I have to work here like in Germany but things are better for my wife and children, and that's what it's like for everyone I've met here, the women have nothing to do except cook the food and keep things clean, that's all the servant girls have to do too, but the men have to eat their bread in the sweat of their brow, although you don't have to work from dawn to dusk, a good worker can do his day's work in 10 hours, earn one dollar and live well on that with a wife and children, and have such good food and drink like the best burgher in Lengerich.

German migrants were often farmers or skilled artisans, and most came with at least some money. Irish immigrants, who flooded into the United States during and after the potato famine of 1845–47, had far poorer prospects than arrivals from Germany. Between 1846 and 1850, nearly six hundred thousand famine migrants reached the United States. A newspaper report from Amherst, New Hampshire, in 1849 described the situation of the new arrivals and the devastation they left behind. The mass migration of Germans and Irish marked the beginning of a new era in northern society. Cities and the working class became increasingly marked by the immigrant presence, and new arrivals provided the labor force needed for accelerating industrial expansion.

The increasing numbers of destitute and unemployed Irish immigrants in our midst give abundant token that the accounts which reach us of suffering and starvation in Ireland are not exaggerated. In this and the adjoining cities the applications for relief and for work are more numerous . . . than ever before. And the prospect is, that this influx of immigration . . . will continue to increase at a ratio restricted only by the lack of vessels to convey to our shores the thousands who are preparing to come.

The details in some of the Irish papers are terrible. A letter from Ballingford gives a fearful picture of affairs in that section of the country. People are dying by the wayside from exhaustion produced by the want of food; and it is affirmed that dead bodies actually strew the fields and ditches for want of persons to bury them. In the workhouse the cholera had appeared and made terrible havoc. . . . It was recently stated by the County Surveyor for Meyo [Mayo County] . . . that in that county alone fifty thousand acres of ground, heretofore in cultivation . . . have been abandoned. In 1845, the population was 400,000 and upwards. It has since decreased to 300,000. Of the deficit 100,000, about 50,000 died through the effects of the famine, 30,000 emigrated to the colonies, and the remaining 20,000 fled to the neighboring counties of England and Scotland. Of the 300,000 still in Mayo, there are only 20,000 families capable of supporting themselves.

Emigrant Landing in New-York, an 1858 illustration from *Harper's Weekly*, captures the disorder of a ship filled with immigrants arriving in New York. As a crowd of newcomers disembarks, two boys fight at center and a porter knocks over a well-dressed man at right. The clothing and facial hair of the two men conversing, far left, mark them as foreigners (probably Germans); most of the figures in the picture wear the clothes of peasants and workers.

A SLAVE FATHER SOLD AWAY FROM HIS FAMILY.

CHAPTER 5

Masters and Slaves

When James Henry Hammond married Catherine Fitzsimons in June 1831, he became the legal owner of all her property, which included over ten thousand acres and 147 slaves. Soon after he and his bride moved into their new home plantation, Hammond concluded that the previous managers had run the place into the ground, and he set about putting the plantation on a new footing. More than anything else, he sought to exert more complete control over the men and women he called his property. For years, the enslaved workers had been given a specific task to do each day, worked with minimal supervision, and quit for the day when their work was done. Hammond called an end to this system, declaring that slaves would henceforth work in gangs from dawn to dusk, under the constant supervision of a driver. Black plantation residents had for a long time engaged in a separate and half-hidden religious life. Hammond vowed to "break up negro preaching & negro church" and decreed that his servants must attend services overseen by white ministers. His slaves had long turned to black medical practitioners when they were sick, but Hammond appointed himself plantation doctor and sought to place them on a new health-care regime. He even sought to control their names, naming all slave children born on his land and giving new names to many of the slaves he bought.

Hammond's slaves had other ideas. The old task system of labor provided them with autonomy at work and free time to hunt, tend their gardens, and spend time with their families. When he put them in gangs, they left "all the weeds and bunches of grass" growing around the cotton, left much of the cotton unpicked, injured Hammond's mules, and

"A slave father sold away from his family," from an 1860 abolitionist children's book, depicts the practice that incurred the deepest grievances among slaves: the breakup of families through sale. Although many masters made some effort to keep slave families united, they had no qualms against selling enslaved children who had reached the age of ten or twelve. Northern audiences were deeply offended by the breakup of slave families, and abolitionists publicized the practice widely.

destroyed his plough. Eventually they wore him down. Despite frequent and vigorous whippings, Hammond returned to task work by 1850. Nor were black plantation residents about to give up their separate religious life without a fight. Although they could not get around the requirement that they attend services with white ministers, they continued to hold their own religious meetings in secret despite severe punishments if they were caught. Many continued to rely on "negro Doctors" and did their best to evade Hammond's treatments. They supplemented the food rations their master gave them with food from plantation stores and the master's kitchen, secretly slaughtered and ate the pigs on the plantation, and took so many potatoes from the field that Hammond never bothered to harvest the crop.

In one respect, Hammond was unusual. Most slave owners owned fewer than five slaves, worked alongside their human property, and sought a moderate prosperity rather than great wealth. Most white southerners owned no slaves at all. But Hammond's servants were not so unusual. Most enslaved people lived on plantations with twenty or more slaves. The conflict between Hammond and the people he owned was typical of larger plantations. Masters sought unchecked power over their human property and tried to arrange plantation work and life to maximize their profits and ensure black subordination. Enslaved people had their own ideas about Christianity, the pace of work, the distribution of material goods, the proper relationship between masters and servants, and the justice of slavery. Despite the enormous inequalities of power between them and their masters, they used what tools they had to try to enforce those ideas. They often did so collectively, thereby creating and strengthening a largely separate black community and culture.

This conflict took place on a rapidly shifting terrain. In 1789, most enslaved people lived and worked in the Atlantic seaboard states. The main crops were tobacco and rice. In many areas, plantation agriculture was in decline, due to soil exhaustion and low prices for plantation products. By the mid-1840s, most slaves worked west of Appalachia, in states like Mississippi and Alabama that had been wrenched from Indian tribes. The vast majority grew short-staple cotton. Slave-based agriculture was booming, as world demand for cotton expanded and prices remained high. The cotton boom and western migration colored the lives of most masters and most slaves. They promised high profits for masters but brought untold hardship for slaves, as migration broke up many families and subjected hundreds of thousands of indi-

TO BE SOLD, on board the Ship *Bance-Island*, on tuesday the 6th of *May* next, at *Ashley-Ferry*; a choice cargo of about 250 fine healthy

NEGROES,

just arrived from the Windward & Rice Coast. —The utmost care has already been taken, and shall be continued, to keep them free from the least danger of being infected with the SMALL-POX, no boat having been on board, and all other communication with people from *Charles-Town* prevented.

Austin, Laurens, & Appleby.

N. B. Full one Half of the above Negroes have had the SMALL-POX in their own Country.

This advertisement, probably from the 1780s, announces a slave auction aboard a ship fresh from Africa. The passage from western Africa to North America was a horrifying one that killed a large proportion of the people being transported. Congress abolished the transatlantic slave trade in 1808, but smuggling continued to bring Africans to the United States.

viduals to the hardships of carving plantations and farms out of forest. This conflict of interest—greater earnings for masters meant dislocation and suffering for slaves—heightened the conflict that lay at the heart of slavery.

The Struggle for Control

Many enslaved people seized the opportunity created by the chaos of the Revolution to win their freedom. The largest number did so by joining the British army, but many bondsmen and bondswomen ran away in groups and formed independent "maroon" villages in remote areas. In a book narrating his travels in the United States in 1783–84, the German Johann David Schoepf described the maroon communities of the Great Dismal Swamp of North Carolina and Virginia.

A famous region, by which the road from Suffolk to Cunningham's passes, is the Dismal Swamp. . . . This swamp . . . is a thick, boggy, impenetrable wilderness, in length 40–50 miles from north to

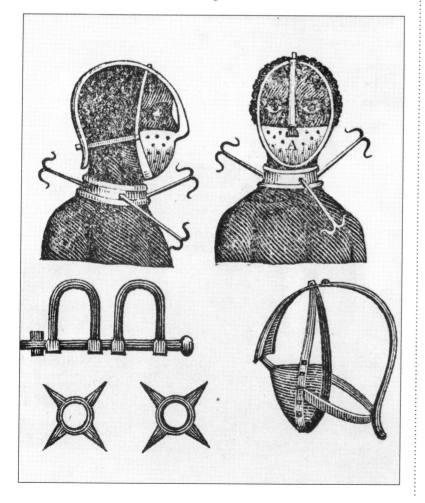

The revolutionary period saw a significant increase in slave resistance, and masters and officials responded with harsh repression. This print displays some of the restraints used to punish recalcitrant slaves.

Maroon villages raided nearby plantations for livestock and supplies and enticed those still in bondage to join them. Southern governors and military commanders were under considerable pressure to defeat and reenslave the escapees, but maroons were often difficult to defeat. In a 1787 letter, Governor Thomas Pinckney of South Carolina ordered Arnoldus Vanderhorst, commander of the Berkley County Militia, to march on a maroon village. The maroons were ultimately defeated.

Sir, Having received information that a party of runaway Negro men, many of whom are armed, are become very troublesome and dangerous to the plantations in the vicinity of Stono and it being represented that they are too numerous to be quelled by the usual parties of patrol, you will be pleased to order a command from your regiment of such part of the militia of the neighborhood as you may judge sufficient effectually to apprehend or disperse such slaves as fall within the above description.

Manumit
To manumit a slave was to free him or her as an individual.

Mustizo
Just north of Spanish Florida, Georgians adopted the Spanish term *mestizo*, which usually referred to a person of mixed European and American Indian ancestry. The term could also, as in this case, refer to persons of mixed African and American Indian descent.

south, and 20–25 miles wide. . . . Few people venture in, and fewer still know anything of what there is except by hearsay. . . .

[S]mall spots are to be found here and there which are always dry, and these have often been used as places of safety by runaway slaves, who have lived many years in the swamp, despite all the snares set for them by their masters, even if planters living near-by, for they are chary of going in. So these negro fugitives lived in security and plenty, building themselves cabins, planting corn, raising hogs and fowls which they stole from their neighbors, and naturally the hunting was free where they were.

In the decades after the Revolution, southern slave owners and political officials struggled to gain control over enslaved people. One way they did so was by passing laws that limited the autonomy of slaves and free African Americans and that provided harsh punishments for crimes against white people. The laws themselves provided evidence of resistance by slaves and free blacks, as legislators tended to outlaw behavior that people were already engaging in. The laws were also evidence of a new racial regime, as they subjected slaves and free African Americans to the same restrictions. They created separate sets of rights and disabilities for whites and nonwhites. The following laws were passed by the Georgia legislature between 1800 and 1810.

From and after the passing of this act, it shall not be lawful for any person or persons to manumit or set free any negro slave or slaves, any mulatto, mustizo, or any other person or persons of colour, who may be deemed slaves at the time of the passing of this act, in any other manner or form, than by an application to the Legislature for that purpose. . . .

If any person or persons shall purchase from a slave, any produce whatsoever, such person or persons shall, for every such offense, forfeit and pay the sum of thirty dollars.

If the owner or owners of any slave, shall permit such slave for a consideration or otherwise to have, hold, and enjoy the privilege of labouring, or otherwise transacting, business for himself, her or themselves, except on their own premises, such owner or owners shall, for every such weekly offence, forfeit and pay the sum of thirty dollars. . . .

From and after the passing of this act, if any person or persons, shall raise or attempt or endeavour to raise any insurrection of slaves, or shall counsel, advise, aid or abet any such insurrection, or shall excite, promote, instigate, or stir up or endeavor to excite, promote, instigate, or stir up any such insurrection, every person or persons so offending, shall on conviction thereof, be adjudged guilty of felony, and shall suffer death without benefit of clergy. . . .

If any slave, free negro, Indian, mulatto or mustizo, (indians in amity with the United States excepted) shall be guilty of homicide of any sort, upon any white person, except by misadventure, or if a slave, in defence of his or her owner, or other person under whose care and government such slave shall be, or shall raise or attempt to raise any insurrection, or commit or attempt to commit any rape on any white person whomsoever, every such offender or offenders, his and their aiders and abettors, shall upon conviction thereof, suffer death; or if any slave, free negro, indian, mulatto, or mustizo, (except as before excepted) shall willfully and maliciously kill any slave, free negro, indian, mulatto, or mustizo, or shall break open, burn or destroy any dwelling house or other building whatsoever, or set fire to any rice, corn, or other grain, tar-kiln, barrel or barrels of pitch, tar, turpentine, rosin, or any other goods or commodities whatsoever, or shall steal any goods or chattels whatsoever, or inveigle, delude or entice any slave or slaves to run away, whereby the owner or owners of such slave or slaves, shall, might, or would have lost or been deprived of such slave or slaves, every such slave, free negro, indian, mulatto, or mustizo, and his and their accomplices, aiders and abettors, shall upon conviction as aforesaid, suffer death. . . .

From and after the first day of January next, all free negroes, mulattoes or mustezoes, who may then or any time thereafter, reside within the corporate limits of the cities of Savannah and Augusta, shall be subject to the same police regulations, and restrictions as slaves are or may be by the laws of this state, and any person who shall hire or let any house or tenement to any free negro, mulattoe or mustezoe within the limits of said cities, without permission from the city council thereof, shall be subject to the same penalties as if such house or tenement had been let or hired to a slave. . . .

That the commissioners of the towns of Washington, Lexington and Milledgeville, be and they are hereby vested with the same powers, as to the regulation of such free persons as above described, within their respective jurisdictions,

Whereas the permitting of free negroes and persons of color to rove about the country in idleness and dissipation, has a dangerous tendency. . . .

Be it therefore enacted . . . That the justices of the peace with any three freeholders of the district, be, and they are hereby vested with power to bind out to service, any male free negroes or persons

In an effort to control both slaves and free black people, some southern cities required that African Americans wear badges, such as this 1823 servant's badge from Charleston, South Carolina, identifying them as free or enslaved.

of color, over the age of eight years, until he arrives to the age of twenty one years, to artisans or farmers; Provided, such free person or persons of color have no guardian.

With the law and the military backing them, slave owners succeeded in crushing open resistance on the part of enslaved people. With that victory assured, they sought to regulate every element of plantation life. Owners with one or a few slaves sought to enforce this control personally, but the owners of large plantations usually established written rules, which were enforced by overseers (plantation managers) and drivers (enslaved people who oversaw the work of small groups of other slaves). In the mid-1830s, James Henry Hammond of South Carolina wrote instructions to his overseer concerning the regulation and treatment of slaves.

The Overseer must see that all the negroes leave their houses promptly after hornblow in the morning. Once, or more, a week he must visit every house after horn blow at night to see that all are in. . . .

The negroes must be made to obey & to work, which may be done by an Overseer, who attends regularly to his business, with very little whipping. Much whipping indicates a bad tempered, or inattentive manager, & will not be allowed. The Overseer must never on any occasion—unless in self defence—kick a negro, or strike with his hand, or a stick, or the butt-end of his whip. No unusual punishment must be resorted to without the Employer's consent. He must never threaten a negro, but punish offences immediately on knowing them; otherwise he will soon have run-aways. . . .

Allowances are given out once a week. No distinction is made among work-hands, whether they are full-hands or under, field hands or adjuncts about the yard, stables, &c.

Negroes are improvident with a longer interval between allowances many will consume, waste or barter their provisions before it closes & must commit thefts, or have insufficient & unwholesome food during a portion of their time; demoralizing & rendering them physically incapable of doing full work, . . . They should, also, be brought into that contact with the master, at least once a week, of receiving the means of subsistence from him.

Each work-hand gets a peck of meal every Sunday morning. . . . Every negro must come in person for meal allowance, & in clean clothes. . . .

Each work hand gets 3 lbs. of bacon or pickled pork every Monday night. Fresh meat may be substituted at the rates of 3 ½ lbs. of fresh pork, (uncured, but salted) or 4 lbs. of beef or mutton, or 4 ½ of pork offal. . . .

Allowances
"Allowances" were regular (often weekly or monthly) distributions of food to slaves.

Each man gets in the fall 2 shirts of cotton drilling, a pair of woolen pants & a woolen jacket. In the Spring 2 shirts of cotton shirting & 2 pr of cotton pants. . . .

Each woman gets in the fall 6 yds. of woolen cloth, 6 yds. of cotton drilling & a needle, skein of thread & ½ doz buttons. In the Spring 6 yds. of cotton shirting & 6 yds. of cotton cloth similar to that for men's pants, needle, thread & buttons.

Each worker gets a stout pr. of shoes every fall, & a heavy blanket every third year.

There is a separate building [in] the charge of a trusty nurse, where the children are kept during the day. Weaned children are brought to it at the last horn-blow in the morning—about good day light. The unweaned are brought to it at sunrise, after suckling, & left in cradles in charge of the nurse. . . .

Sucklers are not required to leave their houses until sun-rise, when they leave their children at the children's house before going to field. The period of suckling is 12 mos. . . .

They are allowed 45 minutes at each morning to be with their children. They return 3 times a day until their infants are 8 mos. old—in the middle of the fore-noon, at noon, & in the middle of the afternoon: till the 12th mo. but twice a day, missing at noon: during the 12th mo. at noon only. On weaning, the child is removed entirely from its Mother for 2 weeks, & placed in charge of some careful woman without a child, during which time the Mother is not to nurse at all. . . .

No negro will be allowed to remain at his own house when sick, but must be confined to the hospital. Every reasonable complaint must be promptly attended to, & with any marked or general symptom of sickness, however trivial, a negro may lie up a day or so at least. . . .

The first morning horn is blown an hour before day-light. All work-hands are required to rise & prepare their cooking, & c. for the day. The second horn is blown just at good daylight, when it is the duty of the driver to visit every house & see that all have left for the field. . . . At 12 P.M. the gang stop to eat dinner. At 1 P.M. through the greater part of the year, all hands return to work. In summer the intermission increases with the heat to the extent of 3 ½ hours. At 15 minutes before sun-set the plow-hands, & at sun-set the rest, knock off work for the day. No work must ever be required after dark. No negro will be allowed to go hunting at night. The negroes are allowed to visit among themselves until the night horn is blown, after which no negro is to

I have ever maintained the doctrine that my negroes have no time Whatever, that they are always liable to my call without questioning for a moment the propriety of it. . . . If I furnish my negro with every necessary of life, without the least care on his part—if I support him in sickness, however long it may be, and pay all his expenses, though he does nothing—if I maintain him in his old age, when he is incapable of rendering either himself or myself any service, am I not entitled to an exclusive right to his time [and] good feelings[?]

—The plantation rules of Bennet Barrow, Louisiana slave owner, 1838 be seen out of his house, & it is the duty of the driver to go around & see that he is in it. The night horn is blown at 8 ½ P.M. in winter, & 9 P.M. in summer.... The head driver is the most important negro on the plantation, & is not required to work like the other hands. He is to be treated with more respect than any other negro by both master & overseer.... He is required to maintain proper discipline at all times. To see that no negro idles or does bad work in the field & to punish it with discretion on the spot....

Marriage is to be encouraged as it adds to the comfort, happiness & health of those who enter upon it, besides insuring a greater increase. Permission must always be obtained from the master before marriage, but no marriage will be allowed with negroes not belonging to the master. When sufficient cause can be shewn on either side, a marriage may be annulled, but the offending party must be severely punished. When both are in wrong both must be punished, & if they insist on separating must have 100 lashes apiece.... For first marriage a bounty of $5.00 to be invested in household articles, shall be given. If either has been married before, the bounty shall be $3.50....

All are privileged & encouraged to go to Church on Sundays, but no religious meeting is allowed on the plantation beyond singing & praying, & at such times as will not conflict with the plantation hours, & always with the permission of the Master or Overseer....

All visiting with strange negroes is positively forbidden. Negroes living at one plantation & having wives at the other can visit them only between Saturday night & Monday morning, & must get a pass card at each visit.... The card is the recognized & required permit in all visiting & any negro leaving the plantation without it, or off the most direct route, shall be punished off detection by the Overseer, & is liable to punishment from anyone meeting him....

Each work-hand is allowed to go to Town once a year (the women always selecting some of the men to go for them) on a Sunday before crop gathering & Christmas. Not more than 10 shall be allowed to go the same day....

Adjoining each negro house is a piece of ground convenient for a fowl-yard & garden.... Negroes may have patches in various parts of the plantation (always getting permission from the master) to cultivate crops of their own.... Negroes are not allowed to grow crops of corn or cotton for themselves, nor to have any cattle or stock of any kind of their own.

At Christmas a holyday of three or four days is given. On that day, if not a Sunday, a barbacue is given, beef or mutton &

pork, coffee & bread being bountifully provided. . . . There is also a barbacue & one day's holyday in August. No strange negroes are allowed to attend, nor shall any of the neighbors be invited by the Overseer without the Employer's consent. . . .

The following is an order in which offences must be estimated & punished: 1st Running away.—2nd Getting drunk or having spirits.—3rd Stealing hogs.—4th Stealing.—5th Leaving plantation without permission.—6th Absence from house after horn blow at night.—7th Unclean house or person.—8th Neglect of tools.—9th Neglect of work.—The highest punishment must not exceed 100 lashes in one day & to that extend only in extreme cases. The whip lash must be one inch in length or a strap of one thickness of leather 1 ½ inches in width, & never severely administered. In general 15 to 20 lashes will be a sufficient flogging. The hands in every case must be secured by a cord. *Punishment must always be given calmly & deliberately & never when angry or excited.*

The World of the Enslaved

The extent to which slave owners succeeded in controlling their slaves has long been a matter of discussion and debate among historians. One area where slaves sought autonomy and masters sought control was in religious life. The Second Great Awakening engulfed the slave states with as much religious fervor as it did the North. Where evangelicalism inspired social experimentation and reform in the North, among southern whites it stimulated social conservatism, especially concerning slavery. Peter Randolph, an enslaved man in Virginia, described in his autobiography the version of Christianity that a neighboring master sought to instill in his human property.

Mr. James L. Goltney was a Baptist preacher, and was employed by Mr. M. B. Harrison to give religious instruction to his slaves. He often used the common text: "Servants, obey your masters." . . . "It is the devil," he would say, "who tells you to try and be free." And again he bid them be patient at work, warning them that it would be his duty to whip them, if they appeared dissatisfied,—all which would be pleasing to God! "If you run away, you will be turned out of God's church, until you repent, return, and ask God and your master's pardon."

The proliferation of printing presses during the early republic created an opportunity for even poor people to enter public discussion. One printed medium favored by the poor was the autobiography. Before the Civil War, most slave autobiographies were written by runaways, who published their stories as a personal witness to the brutalities of slavery. After the Civil War, autobiographies served a wider variety of purposes. Peter Randolph's 1893 narrative, pictured here, bore witness to his religious life and leadership.

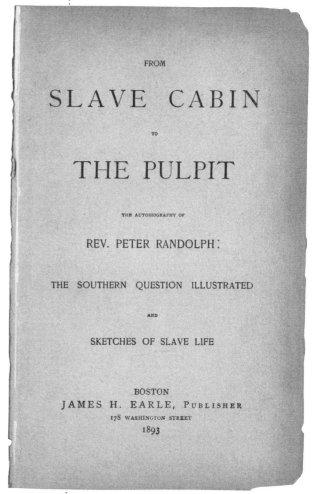

FROM

SLAVE CABIN

TO

THE PULPIT

THE AUTOBIOGRAPHY OF

REV. PETER RANDOLPH:

THE SOUTHERN QUESTION ILLUSTRATED

AND

SKETCHES OF SLAVE LIFE

BOSTON
JAMES H. EARLE, PUBLISHER
178 WASHINGTON STREET
1893

Enslaved men and women adopted Christianity, but a Christianity that was dramatically different from the religion preached to them by slave owners and white ministers. At considerable risk, slaves established a religious community and religious practices that were entirely autonomous from white people. In his autobiography, Peter Randolph described the autonomous religious services of the enslaved people in his neighborhood. His description reveals a great deal about how slaves ordered their relationships with one another.

Not being allowed to hold meetings on the plantation, the slaves assemble in the swamps, out of reach of the patrols. They have an understanding among themselves as to the time and place of getting together. This is often done by the first one arriving breaking boughs from the trees, and bending them in the direction of the selected spot. Arrangements are then made for conducting the exercises. They first ask each other how they feel, the state of their minds, &c. The male members then select a certain space, in separate groups, for their division of the meeting. Preaching in order, by the brethren; then praying and singing all round, until they generally feel quite happy. The speaker usually commences by calling himself unworthy, and talks very slowly, until, feeling the spirit, he grows excited, and in a short time, there fall to the ground twenty or thirty men and women under its influence. . . .

The slave forgets all his sufferings, except to remind others of the trials during the past week, exclaiming, "Thank God, I shall not live here, always!" Then they pass from one to another, shaking hands, and bidding each other farewell, promising, should they meet no more on earth, to strive and meet in heaven, where all is joy, happiness and liberty. As they separate, they sing a parting hymn of praise.

Christianity gave enslaved people a moral system of their own, free from the influence of masters. It provided them a framework with which to pass judgment not only on themselves and other slaves but on their masters, other white people, and slavery itself. The Christianity that enslaved people developed brought moral order in a chaotic and violent existence, hope and love in an environment that often bred despair, and a personal moral authority that overturned the earthly hierarchies maintained by slaveholders. In personal testimony told to J. P. Clark, a white neighbor, in 1854, Thomas Anderson, an enslaved man from Hanover County, Virginia, described his experience of conversion and his confrontation with his master, who opposed his religion. The events took place in the first decade of the nineteenth century.

I became very wicked, and remained so till I arrived at the age of nineteen, at which time I was singularly led to attend a religious meeting held by the Baptists . . . , when I was awakened to a sense of my condition from these words, dropped from a humble minister: "The wicked have no hope beyond the grave, while the righteous have a hope beyond Jordan's cold stream; and after they have crossed Jordan they have gone home to a God of pity, to a God of compassion, to a God of sovereign mercy." These words took a deep hold in my soul. And this prepare me to seek such a friend. And after searching a long season of time, the Friend of Sinners appear and fill my heart with love. He give me peace of soul and confidence of mind; then I could gladly tell this glorious Savior's mine. This destroyed all earthly fear, and prepared me to rest in hope. . . .

Now, I would be glad for all the world to know that after I was awakened, as I have described, that love, in place of fear, fill my heart. May be I better say here that very often, when I goin' on in wickedness, something tell me this wicked, and I feel very bad. At that time I did not know that it was that the good Spirit talking with me; yet I know all the time that I was doing wrong, 'cause I feel guilty, and that make me afraid. But when I give all up to serve the Lord, He promise He help whenever I need him. And soon after, He try my faith very strong. My master who owned me at that time having no knowledge of God or godliness, supposed my religion was all a fancy, and said he could and would whip it out of me. He took me up and tie me, and scourged me until feeling of flesh was almost gone. At length I fall I before him and lift up my cries to heaven, and ask my great Creator "What have I done?" My master cursed me, and said: "Will you preach to me?" But I now feel glad that I could suffer patiently for my new Master. And my manner at that time take master's strength away; and before he left me he untie me and let me off. But in about three hours he come again, and threaten me with fresh scourging. And though I was very weak from the beating I got, our Lord make me feel very strong, and this prepare me to answer: "You have whipped out all fear, and I am not afraid of you no more. You can take a gun and shoot me or kill me, as you please, and all for nothing; and that is all you can do: for I know I have a life you cannot touch, and the fear of you will not keep me from doing anything my new Master tells me to do. And if He let you take this poor bruised body of flesh, I feel it ain't worth much;" and I feel strength to say something like this: "Thy will, O God! be done, and not mine!" After this my old master was conquered, and never whip me again, and left me in the hands of Jehovah. This give me confidence to talk to the white or the black folks, and tell what the Lord has done for my poor soul.

Drawing heavily on the book of Exodus and the Hebrew prophets, slave Christianity contained a distinctly antislavery message. Peter Randolph, a Virginia slave, described the comfort that his mother derived from prayer after his brother Benjamin was sold away from the area.

Thanks be unto God, prayer can ascend, and will be listened to by Him who answereth prayer! To him who crieth unto Him day and night, he will listen, and send His angel of peace to quiet his troubled heart, with the assurance that the downtrodden shall be lifted up, the oppressed shall be delivered from his oppressor, all captives set free, and all oppressors destroyed, as in ancient times. . . .

After this a great many come to me about religion, some good and some bad folks: for it was generally known that a great change had come over Tom.

Enslaved people sought to carve out autonomy and masters sought control over slaves' family life as well. Marriage and childbearing were usually promoted by masters, who knew that they encouraged stability among slaves, discouraged running away, and produced new slaves. But masters had the power to destroy families or to make familial love a source of anguish. In his 1849 autobiography, Henry Bibb, who escaped to the North, described his marriage and his efforts to preserve the integrity of his family, often in opposition to his masters. His description of his wedding provides a glimpse into community life among the enslaved. His account illustrates both the ways in which westward migration disrupted slave life and the resources that slaves and masters brought to their conflict with one another.

There is no legal marriage among the slaves of the South; I never saw or heard such a thing in my life, and I have been through seven of the slave states. A slave marrying according to law, is a thing unknown in the history of American slavery. . . .

Our marriage took place one night during the Christmas holydays; at which time we had quite a festival given us. . . . Notwithstanding our marriage was without license or sanction of law, we believed it to be honorable before God, and the bed undefiled. Our Christmas holydays were spent in matrimonial visiting among our friends. . . .

Some months after our marriage, the unfeeling master to whom I belonged, sold his farm with the view of moving his slaves to the State of Missouri, regardless of the separation of husbands and wives forever; but for fear of my resuming my old practice of running away, if he should have forced me to leave my wife, by my repeated requests, he was constrained to sell me to his brother, who lived within seven miles of Wm. Gatewood, who then held Malinda as his property. I was permitted to visit her only on Saturday nights, after my work was done, and I had to be at home before sunrise on Monday mornings or take a flogging. He proved to be so oppressive, and so unreasonable in punishing his victims, that I soon found I should have to run away in self-defense. But he soon began to take the hint, and sold me to Wm. Gatewood the owner of Malinda. With my new residence I confess that I was much dissatisfied. Not that Gatewood was a more cruel master than my former owner—not that I was opposed to living with Malinda, who was then the centre and object of my affections—but to live where I must be eye witness to her insults, scourgings, and abuses, such as are common to be inflicted upon slaves, was more than I could bear. . . . Not many months after I took up my residence on Wm. Gatewood's plantation, Malinda made me a father. The dear little girl was called Mary Frances. She was nurtured and caressed by her mother and father, until she was large enough to creep over the floor after her parents, and climb up by a chair. . . . Malinda's business was to labor out in the field the greater part of her time, and there was no one to take care of poor little Frances, while her mother was toiling in the field. She was left at the house to creep under the feet of an unmerciful old mistress, whom I have known to slap with her hand the face of little Frances, for crying after her mother, until her little face was left black and blue. I recollect that Malinda and myself came from the field one summer's day at noon, and

THE BROOMSTICK WEDDING.

poor little Frances came creeping to her mother smiling, but with large tear drops standing in her dear little eyes, sobbing and trying to tell her mother that she had been abused, but was not able to utter a word. Her little face was bruised black with the whole print of Mrs. Gatewood's hand. This print was plainly to be seen for eight days after it was done. . . .

On this same plantation I was compelled to stand and see my wife shamefully scourged and abused by her master; and the manner in which this was done, was so violently and inhumanly committed upon the person of a female, that I despair in finding decent language to describe the bloody act of cruelty. My happiness or pleasure was then all blasted. . . .

Slave-owning men's control over their slaves' bodies gave them the power to use their female slaves for sex. Many took full advantage of this power. Harriet Jacobs, a Virginia slave who later ran away to freedom, recorded her master's efforts to coerce her into sex—efforts that

The 1897 illustration *Broomstick Wedding* depicts the most common wedding ceremony used among enslaved people. Slaves were not permitted to become legally married, but they sanctified their marriages by jumping over a broomstick, a ritual that signified their jumping into a domestic partnership. The couple in the wedding are dressed in formal clothes handed down by their master and mistress; the preacher presiding over the ritual is a fellow slave.

she, unlike most female slaves who faced a determined master, successfully resisted.

I now entered on my fifteenth year—a sad epoch in the life of a slave girl. My master began to whisper foul words in my ear. Young as I was, I could not remain ignorant of their import. I tried to treat them with indifference or contempt. . . . He was a crafty man, and resorted to many means to accomplish his purposes. Sometimes he had stormy, terrific ways, that made his victims tremble; sometimes he assumed a gentleness that he thought must surely subdue. . . . He told me I was his property; that I must be subject to his will in all things. My soul revolted against the mean tyranny. But where could I turn for protection? . . . There is no shadow of law to protect her from insult, from violence, or even from death. . . .

. . . My master met me at every turn, reminding me that I belonged to him, and swearing by heaven and earth that he would compel me to submit to him. If I went out for a breath of fresh air, after a day of unwearied toil, his footsteps dogged me. If I knelt by my mother's grave, his dark shadow fell on me even there. The light heart which nature had given me became heavy with sad forebodings. The other slaves in my master's house noticed the change. Many of them pitied me; but none dared to ask the cause. They had no need to inquire. They knew too well the guilty practices under that roof; and they were aware that to speak of them was an offence that never went unpunished. . . .

I had entered my sixteenth year, and every day it became more apparent that my presence was intolerable to Mrs. Flint. Angry words frequently passed between her and her husband. . . . In her angry moods, no terms were too vile for her to bestow upon me. . . .

After repeated quarrels between the doctor and his wife, he announced his intention to take his youngest daughter, then four years old, to sleep in his apartment. It was necessary that a servant sleep in the same room, to be on hand if the child stirred.

I was selected for that office, and informed for what purpose that arrangement had been made. By managing to keep within sight of people, as much as possible, during the daytime, I had hitherto succeeded in eluding my master, though a razor was often held to my throat to force me to change this line of policy. At night I slept by the side of my great aunt, where I felt safe. He was too prudent to come into her room. She was an old woman, and had been in the family many years. Moreover, as a married man, and a professional man, he deemed it necessary to save appearances in some degree. . . .

The secrets of slavery are concealed like those of the Inquisition. My master was, to my knowledge, the father of eleven slaves. But did the mothers dare to tell who was the father of their children? Did the other slaves dare to allude to it, except in whispers among themselves? No, indeed! They knew too well the terrible consequences.

Resistance, Repression, and Rebellion

Another source of conflict between masters and enslaved people was the pace of work. In an 1846 letter to his sister, the planter John B. Lamar of Georgia described the foot-dragging of his slave Ned.

With reference to the building of your negro house, I expect it would be best under the circumstances to . . . let some one find all the materials & do the work at a specific price. . . .

My man Ned the carpenter is idle or nearly so at the plantation. He is fixing gates & . . . trying to fool himself into the belief that he is doing something. But on considering his general character for intemperance & disobedience, & quarrelsomeness I have concluded it would be best to pay a little too much for the house, rather than inflict him on you at this time. . . . He is an eye servant. If I was with him I could have the work done soon & cheap, but I am afraid to trust him off where there is no one he fears. He is doing literally nothing at home, and sparing him would not be a cents expense as to that, but I conclude that you do not feel like being annoyed, just now, as I fear & almost know he would annoy you, by getting drunk and raising a row on the lot. I shall sell the rascal the first chance I get.

Eye servant

"Eye servant" was a term used by masters to describe slaves they believed would only work well when watched by a master, overseer, or driver.

Another way in which enslaved men and women defied expectations was in taking goods, especially food, that legally belonged to their masters. In his 1859 autobiography, Austin Steward, an enslaved Virginian who escaped to the North, describes an instance of slave theft that occurred sometime in the first decade of the nineteenth century.

Col. A[lexander] gave his slaves the liberty to get up a grand dance. Invitations were sent and accepted, to a large number of slaves on other plantations, and so, for miles around, all or many of the slaves were in high anticipation of joining in the great dance, which was to come off on Easter night. . . .

The slaves on Col. A's plantation had to provide and prepare the supper for the expected vast "turn out," which was no light matter;

Born a slave in Virginia, Austin Stewart was moved with several other slaves by his master to a new home in upstate New York in the years before the War of 1812. There, Stewart sought out the leaders of the local antislavery society, who informed him that he was free under New York law. Stewart left his master and hired himself out for wages. Austin's portrait, taken during the 1850s, emphasizes his status as a free and respectable man. He is dressed in the vest, jacket, and ascot favored by the middle class.

and as slaves like on such occasions to pattern as much as possible after their master's family, the result was, to meet the emergency of the case, they *took*, without saying, "by your leave, Sir," some property belonging to their master, reasoning among themselves, as slaves often do, that it can not be *stealing*, because "it belongs to massa, and so do *we*, and we only use one part of his property to benefit another. Sure 'tis all massa's." And if they do not get detected in this removal of "massa's property" from one location to another, they think no more of it.

Col. Alexander's slaves were hurrying on with their great preparations for the dance and feast; and as the time drew near, the old and knowing ones might be seen in groups, discussing the matter, with many a wink and nod; but it was in the valleys and by-places where the younger portion were to be found, rather secretly preparing food for the great time coming. This consisted of hogs, sheep, calves; and as to master's *poultry*, that suffered daily. Sometimes it was missed, but the disappearance was always easily accounted for, by informing "massa" that a great number of hawks had been around of late; and their preparation went on, night after night, undetected.

"Taking," foot dragging, and pressuring a master to respect one's family ties were all forms of resistance that stopped short of open defiance. Not so with running away. Most enslaved people who ran away went only a short distance and stayed away only for a short period of time. Relatively few were willing to cut their ties to home, kin, and friends and embark on a dangerous journey to an unknown destination. For most runaways, escaping was a response to a particular grievance or unbearable situation. In his autobiography, Peter Randolph, of Virginia described his brother Benjamin's short-term escape and his master's response.

My oldest brother . . . was owned by C. H. Edloe, the same person who owned me. Benjamin was a very bright young man, and very active about his work. He was fond of laughing and frolicking with the young women on the plantation. This Lacy, the overseer, did not like; and therefore was always watching Benjamin, seeking an occasion to have him whipped. At one time, a pig had been found dead. The little pig could not tell why he was dead, and no one confessed a knowledge of his death; consequently, Lacy thought so great a calamity, so important a death, should be revenged. He advised Edloe to have every slave whipped. Edloe consented, expecting, probably, to prevent, by such cruelty, any other pig from dying a natural death. Lacy . . . took his rawhide, with a wire attached to the end of it, and gave each man twenty lashes on the bare back. . . .

The wounds of these poor creatures prevented them from performing their daily tasks. They were, indeed, so cut up, that pieces came out of the backs of some of them. . . . My brother Benjamin was one of the slaves so savagely beaten. One morning, Lacy—perhaps thinking piggy's death was not wholly avenged—proposed again to whip my brother; but Benjamin did not agree with him as to the necessity of such proceedings, and determined not to submit; therefore, he turned his back upon Lacy, and his face to the woods, making all possible speed towards the latter. . . . For seven months, he lived in the swamps of Virginia, while every effort was made to catch him, but without success. . . . My mother and myself used to carry him such food as we could procure to keep him alive. . . . The overseer had threatened that if he ever saw him, he would shoot him, as quick as he would a wild deer. All the other overseers had made the same threats.

Edloe, not thinking it best to take Benjamin on to his plantation (provided he could catch him), sold him to another man, who . . . sent for him to come out of the swamp and go with him. Benjamin went home to his new master, and went faithfully to work for him—smart young man that he was! . . .

Benjamin continued to serve his new master, until he was suddenly bound and carried to Petersburgh, Virginia, and sold to a negro-trader, who put him in a slave-pen . . . to be carried into bondage further South. . . .

Those who tried to run away for good were a small minority of enslaved people. But their numbers added up: perhaps a thousand fugitives made it to the North every year during the 1840s and 1850s. Their political impact was significant as well. Many self-liberated men and women became militant opponents of slavery once they reached the North, and by the 1840s they became a significant source of political conflict between the North and the South. Joseph Taper escaped bondage in Frederick County, Virginia, with his wife and children in 1837 and moved to Canada two years later. In an 1840 letter to his former master, he spoke freely for the first time about slavery and his aspirations for freedom.

I now take this opportunity to inform you that I am in a land of liberty, in good health. . . .

Since I have been in the Queens dominions I have been well contented. Yes well contented for here, man is as God intended he should be, that is, all are born free & equal. This is a wholesome law, not like the Southern laws which puts man made in the image of God, on level with brutes. O, what will become of the people, &

Malachi

Malachi 3:5, from the Old Testament (King James Version): "And I will come near to you to judgment; and I will be a swift witness against the sorcerers, and against the adulterers, and against false swearers, and against those that oppress the hireling in his wages, the widow, and the fatherless, and that turn aside the stranger from his right, and fear not me, saith the LORD of hosts."

where will they stand in the day of Judgment. Would that the 5th verse of the 3d chapter of Malachi were written as with the bar of iron, & the point of a diamond upon every oppressors heart that they might repent of this evil, & let the oppressed go free. . . .

We have good schools, & all the colored population supplied with schools. My boy Edward who will be six years next January, is now reading, & I intend keeping him at school until he becomes a good scholar.

I have enjoyed more pleasure with one month here than in all my life in the land of bondage. . . .

My wife and self are sitting by a good comfortable fire happy, knowing that there are none to molest or make afraid. God save Queen Victoria. The Lord bless her in this life, & crown her with glory in the world to come is my prayer.

The Resurrection of Henry Box Brown at Philadelphia portrays one of the most celebrated slave escapes in American history: that of Henry "Box" Brown, who had a friend ship him in a crate from Richmond, Virginia, to Philadelphia in 1849. The lithograph depicts Brown as being uncrated by the prominent abolitionist Frederick Douglass and three others, but in reality only one man freed Brown from his box.

Enslaved people used violence against their masters only rarely, but they did so frequently enough for masters everywhere to fear them. A newspaper account from Raleigh, North Carolina, in 1822 reports one group of slaves' attempt to kill their owner's family.

SHOCKING OCCURRENCE. Some negroes of the family of Gen. G. L. Davidson, Iredell county, in this state, unwilling to go to Alabama with the General and his family, who were about to remove there, took the desperate resolution of destroying them by poison, and shocking to relate, effected their purpose on two of the General's daughters. . . .

The poison used, it is believed, was Hemlock, which was furnished by an old negro in the adjoining county of Cabbarus, and had been tried some months before the proper dose was given, to effect the horrid purpose. This has been since ascertained from the frequent sickness of the two ladies, which could not, at the time be accounted for. It is said a dose was ready for the General himself, the administering of which was prevented by the discovery of the horrid plot. Five negroes concerned in this affair, are at present in confinement in Iredell jail.

Open rebellion was even rarer than murder. The reason was simple: white people had all the guns, and slave rebels were sure to be killed. Still, enslaved people did occasionally rebel. The largest slave insurrection between the Revolution and the Civil War was the 1831 rebellion in Southampton County, Virginia, led by Nat Turner, a field hand and lay preacher. Deeply intelligent and charismatic, Turner was a religious seeker whose gifts of prophecy were admired and sought out by fellow slaves and local whites. At the rebellion's height, Turner had about eighty followers, and they killed about sixty white people before being dispersed by the militia. Many of Turner's followers were killed on the spot; others were, like Turner himself, arrested, tried, and hung. Before his trial, he gave testimony to Thomas Gray, a white reporter, about the rebellion and the religious experiences that motivated it. Long convinced that God had chosen him for some great work, in the late 1820s Turner received a series of visions revealing what that work would be. Despite their rarity, slave rebellions served as a stark reminder of the ever-present conflict between masters and their human property, and of enslaved people's ongoing hope for freedom.

I had a vision—and I saw white spirits and black spirits engaged in battle, and the sun was darkened—the thunder rolled in the Heavens, and blood flowed in streams—and I heard a voice saying, "Such is your luck, such you are called to see, and let it come rough or smooth, you must surely bear it." I now withdrew myself as much as my situation would permit, from the intercourse of my fellow servants, for the avowed purpose of serving the Spirit more fully. . . . Shortly afterwards, while laboring in the field, I discovered drops of blood on the corn as though it were dew from heaven—and I communicated it to many, both black and white, in the neighborhood—and I then found on the leaves in the woods hieroglyphic characters, and numbers, with the forms of men in different attitudes, portrayed in blood, and representing the figures I had seen before in the heavens. And now the Holy Ghost had revealed itself to me, and made plain the miracles it had shown me—For as the blood of Christ had been shed on this earth, and had ascended to heaven for the salvation of sinners, and was now returning to earth again in the form of dew—and as the leaves on the trees bore the impression of the figures I had seen in the heavens, it was plain to me that the Savior was about to lay down the yoke he had borne for the sins of men, and the great day of judgement was at hand. . . . And on the 12th of May, 1828, I heard a loud noise in the heavens, and the Spirit instantly appeared to me and said the Serpent was loosened, and Christ had laid down the yoke he had borne for the sins of men, and that I should take it on and fight against the Serpent, for the time was fast approaching when the first should be last and the last should

HORRID MASSACRE IN VIRGINIA.

The Scenes which the above Plate is designed to represent, are—Fig 1. a Mother intreating for the lives of her children.—2. Mr. Travis, cruelly murdered by his own Slaves.—3. Mr. Barrow, who bravely defended himself until his wife escaped.—4. A comp. of mounted Dragoons in pursuit of the Blacks.

Horrid Massacre in Virginia, an 1831 woodcut, represents a composite of several events in Nat Turner's insurrection. The larger scenes above depict the insurrection; the smaller, bottom scenes portray the Virginia militia's defeat of it.

be first. . . . And by signs in the heavens that it would make known to me when I should commence the great work. . . . And on the appearance of the sign (the eclipse of the sun last February) I should arise and prepare myself, and slay my enemies with their own weapons. And immediately on the sign appearing in the heavens, . . . I communicated the great work laid out for me to do, to four in whom I had the greatest confidence (Henry, Hark, Nelson, and Sam). . . . Many were the plans formed and rejected by us. . . .

On Saturday evening, the 20th of August, it was agreed between Henry, Hark and myself, to prepare a dinner for the next day for the men we expected, and then to concert a plan. . . . They prepared in the woods a dinner, where, at three o'clock, I joined them. . . .

I saluted them on coming up, and asked Will how came he there, he answered, his life was worth no more than others, and his liberty as dear to him. I asked him if he thought to obtain it? He said he would, or lose his life. . . . It was quickly agreed we should commence at home (Mr. J. Travis') on that night, and until we had armed and equipped ourselves, and gathered sufficient force, neither age nor sex was to be spared (which was invariably adhered to.) We remained at the feast, until about two hours in the night, when we went to the house. . . . Hark got a ladder and set it against the chimney, on which I ascended, and hoisting a window, entered and came down stairs, unbarred the door, and removed the guns from their places. . . . Armed with a hatchet, and accompanied by Will, I entered my master's chamber, it being dark, I could not give a death blow, the hatchet glanced off his head, he sprang from the bed and called his wife, it was his last word, Will laid him dead, with a blow of his axe, and Mrs. Travis shared the same fate, as she lay in bed. The murder of his family, five in number, was the work of a moment. . . . We got here four guns that would shoot and several old muskets, with a pound or two of powder. . . . I . . . marched them off to Mr. Salathul Francis', about six hundred yards distant. Sam and Will went to the door and knocked. Mr. Francis . . . got up and came to the door. . . . He was dispatched by repeated blows on the head; there was no other white person in the family. . . . We started from there for Mrs. Reese's . . . , where finding the door unlocked, we entered, and murdered Mrs. Reese on her bed, while sleeping; her son awoke, but it was only to sleep the sleep of death. . . . A general destruction of property and search for money and ammunition, always succeeded the murders. By this time my company amounted to fifteen, and nine men mounted. . . . Having murdered Mrs. Waller and ten children, we started for Mr. William Williams'—having killed him and two little boys that were there. . . . I then started for Mr. Jacob Williams, where the family were murdered. . . . Mrs. Vaughan was the next place we visited—and after murdering the family there, I determined on starting for Jerusalem—Our number amounted now to fifty or sixty, all mounted and armed with guns, axes, swords and clubs. . . .

CHAPTER **6** • **PICTURE ESSAY**

Picturing Families

Look at Papa, a lithograph from the 1840s, embraces many elements of the domestic ideology that was now dominant among northern, white, middle-class families. Like most middle-class men in the antebellum era, the father is absent from home. The mother is the child's caretaker, and she instructs him in the habits of familial affection. The child takes naturally to the lesson, reaching out to his absent father.

Almost everyone who lived in the early nineteenth century agreed that families were the foundation stones upon which society was built. Strong, orderly families, they believed, were essential to the health of the social order. The early nineteenth century was hardly marked by order within families, however, especially in the North. Collective labor declined among the middle and working classes as men's work moved to counting-houses, banks, stores, and workshops outside their homes. Northern, middle-class men and women embraced a new ideal of family life that stressed the natural separateness of home and work, emphasized the importance of nurturing children, and celebrated the special characteristics that fitted women to govern domestic life. Many rejected this "cult of domesticity," however. The early nineteenth century was marked by ongoing conflict over what constituted proper family relationships and behavior. The period was also marked by persistent fears that families were becoming disordered, leaving wider disorder in their wake.

One of the ways in which Americans expressed their ideas about proper family life (or gave vent to their anxiety about the ways in which families were changing) was through visual images. Prosperous men and women commissioned family portraits, through which they trumpeted their conformity to family ideals. Advocates of the new domesticity used cheaper engravings and lithographs to promote their vision of family life. Skeptics used the same technology to challenge domestic ideology. Reformers of various stripes sought to appeal to their audiences' anxiety about family breakdown, arguing through pictures as well as words that the evils they sought to abolish were destroying families.

Visual depictions of families are unreliable documents about how families really looked, behaved, or lived, because they sought to depict their subjects in idealized ways—or represented them as blatantly violating norms of family life. But they are wonderful documents for understanding what people thought family life ought to be. Whether it is an oil painting, a cheap engraving, or an example of the new photographic technology, an image of a family provides a window onto family ideals and anxieties. Everything in a family picture tells us something about the standards and fears of the person who made or commissioned it. Who is included or excluded says a great deal about what a proper (or improper) family looked like. The posture, gesture, and direction of the gaze of the picture's subjects convey a great deal about the appropriate emotional content of family life and about the relationships of authority in a family. The subjects' clothing, the home, the physical objects depicted—all say something about how families ought to live.

Before the Industrial Revolution, most people thought of families as productive units—as ways to organize labor. Before 1820, almost all representations of farm and artisanal families reflected this conception, showing them at work. As in real life, even the young girls depicted in *Field of Onions at Wethersfield* are part of the workforce. No man is present, because women had practical control over their own and their daughters' labor. The artist dresses all the females the same way, with nothing in a young girl's clothing to mark her as a child. Each figure is single-mindedly focused on her work.

From the 1790s on, increasing numbers of middle-class men left home to go to work. Homes became spaces occupied primarily by women and children, with adult men coming and going. Increasingly, domestic writers and the middle-class people who read them came to see homes not as sites of labor but as sites of child nurture, instruction, and play—all presided over by the wife and mother. *The Sargent Family*, painted by an anonymous artist in 1800, portrays a father arriving home (or leaving it—the front door is open, and he is wearing a cloak and hat) and being greeted affectionately by his two oldest children. Where the girls in *Field of Onions at Wethersfield* are all dressed like their mother, the children in this painting are dressed in special children's clothes. While most middle-class women did plenty of physical labor, cleaning, sewing, and making household items like candles and soap, Mrs. Sargent's work is portrayed as looking after her children. The materials of family amusement are present: a toy, birds in cages, and a family dog. Where the figures in *Field of Onions* focus solely on their work, here the children focus on their parents, their play, and each other.

Domestic writers of the early nineteenth century depicted the nurturing and instruction of children as woman's highest calling and argued that this calling required women to be educated. This engraving, *Maternal Instruction*, from an 1845 women's magazine, portrays a mother teaching her youngest daughter to read while her older daughter looks on, leaning toward her mother in a gesture of affection. True to middle-class taste in home decoration in the 1840s, the room, the clothing, and the furnishings are all darker, heavier, and more ornate than those in *The Sargent Family*. Only a very prosperous family could afford such furnishings or dresses.

MATERNAL INSTRUCTION.

Engraved expressly for Godey's Lady's Book.

Many Americans were skeptical of the new domesticity. John Lewis Krimmel's *Home and Away*, a pair of engravings from about 1820, offers a burlesque of girls' education—a central element in domestic thought. In the first picture, the young woman is leaving her home for one of the female academies that multiplied after 1790. The family members are well dressed; her father, sitting at a small desk, is counting his ample supply of money. Emblems of rural productivity are everywhere: a spinning wheel, a book on farming, a farmer's almanac.

Krimmel's second image depicts the same household after the young woman has returned from school. The desk has been replaced by a piano—a universal marker of women's nonproductive, "ladylike" accomplishment. The young woman's dress and hair, once simple, now conform to high fashion. The almanac, the book on farming, and the spinning wheel have been replaced by fashionable pictures and, in common with the *The Sargent Family*, a bird in a cage and a little dog. The girl's father stares at an unpaid bill. The room, once open and airy, is dark and cluttered, in a parody of middle-class decorating schemes like those in *Maternal Instruction*. The girl and her beau, once affectionate, are now arguing.

Depictions of the family life of enslaved people in the American South are extremely rare. Far more common are portraits of slave-owning families that include a household slave. This daguerreotype, taken around 1848, shows a slave owner, his two daughters, and the children's nurse. The father, dressed in fine clothing and slouching, dominates the picture while his older daughter leans into him, holding his lapel. Both father and daughter look directly into the camera with an air of authority. The nurse stares straight ahead with a pinched expression. Her clothing, while of better quality than that of most enslaved people, is far less fine than that of her master and mistresses. The introduction of photography brought a new convention to the family portrait: the figures in the portrait did not focus their attention on one another, but on the camera.

Pictorial views of American Indian families are rare, and those that exist follow a shared set of conventions. Karl Bodmer's *Interior of the Hut of a Mandan Chief*, painted around 1834, reveals the home of a Mandan family—members of a people who lived in giant towns on the Great Plains. Bodmer was more interested in highlighting the exotic (and to American and European eyes, savage) material conditions in which they lived—the skins and weapons, the crudeness of the structure, the lack of furniture, and the presence of horses (far left) inside the home—than in portraying the family itself. In his painting, the family becomes just another fixture in the interior landscape. The faces are indistinct, when they are shown. The affection between family members, a central element in northern, middle-class family portraits, is nowhere to be seen. Although most Indian families (including those of the Mandan) were centered on the mother, with the children's lineage and identity traced through her, Bodmer places the men at the center of the family. The women are portrayed from the back; only the men's and children's faces can be seen.

Although multiple generations of a single Anglo family often lived together during the early nineteenth century, Anglo family portraits almost always depicted only nuclear families—father, mother, and children. Not so in "Mexican Family," taken by an unknown photographer in one of the areas occupied by American troops during the Mexican War. This photograph includes a large extended family, including at least three generations and what appear to be several adult sisters or sisters-in-law. Markers of the family's economic status can be seen in the elegant clothes and the book being read by the woman on the left.

Unlike slaveholders, abolitionists frequently published images of the families of enslaved people. They almost always depicted such families as distressed or broken up by the actions of the slaveholder. This engraving, titled *The Domestic Slave Trade*, portrays an enslaved mother kneeling and crying on the shore as slave traders take her children away in a boat.

Southern white artists embraced large planters' belief that slaves were part of an extended plantation family, governed by a benign patriarch. This proslavery cartoon from 1841 illustrates a slave owner's family as it visits the slave quarters. Everywhere there is evidence of happy families. The dignified and well-dressed old couple have a healthy baby at their feet. Younger couples dance to a fiddler in the background. While a smiling slave holds a white child, the old slaves bless their owner for feeding them, clothing them, and caring for them when they are sick or old. Significantly, the only figure characterized as exercising a father's authority is the master, who swears that "while a dollar is left me, nothing shall be spared to increase their comfort and happiness."

Temperance advocates also stirred up anxieties about destroyed families. *The Drunkard's Progress*, an 1826 temperance broadside, chronicles the downfall of an alcoholic. In the first scene, early in the father's drinking, the home is clean and orderly and its members are well dressed. But a cow is breaking through the fence outside. The third scene depicts the family's changed circumstances once the father has become a "confirmed drunkard." Their clothing is now ragged; the home is run-down; the father is violent, the mother crying; and notice of an upcoming sheriff's sale of the family's property is on the wall and the floor. In the final scene, the family leaves its home, which is about to be sold at auction, for the almshouse.

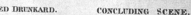

CHAPTER 7

The Triumph of Partisan Democracy

A gentleman in a top hat stands right behind a farmer in a straw hat in Washington, D.C. Alongside elegantly dressed ladies and gentlemen, common people attended Andrew Jackson's first inauguration at the White House in 1829. The presence of large numbers of such common people at an inauguration was new, befitting the installation of a president who had come to power through large-scale democratic mobilization. Artist Robert Cruikshank gave his work the comic title *President's Levee, or All Creation Going to the White House*.

Nobody had ever seen anything like it. For the entire previous day, people had poured into Washington, D.C., to see their new president, Andrew Jackson, sworn in. By ten in the morning of the inauguration, the streets were jammed. Up to this point, presidential inaugurations had been quiet affairs. Now, according to Margaret Bayard Smith, a leading member of the capital's gentry, the streets were jammed with fancy carriages and farmer's carts, "filled with women and children, some in finery and some in rags." After the new president swore his oath and gave his speech, a long procession of "country men, farmers, gentlemen, . . . boys, women and children, black and white" followed him to the White House and descended upon the presidential reception. The crowd smashed several thousand dollars' worth of glass and china in the rush to get at the refreshments. Jackson was nearly crushed as the crowd pressed in on him to shake his hand. Men and boys in muddy boots entered through windows and climbed on the furniture to get a peek at the new president. Everyone agreed that the crowd at the inaugural signaled something radically new in American politics. Margaret Bayard Smith, the wife of a Maryland senator, believed that the days in which elites controlled politics were over. "It was the People's day, and the People's President and the People would rule."

Like most conservatives, Mrs. Smith exaggerated. Andrew Jackson's inauguration did not usher in anything like direct popular rule. But it did signal a new political order in which ordinary people played a far more prominent role. This change had been a long time coming. Since the 1790s, ordinary people had fought to secure their rights to

149

speak their views, oppose the actions of their rulers, and participate in electoral politics. Fierce partisanship erupted, even as political leaders disdained partisanship, and local activists developed new methods of drawing ordinary voters into the political process. In the 1820s and 1830s, this struggle entered a new phase. Poor white men won the vote. Middling-born, self-made political leaders won control over the political parties. These men extended the democratic practices and institutions that had been pioneered before 1815, and they developed new ones. Political leaders preached a new, democratic message that celebrated partisanship and emphasized ordinary white men's capacity to wield political power. American politics would never be the same.

Creating a White Male Electorate

One of the most important elements of the new political order was expanded suffrage. By the 1810s, the number of adult men who did not meet property requirements to vote was expanding dramatically. In the cities, a growing number of men worked for wages or salaries but owned no land. In the West, large numbers of recent arrivals were squatters or had mortgaged their land; neither group legally owned their farms. As their numbers grew, these propertyless men began to challenge their exclusion from the suffrage. Most states were flooded with petitions like this one sent by landless citizens of Richmond to the Virginia constitutional convention of 1829–30.

Memorialist
A memorialist was a person who presented a statement of facts in the form of a petition.

Your memorialists . . . belong to that class of citizens, who not having the good fortune to possess a certain portion of land, are, for that cause only, debarred from the enjoyment of the right of suffrage. Experience has but too clearly evinced . . . by how frail a tenure they hold every other right, who are denied this, the highest prerogative of freedmen. . . . Comprising a very large part, probably a majority of male citizens of mature age, they have been passed by, like aliens or slaves, as if destitute of interest, or unworthy of a voice, in measures involving their political destiny. . . .

The existing regulation of suffrage . . . instead of the equality nature ordains, creates an odious distinction between members of the same community; robs of all share, in the enactment of the laws, a large portion of the citizens bound by them, and whose blood and treasure are pledged to maintain them. . . .

The object . . . meant to be obtained [by a property qualification for voting] was . . . to admit the meritorious, and reject the unworthy. But the same qualifications that entitle [the citizen] to assume the management of his private affairs, and to claim all other privileges of citizenship, equally entitle him, in the judgment of your memorialists, to be entrusted with this, the dearest of all his privileges. . . . They cannot discern in the possession of land any evidence of peculiar merit. . . . To ascribe to a landed possession, moral or intellectual endowments, would truly be regarded as ludicrous, were it not for the gravity with which the proposition is maintained, and still more for the grave consequences flowing from it. Such possession no more proves him who has it, wiser or better, than it proves him taller or stronger, than him who has it not. . . .

Virtue, intelligence, are not among the products of the soil. Attachment to property, often a sordid sentiment, is not to be confounded with the sacred flame of patriotism. The love of country . . . is engrafted in our nature. It exists . . . among all classes. . . .

If the landless citizens have been . . . driven from the polls, in time of peace, they have . . . been . . . summoned, in war, to the battle-field. Nor have they disobeyed the summons, or, less profusely than others, poured out their blood in the defense of that country which is asked to disown them. Will it be said they owe allegiance to the Government that gives them protection? Be it so: and . . . if privileges are really extended to them . . . have they not an interest, a deep interest, in perpetuating the blessings they enjoy, and a right, consequently, to guard those blessings, not from foreign aggression merely, but from domestic encroachment?

But, it is said, yield them this right, and they will abuse it: property, that is, landed property will be rendered insecure, or at least overburthened, by those who possess it not. . . . If we are sincerely republican, we must give our confidence to the principles we profess. We have been taught by our fathers, that all power is vested in, and derived from, the people; not the freeholders; that the majority of the community . . . have . . . the political right of creating and re-moulding at their will, their civil institutions. Nor can this right be any where more safely deposited. The generality of mankind, doubtless, desire to become owners of property; left free to reap the fruits of their labors, they will seek to acquire it honestly. It can never be their interest to overburthen, or render precarious, what they themselves desire to enjoy in peace. . . .

The interests of the many deserve at least as much to be guarded as those of the few. . . . What security . . . is there against the injustice of the freeholders? . . . What is there to prevent their imposing

Since the Revolution, almost all states gave the vote only to adult male owners of land who met certain residency requirements. Voting requirements in New York, established during its constitutional convention in 1777, were typical.

Every male inhabitant of full age, who shall have personally resided within one of the counties of this State for six months immediately preceding the day of election, shall, at such election, be entitled to vote for representatives of the said county in assembly; if during the time aforesaid, he shall have been a freeholder, possessing a freehold of the value of twenty pounds, within the said county, or have rented a tenement [rented real estate] therein of the yearly value of forty shillings, and been rated and actually paid taxes to this State. . . .

Freeholder

A "freehold" was ownership of land; a "freeholder" was a person who owned land.

upon others undue burthens, and conferring on themselves unjust exemptions? Supplying the public exigencies by a . . . tax exclusively or oppressively operating on the other portions of the community? Exacting from the latter, in common with slaves, menial services? . . . Denying to the children of all other classes admission to the public seminaries of learning? . . .

For obvious reasons, by almost universal consent, women and children, aliens and slaves, are excluded. It were useless to discuss the propriety of a rule that scarcely admits of diversity of opinion. What is concurred in by those who constitute the society, the body politic, must be taken to be right. But the exclusion of these classes for reasons peculiarly applicable to them, is no argument for excluding others to whom no one of those reasons applies. . . .

They alone deserve to be called free . . . who participate in the formation of their political institutions, and in the control of those who make and administer the laws.

Between the 1810s and the 1850s, every state held at least one convention to revise its constitution. In these conventions, petitioners like the non-freeholders of Richmond found many supporters who adopted their reasoning. They also found opponents. Warren Dutton, a delegate to the Massachusetts constitutional convention in 1820, laid out the standard argument against an expanded suffrage in a speech to the convention.

Mr. DUTTON said . . . the resolution . . . introduced a new principle into the constitution. It was universal suffrage. There were two ways of considering it. 1st. As a matter of right. 2d. As a matter of expediency. As to the right, he inquired why paupers were excluded at all, if it was a common right; and if it was not, then there was the same right in the community to exclude every man, who was not worth two hundred dollars, as there was to exclude paupers, or persons under twenty-one years. In truth there was no question of right; it was wholly a question of expediency. He thought it expedient to retain the qualification in the constitution. It was in the nature of a privilege, and as such, it was connected with many virtues, which conduced to the good order of society. It was a distinction to be sought for; it was the reward of good conduct. It encouraged industry, economy, and prudence; it elevated the standard of all our civil institutions, and gave dignity and importance to those who chose, and those who were chosen. . . . He maintained that in this country, where the means of subsistence were so abundant, and the demand for labor so great, every man of sound body could acquire the necessary qualification. If he failed

Most (but not all) supporters of ending property qualifications for the vote wished to narrow the electorate in another way: by race. In a speech to the New York constitutional convention of 1821, John Z. Ross, an advocate of giving propertyless white men the vote, argued for withholding that privilege from African Americans.

The right of suffrage is extended to white men only. But why, it will probably be asked, are blacks to be excluded? I answer, because they are seldom, if ever, required to share in the common burthens or defense of the state. There are also additional reasons; they are a peculiar people, incapable, in my judgment, of exercising that privilege with any sort of discretion, prudence, or independence. They have no just conceptions of civil liberty. They know not how to appreciate it, and are consequently indifferent to its preservation.

Under such circumstances, it would hardly be compatible with the safety of the state, to entrust such a people with this right. . . .

to do this, it must be, ordinarily, because he was indolent or vicious. . . . He also considered it as unreasonable, that a man who had no property should act indirectly upon the property of others. . . . It was . . . wholly inequitable in its nature, that men without a dollar should, in any way, determine the rights of property, or have any concern in its appropriation. He also contended, that the principle of the resolution was anti-republican. It greatly increased the number of voters, and those of a character most likely to be improperly influenced and corrupted. It enlarged the field of action to every popular favorite, and enabled him to combine greater numbers. The time might come, when he would be able to command, as truly as ever a general commanded an army, sufficient numbers to affect or control the government itself. In that case, the form of a republican constitution might remain, but its life and spirit would have fled. The government would be essentially a democracy, and between that and a despotism there would be but one step.

In every state except Virginia, Louisiana, and Rhode Island, the opponents of a property qualification for the vote triumphed by 1840. But most new state constitutions added more stringent residency requirements and other restrictions on who could vote. All but five states restricted or prohibited voting by African Americans. The result, nationwide, was the creation of a political community made up of almost all adult white men. The New York convention of 1821 tightened residency requirements for the vote, but its enfranchisement of propertyless white men dramatically expanded the electorate.

Every male citizen of the age of twenty-one years, who shall have been an inhabitant of this State one year preceding any election, and for the last six months a resident of the town or county where he may offer his vote; and shall have, within the year next preceding the election, paid a tax to the State or county, assessed upon his real or personal property; or shall by law be exempted from taxation; or being armed and equipped according to law, shall have performed within that year military duty in the militia of this State; or who shall be exempted from performing militia duty in consequence of being a fireman in any city, town, or village in this State; and also, every male citizen of the age of twenty-one years, who shall have been, for three years preceding such election, an inhabitant of this State; and for the last year a resident in the town or county where he may offer his vote; and shall have been, within the last year, assessed to labor upon the public highways, and shall have performed the labor, or paid an equivalent therefore, according to law, shall be entitled to vote in the town or ward where he actually resides, and not else-where, for all officers that now are, or hereafter may be, elective by the people; but no man of color, unless he shall have been for three years a citizen of this State, and for one year next preceding any election shall be seized and possessed of a freehold estate of the value of two hundred and fifty dollars, over and above all debts and incumbrances charged thereon, and shall have . . . paid a tax thereon, shall be entitled to vote in any such election. . . .

Laws may be passed excluding from the right of suffrage persons who have been or may be convicted of infamous crimes.

Re-creating Party Politics

The second great political innovation of the 1820s and 1830s was the creation of powerful political parties, and their gradual domination of virtually every aspect of electoral politics. Competition between the Federalist and Republican parties ended after 1815 with the collapse of the Federalists. For the next decade and a half, politics was defined by competition between warring factions of the Republican Party. This situation began to change in the 1820s, as political leaders in several states began to work toward a revival of party competition. Their efforts began to bear fruit on a national level in 1828, when Andrew Jackson, a popular military hero, ran for president against the incumbent John Quincy Adams. In 1827, Martin Van Buren, a New York politician who was managing Jackson's national presidential campaign, wrote to Thomas Ritchie, leader of the powerful Virginia faction known as the Junto, making his case for using Jackson's candidacy to revive old party divisions.

Dear Sir,

You will have observed an article in the [Albany, NY] Argus upon the subject of a national convention. . . . The following may, I think, justly be ranked among its probable advantages. First, it is the best and probably the only practicable mode of concentrating the entire vote of the opposition and of effecting what is of still greater importance, the substantial reorganization of the old Republican Party. 2nd. . . . I have long been satisfied that we can only get rid of the present, and restore a better state of things, by combining Genl. Jackson's personal popularity with the portion of old party feeling yet remaining. . . . 3rd the call of such a convention, its exclusive Republican character, and the refusal of Mr. Adams and his friends to become parties to it, would draw anew the old Party lines and the subsequent contest would reestablish them. . . .

Concentrate

To "concentrate" the votes of a party was to focus them on one candidate, rather than allowing them to be split up among several candidates.

We must always have party distinctions and the old ones are the best of which the nature of the case admits. Political combinations between the inhabitants of the different states are unavoidable and the most natural and beneficial to the country is that between the planters of the South and the plain Republicans of the North. The country has once flourished under a party thus constituted and may again. It would take longer than our lives (even if it were practicable) to create new party feelings to keep those masses together. If the old ones are suppressed, geographical divisions founded on local interests, or what is worse prejudices between free and slave holding states will inevitably take their place. Party attachment in former times furnished a complete antidote for sectional prejudices by producing counteracting feelings. It was not until that defense had been broken down that the clamour against Southern Influence and African Slavery could be made effectual in the North. . . . Formerly, attacks upon Southern Republicans were regarded by those in the North as assaults upon their political brethren and resented accordingly. This all powerful sympathy . . . can and ought to be revived and the proposed convention would be eminently serviceable in effecting that object.

Lastly the effect of such a nomination on Genl. Jackson could not fail to be considerable. His election, as the result of his military services without reference to party . . . would be one thing. His election as the result of a combined and concerted effort of a political party, holding in the main, to certain tenets and opposed to certain prevailing principles, might be another and a far different thing.

This Jacksonian broadside from the 1828 election in Virginia reveals some of the aspirations that helped propel Jackson into the presidency. The American eagle holds the Great Seal of Virginia. In that seal, the Roman goddess Virtus stands astride a dead tyrant; the state's motto declares *Sic Semper Tyrannis*—"Thus always to tyrants." The image and phrase fit well with the Jackson men's insistence that the federal government had been taken over by an undemocratic and self-perpetuating elite. The party's candidates, unlike their opponents, were "no favored few, booted and spurred, ready to ride us." The broadside promised "No bargain, sale or management," referring to their belief that John Quincy Adams had won the presidency in 1824 through a "corrupt bargain" with Henry Clay. The poster emphasized Jackson's status as a war hero, promising "Justice and equality to all—and honor and gratitude to the man who has filled the measure of his country's glory." With appeals like these, Jackson men throughout the United States adopted the most advanced techniques of the Jeffersonians—conventions, public appeals through print, party tickets. They also sought to increase their appeal by associating their entire party with the war hero Jackson.

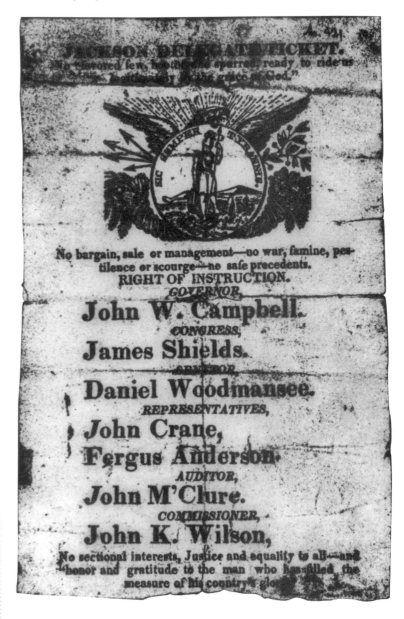

In the twelve years after the 1828 campaign, Van Buren and his allies were spectacularly successful in reviving party divisions. One key to that success was grassroots organizing. Jacksonian party activists (who now called themselves Democrats) built upon the organizing tactics of the Republicans, extending them to the majority of localities in the country and backing them up with larger, more disciplined party organizations. A "Plan of Organization" sent by the New York Democratic State Committee to the state's Democratic County Committees in 1844 describes the structure of the state's Democratic organization and shows how party activists mobilized popular support.

PLAN OF ORGANIZATION

I. *A State Committee of Organization*, whose duty will be to cause the establishment of County Committees, to correspond frequently with them, and to supervise and stimulate the general working of the organization. . . .

II. *A County Committee of Organization*, of three or five young and active men, who will agree to perform the duties assigned to them. These duties will be:—

   1. To see that Democratic Associations are promptly formed in every town, and to send or go personally for that purpose in each town. . . .

   3. To make provision for furnishing these Associations with tracts, documents, &c., for gratuitous distribution, besides stimulating them to active efforts to supply themselves as copiously as possible.

   4. To make arrangements for furnishing each town with efficient public speakers as often as convenient, and at least twice within the two months before the election.

   5. To correspond frequently with the town associations or committees, for the purpose of promoting concert of action, and urging upon them the importance of carrying out efficiently the local organization, and also to correspond with the State Committee.

III. *A Democratic Association* in every town or election district, into which efforts should be made to bring every democratic voter. . . . The practical work of the organization to be mainly conducted by their *Executive Committees*, who will also constitute the *Town Committees of Organization*. . . . The duties of the *Town Executive Committee* to be:—

   1. To establish a Committee of Three in every School District, consisting of young, active and zealous men, who will agree and be reliable for the thorough and effective performance of their duty. . . .

   2. To receive the district lists, and form a town list, reporting the result, with corrections from time to time, to the County Committee.

   3. On the day of the election to station one of their number at each poll, with an accurate list of the voters at that poll, *checking the names of the democratic electors as they arrive and vote*, and causing

This broadside sought to mobilize ordinary citizens in the Whig Party's 1840 electoral campaign, announcing one of thousands of public meetings held that year. The drawing depicts the elite-born William Henry Harrison as a man of the people, plowing in ordinary farmer's clothes. Behind him is the mythical log cabin in which they said he was born. Like the Jacksonians in 1828, it associates its candidate with "Reform."

prompt measures to be taken to bring out those who do not come early in the day.

4. To exert themselves actively for the distribution of useful tracts, documents, newspapers and handbills among the people, both in person and through the district committees.

5. To call special meetings of the district committees, and supervise and stimulate them to the performance of their duties.

6. To station proper challengers at the polls, and to be vigilant in adopting all means that may be necessary to ensure the purity of the election.

7. To report at least on the 1st of every month to the County Committee.

IV. *The School District Committees.* Their duties will be:—

1. To prepare an accurate list of all the voters in their school district, classifying them in separate columns as *Democratic, Whig,* or *Doubtful,* with remarks as to the latter class. The utmost effort should be made to get every name upon the list, and count none as democrats but those fully reliable. . . .

2. To receive from the committees above, and to procure for themselves whenever they can . . . useful tracts, documents, newspapers and handbills for circulation. These should be distributed especially among the doubtful, the more moderate and reasonable whigs, and those of the democratic party supposed to incline to apathy. The more and the oftener they are thus served, the better.

3. To act as a Committee of Vigilance for the district, to procure the attendance of the people at public meetings, to endeavor, by reason and argument, to convince the doubting and animate the apathetic.

4. To procure the attendance of the democratic electors at the polls. Before the election, the committees should personally see every democrat in the district, provide means of conveyance for the infirm and aged, and engage all to go early to the polls. Unless the mind has been previously prepared, and calculations for the purpose been made, many individuals will be found who, on the day of election, can not

Whig

A Whig was a member of the Whig Party, which was founded in 1835 to oppose the Democratic Party be induced or will be prevented from attending. It is especially important, too, that all who can should be induced to go *early*, in order to give opportunity to get out those who may fail; for if it be not ascertained until afternoon who are behind, it will then be too late to send for them. And, on the day of election, where there is the least doubt of a voter's attending . . . , he should be sent for at once. . . .

Party Issues, Party Principles

Andrew Jackson's presidency was a defining era, as both the president's supporters (who called themselves Democrats) and his opponents (who created the Whig Party after 1834) clarified their ideological and policy commitments in response to his policies. By far the most controversial and influential issue during Jackson's presidency was whether to renew the charter of the Second Bank of the United States, a private corporation that Congress had created in 1816. The bank was the sole repository for the federal government's money, and largely on the basis of federal deposits, it acted as the main regulator of the money supply, printing its own money, making loans to other banks, and withholding loans from banks that it considered imprudent. In 1831, Congress renewed the federal charter of the bank. Jackson vetoed the recharter. In 1833, he ordered that all federal funds be withdrawn from the bank. The bank could not survive the withdrawal, and it closed. Jackson's 1831 veto message, reprinted in Democratic newspapers across the nation, expressed many of what were becoming the central principles of Jackson's presidency and of the Democratic Party.

The . . . Bank of the United States . . . enjoys an exclusive privilege of banking under the authority of the General government, a monopoly of its favor and support, and, as a necessary consequence, almost a monopoly of the foreign and domestic exchange. The powers, privileges, and favors bestowed upon it in the original charter, by increasing the value of the stock far above its par value, operated as a gratuity of many millions to the stockholders. . . .

Every monopoly and all exclusive privileges are granted at the expense of the public, which ought to receive a fair equivalent. The many millions which this act proposes to bestow on the stockholders of the existing bank must come directly or indirectly out of the earnings of the American people. . . .

This act does not permit competition in the purchase of this monopoly. It seems to be predicated on the erroneous idea that the

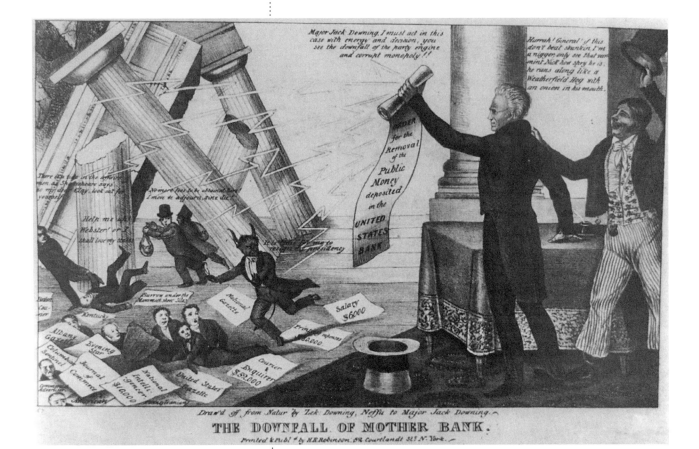

THE DOWNFALL OF MOTHER BANK.

As Jackson brandishes his 1833 order to withdraw all federal funds from the United States Bank, it emits lightning bolts that cause the bank to collapse. Jackson says, "You see the downfall of the party engine and corrupt monopoly," while his companion, the fictional folk philosopher Major Jack Downing, cheers him on. Nicholas Biddle, the president of the bank (depicted as the devil), runs from the collapsing building, as do the bank's political allies. Strewn across the floor are the names of the newspapers that supported the bank and the amount of money that the bank had given to each one—a reference to the bank's practice of subsidizing friendly newspapers. Also on the floor is a paper labeled "Salary $6000"—an allusion to the bank's habit of hiring friendly politicians to well-paid positions.

present stockholders have a prescriptive right not only to the favor but to the bounty of Government. It appears that more than a fourth part of the stock is held chiefly by foreigners and the residue is held by a few hundred of our own citizens, chiefly of the richest class. For their benefit does this act exclude the whole American people from competition in the purchase of this monopoly and dispose of it for many millions less than it is worth. . . .

As little stock is held in the West, it is obvious that the debt of the people in that section to the bank is principally a debt to the Eastern and foreign stockholders; that the interest they pay upon it is carried into the Eastern States and into Europe, and that it is a burden upon their industry and a drain on their currency, which no country can bear without inconvenience and occasional distress. . . .

Is there no danger to our liberty and independence in a bank that in its nature has so little to bind it to our country? The president of the bank has told us that most of the State banks exist by its forbearance. Should its influence become concentrated, as it may under the operation of such an act as this, in the hands of a self-elected directory whose interests are identified with those of the foreign stockholders, will there not be cause to tremble for the purity of our elections in peace and for the independence of our country in war? Their power would be great whenever they might choose to exert it. . . .

[I]t is the exclusive province of Congress and the President to decide whether the particular features of this act are *necessary and proper* in order to enable the bank to perform conveniently and efficiently the public duties assigned to it as a fiscal agent, and therefore constitutional, or *unnecessary* and *improper*, and therefore unconstitutional. . . .

It can not be *necessary* to the character of the bank as a fiscal agent of the Government that its private business should be exempted from that taxation to which all State banks are liable, nor can I conceive it " *proper*" that the substantive and most essential powers reserved to the States shall be thus attacked and annihilated as a means of executing the powers delegated to the General Government. It may be safely assumed that none of those sages who had an agency in forming or adopting our Constitution ever imagined that any portion of the taxing power of the States not prohibited to them

An anti-Jacksonian takes issue with some of the president's policies in this satirical drawing. Jackson and his vice president, Martin Van Buren, lead the "caravan," singing nonsense lyrics from popular songs. They are followed by the devil playing a fiddle. In a reference to Jackson's history as an Indian fighter and his presidential policy of Indian removal, the parade concludes with a wagon carrying a number of Indians in a cage. A flag inscribed "Rights of Man," topped by a liberty cap, flies over the cage. Inside the cage, one Indian says "Home Sweet Home." In the background, a crowd cheers its hero and holds banners proclaiming his heroism, while a drunk man lies in the mud in the foreground, singing "Hail Columbia, Happy Land." Both details reflect the opposition's view of Jackson as the hero of the unruly and unvirtuous elements of the American lower classes.

THE GRAND NATIONAL CARAVAN MOVING EAST.

nor delegated to Congress was to be swept away and annihilated as a means of executing certain powers delegated to Congress. . . .

It is to be regretted that the rich and powerful too often bend the acts of government to their selfish purposes. Distinctions in society will always exist under every just government. Equality of talents, of education, or of wealth can not be produced by human institutions. In the full enjoyment of the gifts of Heaven and the fruits of superior industry, economy, and virtue, every man is equally entitled to protection by law; but when the laws undertake to add to these natural and just advantages artificial distinctions, to grant titles, gratuities, and exclusive privileges, to make the rich richer and the potent more powerful, the humble members of society—the farmers, mechanics, and laborers—who have neither the time nor the means of securing like favors to themselves, have a right to complain of the injustice of their Government. There are no necessary evils in government. Its evils exist only in its abuses. If it would confine itself to equal protection, and, as Heaven does its rains, shower its favors alike on the high and the low, the rich and the poor, it would be an unqualified blessing. . . .

Nor is our Government to be maintained or our Union preserved by invasions of the rights and powers of the several States. In thus attempting to make our General Government strong we make it weak. Its true strength consists in leaving individuals and States as much as possible to themselves—in making itself felt, not in its power, but in its beneficence; not in its control, but in its protection; not in binding the States more closely to the center, but leaving each to move unobstructed in its proper orbit.

Jackson's ideas and policies were quickly adopted and elaborated by his party, and they remained the centerpiece of the Democratic program into the 1840s. One of the best summaries of the party's core principles came in 1838 from the pen of John O'Sullivan, the editor of the *United States Magazine and Democratic Review*, a Democratic magazine of politics, literature, and social commentary.

We believe . . . in the principle of *democratic republicanism*, in its strongest and purest sense. We have an abiding confidence in the virtue, intelligence, and full capacity for self-government, of the great mass of our people—our industrious, honest, manly, intelligent millions of freemen.

We are opposed to all self-styled "wholesome restraints" on the free action of the popular opinion and will, other than those which have for their sole object the prevention of precipitate legislation. This latter object is to be attained by the expedient of the division of power, and by causing all legislation . . . to be sifted through the discussions of co-ordinate legislative branches. . . . Yet all should be dependent with equal directness and promptness on the influence of public opinion; the popular will should be equally the animating and moving spirit of them all. . . .

The greatest number are *more likely*, at least, as a general rule, to understand and follow their own greatest good, than is the minority. . . .

A minority is much more likely to abuse power for the promotion of its own selfish interests, at the expense of the majority of numbers—the substantial and producing mass of the nation—than the latter is to oppress unjustly the former. . . .

There does not naturally exist any . . . superiority in a minority class above the great mass of the community, in intelligence and competence for the duties of government. . . . The general diffusion of education; the facility of access to every species of knowledge . . . ; the freedom of the press, . . . in this country at least, make the pretensions of those self-styled "better classes" to the sole possession of the requisite intelligence for the management of public affairs, too absurd to be entitled to any other treatment than an honest, manly contempt. . . .

The best government is that which governs least. No human depositories can, with safety, be trusted with the power of legislation upon the general interests of society so as to operate directly or indirectly on the industry and property of the community. Such power must be perpetually liable to the most pernicious abuse. . . . Legislation has been the fruitful parent of nine-tenths of all the evil . . . by which mankind has been afflicted since the creation of the world. . . . Government should have as little as possible to do with the general business and interests of the people. If it once undertake these functions as its rightful province of action, it is impossible to say to it "thus far shalt thou go, and no farther." . . . It will be perpetually tampering with private interests, and sending forth seeds of corruption which will result in the demoralization of the society. Its domestic action should be confined to the administration of justice, for the protection of the natural equal rights of the citizen, and the preservation of social order. In all other respects, the VOLUNTARY PRINCIPLE, the principle of FREEDOM, suggested to us by the analogy of the divine government of the Creator, and already recognized by us with perfect success in the great social interest of Religion, affords the true "golden rule" which is alone abundantly competent to work out the best possible general result of order and happiness from that chaos of characters, ideas, motives, and interests—human society. Afford but the single nucleus of a system of administration of justice between man and man, and, under the sure operation of this principle, the floating atoms will distribute and combine themselves, as we see in the beautiful natural process of crystallization, into a far more perfect and harmonious result than if government, with its "fostering hand," undertake to disturb, under the plea of directing, the process. The natural laws which will establish themselves and find their own level are the best laws. The same hand was the Author of the moral, as of the physical world; and we feel clear and strong in the assurance that we cannot err intrusting, in the former, to the same fundamental principles of spontaneous action and self-regulation which produce the beautiful order of the latter.

The Whig Party's core principles and policies were summarized by Horace Greeley, editor of the _New York Tribune_, in a pamphlet published during the late 1840s.

Two grand and fruitful ideas attract and divide the political world. On the one hand Liberty, on the other Order, is the watchword of a mighty host, impatient of resistance and eager for universal dominion. . . . An infinity of cruelty and crime has been perpetrated in the abused name of Order, and hardly less in that equally abused of Liberty. But neither of these suffices without the other. Each is indispensable to general contentment, prosperity, and happiness. . . . If without Liberty human existence is bitter and irksome, without Order it is precarious and beset with constant perils. Few men will clear, and plant, and build, without a reasonable assurance that they shall likewise reap, and inhabit, and enjoy. . . . Anarchy or mob-rule is the worst of despotisms,—it is the rule of thousands of savage tyrants instead of one—it is the carnival of unbridled lust, brutality, and ruffianism. As an escape from this, the government even of

The _Log Cabin_ was a spectacularly successful Whig campaign newspaper in the 1840 presidential campaign, one that launched the long and distinguished newspaper career of Horace Greeley. Newspapers were essential to popular mobilization, as they were the main organ for indoctrinating the rank and file in Whig and Democratic doctrines and ways of understanding society and politics. The number of newspapers exploded during the antebellum era, and most of them allied with one party or the other.

Egypt or Naples would be joyfully accepted by all who prefer to walk in the quiet paths of Industry and Virtue.

Now republics have their peculiar perils no less than monarchies. . . . What the sycophant, the courtier, is to the sovereign Prince, the demagogue is to the Sovereign People. The maxim that "The King can do no wrong" is as mischievous in a free state as in any other. Nations, as well as kings, have their weaknesses, their vices, their temptations. . . . They, too, are subject to the illusion of false glory. They are often impelled to kill or to enslave their neighbors under the pretense of liberating them: they are in danger of mistaking the promptings of ambition or covetousness for those of philanthropy or destiny. Nowhere is there greater need of Conservatism than in a young, powerful, and martial Republic. . . . While it is quite possible to err on the side of Order, as well as on that of Liberty, the tendency, the temptation, in a Democracy like ours, is almost wholly on the side of the latter. . . .

The party styling itself Democratic is, as regards Foreign Powers, the more belligerent and aggressive party. It takes delight in shaking its fists in the face of mankind in general. It made all the foreign wars in which our country has been involved since her independence was acknowledged. . . .

No reproach has been more commonly applied to the Whig party by its enemies than that of being a "peace party," and of "taking the side of the enemy;" and nothing could be said, which, rightly regarded, redounds more to its praise. It is easy and popular—in the case of international disputes, to take extreme ground, to insist on all the points which favor our own country and slur over those which make for its antagonist—easy to rouse the dogs of war, and cry havoc amidst the shouts of excited and admiring multitudes. But to urge that there is another side to the picture, which also demands consideration . . . that we have not only endured wrong but done wrong, and that the claims put forth on our behalf are beyond the measure of justice,—this is not the way to win huzzas nor elections, yet it is the course often dictated by duty and genuine patriotism. Honor, then, to that party which has repeatedly dared to stem the mad torrent of revenge and lust of conquest. . . .

Opposed to the instinct of boundless acquisition stands that of Internal Improvement. A nation cannot simultaneously devote its attention to the absorption of others' territories and the improvement of its own. In a state of war, not law only is silent, but the pioneer's axe, the canal-digger's mattock, and the house-builder's trowel also.

Vainly should we hope to clear, and drain, and fence, and fertilize, our useless millions of acres, at the same time that we are intent on bringing the whole vast continent under our exclusive dominion. It is by no accident, therefore . . . that the Democratic party arrays itself against the prosecution of Internal Improvements. We see this evinced in its votes against and vetoes of river and harbor improvement bills, in its repudiations, its hostility to corporations, &c. &c. Individuals in the party will pretend to be in favor of the prosecution of such improvements, but not by the General government, nor by the State government, nor yet by a company of citizens, unless clogged with conditions which render such prosecution morally impossible. . . .

A tariff of duties, wisely adjusted so as to afford both Revenue and Protection, is essential to the national growth and well-being. What do we mean by Protection? Simply the restriction of importations of foreign manufactures to such an extent that their younger and less hardy American rivals may take root and flourish. How far do we propose to prosecute this policy? Until our country's legitimate wants are supplied by her own labor, so far as Nature may have interposed no impediment. . . .

There underlies the practical politics of our time and country a radical diversity of sentiment respecting the appropriate sphere of Government. On the one hand, Republican Government is regarded as the natural friend and servant of the People, whose proper function it is to lighten their burdens, to increase their facilities for intercourse or intelligence, and to contribute in all practicable ways to their progress, comfort, and happiness. On the other, Government is regarded with jealousy and distrust, as an enemy to be watched, and evil to be restricted within the narrowest limits. The mottoes of this latter school are significant: "The world is governed too much,"—"The best government is that which governs least,"—"*Laissez faire,*" ("Let us alone"), &c., &c. Now these maxims seem to me unwisely transferred from Governments directed by despots to Governments controlled by and existing for the People. They are nowhere recognized by the Democracy of Europe, which plainly contemplates the institution of Governments more pervasive and efficient than the world has yet known. Free Education, Insurance by the State, the Right to Labor,—these are but a part of the ideas of like tendency, which the European Democracy stands ready to realize whenever it shall have the power. Its policy is constructive, creative, and beneficent, while that of our self-styled "Democracy" is repulsive, chilling, nugatory,—a bundle of negations, restrictions, and abjurations. Can there be a rational doubt as to which of these is the true Democracy? Who does not see that the fundamental ideas of our party Democracy are as radically hostile to Common Schools, and to tax-sustained Common Roads, as to a Protective Tariff, a National Bank, or to the National Improvement of Rivers and Harbors, if it dare but follow where its principles lead?

Politics Without Parties

Party activists were not the only political innovators at work in the first half of the nineteenth century. The northern states were teeming with political insurgents and reformers, most of whom rejected the Democrats' and the Whigs' way of conducting politics and developed their own political institutions and practices. The Workingmen's Party was one of many political movements that denounced what it saw as the undemocratic tendencies of the major parties and sought to topple them from power by using the methods that the parties had pioneered: grassroots electoral organizing

Although female moral reformers clearly accepted the conventional belief that unmarried, sexually active women were "fallen" and marked by "shame," they also confronted male privilege by attacking the sexual double standard. In 1840 the first annual report of the Female Moral Reform Society articulated the society's position.

The obligation . . . rests on all, and emphatically on *christians*, to treat the violators of the 7th commandment, of both sexes, with strict regard to moral character, and until satisfactory evidence of penitence is obtained, to refuse association with either. . . . Reason and religion, common sense and humanity, alike revolt at the unnatural distinction now made between the sexes in the punishment awarded to this transgression. In the one, it is an unpardonable crime, for which tears of blood can never atone—in the other, it is considered a venial offence for which no repentance is required. Thus impunity in guilt prepares the stronger sex to prey upon the weaker; while the certainty that one false step is irremediable ruin, renders the erring female reckless of consequences, and hardened in iniquity. A remedy for this complicated wrong, is . . . "to treat the vicious man and woman alike while they continue equally guilty in the sight of God."

Advocate

The *Advocate of Moral Reform*, the national newspaper of the Female Moral Reform Society, regularly published the names of men who frequented prostitutes.

and use of print media, such as this cartoon, by an unknown artist, probably from the 1830s. On the left, the devil hands a Tammany man (a member of the dominant organization in the New York City Democratic Party) a ballot box and a newspaper, saying, "Take any, my dear Friend, they will all help you to grind the Workies." On the right, Lady Liberty holds out a ballot box while a working man deposits his ballot, saying, "Now for a noble effort for Rights, Liberties, and Comforts. . . . No more grinding the POOR—But Liberty and the Rights of Man."

The most influential of the political outsiders who challenged the political practices of the major parties were evangelical reformers, whose politics grew out of their commitment to rid the world of sin, preparing for the millennium. Among these reformers were many women. Although the new domestic ideology taught that women were formed by God for domestic life, it also taught that they were endowed with superior moral capacities. Many middle-class white and African American women in the North seized on this belief, campaigning to make the world conform to God's will as they saw it. In the process, they created a new kind of politics. Evangelical politics sought not to win office but to change the world by transforming individual consciences. And it rejected mainstream politicians' exclusion of women and people of color from public life.

Few reform causes won more support from white, middle-class, northern women than the Female Moral Reform Society, founded in New York City in 1834. Dedicated to ending the sins of sexual impurity, fornication, and adultery, the society became a hothouse of female activism, publishing the first female-edited newspaper, the *Advocate of Moral Reform*, in American history. Margaret Prior's published account of her work as a "missionary" for the New York City branch of the society during the 1830s, probably taken from her diary, illustrates some of the daily work of reform. By the late 1830s, the pattern of politics that would define public life for the rest of the nineteenth century was set. Electoral politics and government were dominated by the major political parties, who practiced a democratic, partisan politics that included all adult white men, while vibrant dissident movements thrived outside the world of elections and government, championing causes the major parties disdained and challenging those parties' political methods.

Oct. 24th. A lady called to solicit counsel and assistance. She had an unfaithful husband, and for the sake of her children and herself, she wished to take a judicious course, whatever might be the sacrifice. She had grieved over his guilt, but had sometimes told him his sin might find him out ere he was aware of it. He affected to despise the Advocate, and its disclosures, and often used reproachful language concerning it. She had watched him from time to time, and was well convinced that he made frequent calls at No. ___ , and had seen him enter at this No., on her way to my house. She wished me, if I had sufficient courage, to go with her, that she might meet him there before evidence. We went together, and gained admittance. The person who met us at the door, on inquiry, gave her name, and proved to be the individual whom we wished to see. The paper and tracts were offered and received. The wife then remarked that she came to see her husband, and supposed he was within. His being there was denied, but we followed to her room. Here we found everything in proper order, and the woman put on the appearance of so much innocence, that, to a person not versed in the knowledge of corrupt human nature, she would have seemed above suspicion. However the wife was not easily satisfied, and frankly alleged her charges. Both were much agitated. . . . Finding the point at issue not likely to be settled, I proposed prayer. After we knelt, it was ascertained by the wife that her husband was concealed under the bed. A conversation ensued between them, during which he promised reformation, if his name might not be exposed; but refused to leave his hiding-place, till "that moral reform woman left the room." O! that he may forsake sin and repent, "lest iniquity prove his ruin." . . .

20th. Entered this afternoon forty-four dwellings, and left tracts and papers. This district has been considered so degraded, that the tract agent could find no visitor willing to take it [the district]. Have had the privilege of praying with several, of giving bibles to some, and securing three young girls from a course of sin and shame. . . .

25th. Went by request to see an unfortunate young woman, from a country village not far distant. But a few months since, she left clandestinely the paternal roof, and came to this city with a man who had gained her affections, and promised marriage. Instead of fulfilling his engagements, after her ruin was effected, he provided her a home among the fallen, and here I found her. I was made the bearer of a letter to her from a near relative. She was too much affected to read it, and while it was read to her, wept excessively. She acknowledged the extent of her sin and shame, the kindness of her injured friends, her ingratitude in leaving them—and gave, as her only apology, the regard she felt for her destroyer. She was young, and previous to her fall, had been considered beautiful. At this house and the one adjoining, I conversed with ten young creatures who had been recently induced to come from the country and enter these chambers of death. It was painful and heart-sickening to behold the wreck of so much youth and loveliness.

Tract agent

At the Female Moral Reform Society, a tract agent directed and supervised the workers who distributed the society's tracts.

CHAPTER **8**

Race, Reform, and Sectional Conflict

Prudence Crandall was probably surprised when Sarah Harris, the daughter of an African American farmer in Canterbury, Connecticut, applied for admission to the Canterbury Female Seminary. When Crandall had founded the academy, she had assumed that only white students would attend. But Crandall had been raised as a Quaker and had long regarded slavery as a sin. More recently, she had begun reading The Liberator, *a Boston newspaper committed to bringing about an immediate end to slavery and racial discrimination. So when Harris asked to be admitted, Crandall said yes.*

Crandall admitted Harris in the fall of 1832, a decision that brought both women nothing but trouble. On hearing of Crandall's decision, most white parents withdrew their girls from the academy. Crandall announced that she was reorganizing her school as a teachers' academy for African American women, to open the following fall. Canterbury's white residents issued a storm of protest, and the town council declared the new academy illegal. Crandall opened the school anyway, with students from as far away as Boston and New York. The white townspeople refused to trade with Crandall and her students. The Congregational church banished them from services. Town authorities arrested students as vagrants and paupers. Vandals broke the school's windows and threw manure into its well. In May 1833, white people convinced the state legislature to make it illegal for a school to admit black students from out of state.

Despite the harassment and the new law, Crandall refused to close her school. She was arrested, tried, and convicted. When her conviction was reversed on appeal in July 1834, she announced that classes would resume. In September, a crowd attacked the schoolhouse and tore it down. Only then did Crandall end her fight. She declared the institution closed and moved to New York.

Hundreds, perhaps thousands, of conflicts like the one in Canterbury erupted during the 1830s and 1840s. These conflicts grew out of two contradictory trends. On the one hand, some Americans began to challenge slavery and racial inequality with a new militance. Northern African Americans became more assertive in their decades-old bid for equality and an end to slavery. These activists found allies among a small minority of radical whites, who, inspired by the evangelical drive to bring the world into conformity with God's will, worked to end the sins of slavery and racial discrimination. Unlike earlier antislavery activists, the new abolitionists insisted that slavery should be ended immediately, and without compensation. They carried out their campaign with militant tactics and in a confrontational language of sin and redemption. Although white abolitionists clung to racist attitudes and behaviors—especially paternalism and condescension toward black people—they departed from earlier antislavery practice in making their movement a biracial one. Abolitionists were the only large group in the early republic committed to racial equality and biracial cooperation. In another departure from their abolitionist predecessors, many activists were women, who saw in the campaign against slavery an opportunity to establish themselves as political actors. Although many male abolitionists were deeply committed to women's subordination, they were the only group that allowed both men and women to participate in leadership and to speak in public.

Partly in response to the abolitionist challenge, most white Americans became far more hostile and exclusionary in their stance toward African Americans and Indians. Most white Americans had long considered blacks and Indians inferior, but their thinking on the subject had been vague and, for the most part, separate from their politics. Beginning in the 1810s, and increasingly during the 1830s and 1840s, white Americans embraced more systematic ideas of strict racial hierarchy. At the same time, northerners began a campaign to exclude African Americans from the workplaces, neighborhoods, schools, and places of amusement that white people frequented. Like southern legislatures in earlier decades, northern representatives began grafting racial distinctions into law. From the 1820s through the 1860s, white American city-dwellers repeatedly rioted against abolitionists, black people, and the institutions of the black community. Their violence sought to suppress black self-assertion and challenges to the emerging color line. The new politics of race and slavery was not a strictly northern phenomenon.

Thanks to the cotton gin, the expansion of textile manufacturing, and Indian removal, plantation agriculture was booming in the South, and southerners abandoned their doubts about the morality of slavery. Abolitionists attacked the labor system and the property that underlay that growth, and southern leaders responded with their own militance. The result was a sectional crisis that would not abate until it was resolved in civil war.

A New Antislavery Movement

Abolitionism emerged in part out of a new radicalism in northern African American communities. Spurred by a hardening of white racism in the North, black activists in the 1820s intensified their fight against racism and slavery. Their movement also gained a fervently Christian flavor—a result of evangelism's impact on northern black communities. David Walker was one of the new black activists of the 1820s. The son of a free mother and slave father in North Carolina, he moved during the mid-1820s to Boston, where he ran a used-clothing shop. He became active in the growing black political movement, serving as an antislavery speaker and as an agent for *Freedom's Journal*, the nation's first African American newspaper. In 1828, he wrote his *Appeal to the Colored Citizens of the World*, a pamphlet that went through several editions and was carried by black sailors and read as far away as South Carolina and the Caribbean.

We, (coloured people of these United States of America) are the *most wretched, degraded and abject* set of beings that *ever lived* since the world began, and . . . the white Americans having reduced us to the wretched state of *slavery*, treat us in that condition *more cruel* (they being an enlightened and Christian people), than any heathen nation did any people whom it had reduced to our condition. . . .

Remember . . . to lay humble at the feet of our Lord and Master Jesus Christ, with prayers and fastings. Let our enemies go on with their butcheries, and at once fill up their cup. Never make an attempt to gain our freedom or *natural right*, from under our cruel oppressors and murderers, until you see your way clear—when that hour arrives and you move, be not afraid or dismayed; for be you assured that Jesus Christ the King of heaven and of earth who is the God of justice and of armies, will surely go before you. And those enemies who have for hundreds of years stolen our *rights*, and kept us ignorant of Him and His divine worship, he will remove. . . .

The man who would not fight under our Lord and Master Jesus Christ, in the glorious and heavenly cause of freedom and of God—to be delivered from the most wretched, abject and servile

FREEDOM'S JOURNAL.

" RIGHTEOUSNESS EXALTETH A NATION."

CORNISH & RUSSWURM, Editors & Proprietors.   NEW-YORK, FRIDAY, MARCH 16, 1827.   VOL. I. NO. 1.

This is the masthead of *Freedom's Journal*, the first newspaper in the United States owned and edited by African Americans. The newspaper was one manifestation of a new radicalism and militant stance against slavery and racism among northern African Americans from the late 1820s on.

slavery, that ever a people was afflicted with since the foundation of the world ... —ought to be kept with all of his children or family, in slavery, or in chains, to be butchered by his *cruel enemies*. . . .

Are we MEN!!—I ask you, O my brethren! Are we MEN? Did our Creator make us to be slaves to dust and ashes like ourselves? Are they not dying worms as well as we? . . . Have we any other Master but Jesus Christ alone? . . . What right, then, have we to obey and call any other Master, but Himself? . . .

Ignorance, my brethren, is a mist, low down into the very dark and impenetrable abyss in which, our fathers for many centuries have been plunged. The Christians, and enlightened of Europe, and some of Asia, seeing the ignorance and consequent degradation of our fathers, instead of trying to enlighten them, by teaching them that religion and light with which God had blessed them, they have plunged them into wretchedness ten thousand times more intolerable . . . , and to add to their miseries . . . tell them, that they are an *inferior and distinct race of beings*. . . .

Ignorance and treachery one against the other—a grovelling servile and abject submission to the lash of tyrants . . . are not the natural elements of the blacks, . . . but these are misfortunes which God has suffered our fathers to be enveloped in for many ages, no doubt in consequence of their disobedience to their maker. . . . Any man who is curious to see the full force of ignorance among the coloured people of the United States of America, has only to go into the southern and western states of this confederacy. . . . He may see there a son take his mother . . . and by the command of a tyrant, strip her as naked as she came into the world, and apply the cow-hide to her, until she falls a victim to death in the road! . . . My observer may see fathers beating their sons, mothers their daughters, and children their parents, all to pacify the passions of unrelenting tyrants. He may also see them telling news and lies, making mischief one upon another. . . .

Men of colour, who are also of sense, for you particularly is my APPEAL designed. . . . I call upon you . . . to cast your eyes upon the wretchedness of your brethren, and to do your utmost to enlighten them—*go to work and enlighten your brethren!* . . . Do any of you say that you and your family are free and happy, and what have you to do with the wretched slaves and other people? . . . Look into your freedom and happiness, and see of what kind they are composed!! They are of the very lowest kind—they are the very *dregs!* . . . We are so subjected under the whites, that we cannot obtain the comforts of life, but by cleaning their boots and shoes, old clothes, waiting on them, shaving them &c. . . . I advance it therefore to you . . . that your full glory and happiness, as well as all other coloured people under Heaven, shall never be fully consummated, but with the *entire emancipation of your enslaved brethren all over the world.* . . . I believe it is the will of the Lord that our greatest happiness shall consist in working for the salvation of our whole body. . . .

There is a great work for you to do. . . . You have to prove to the Americans and the world, that we are MEN, and not *brutes*, as we have been represented, and by millions treated. Remember, to let the aim of your labours among your brethren . . . be the dissemination of education and religion. . . .

For coloured people to acquire learning in this country makes tyrants quake and tremble on their sandy foundation. . . . They know that their infernal deeds of cruelty will be made known to the world. Do you suppose one man of good sense and learning would submit himself, his father, mother, wife and children to be slaves to a wretched man like himself, who, instead of compensating him for his labours, chains, hand-cuffs and beats him and family almost to death, leaving life enough in them, however, to work for, and call him master? No! no! He would cut his devilish throat from ear to ear, and well do slave-owners know it. . . .

Americans! . . . Now let us reason—I mean you of the United States, whom I believe God designs to save from destruction, if you will hear. For . . . there are some on the continent of America, who will never be able to repent. God will surely destroy them. . . . Had you not better take our body, while you have it in your power, and while we are yet ignorant and wretched, . . . give us education, and teach us the pure religion of our Lord and Master, which is calculated to make the lion lay down in peace with the lamb . . . , and thus at once, gain our affection while we are ignorant? Remember Americans, that we must and shall be free and enlightened as you are, will you wait until we shall, under God, obtain our liberty by the crushing arm of power? . . . Wo, wo, will be to you if we have to obtain our freedom by fighting. Throw away your fears and prejudices then, and enlighten us and treat us like men, and we will like you more than we do now hate you. . . . Treat us like men, and there is no danger but we will all live in peace and happiness together.

Another important wellspring of abolitionism was evangelism. Having committed themselves to ridding the world of sin, many white evangelicals came to believe that slavery was a sin. William Lloyd Garrison, an evangelical reformer and printer, came to this conclusion through the influence of two groups: English abolitionists, who won abolition in the British Empire in 1826, and the African American activists whom he met while he was living in Baltimore. In 1831, he moved to Boston and opened an antislavery newspaper, the *Liberator*. Garrison quickly won supporters in both the black and white communities of the North, who began creating local antislavery societies. In 1833, activists in those societies—black and white, male and female—met in Philadelphia (where the Continental Congress had adopted the Declaration of Independence fifty-seven years before) and formed the American Anti-Slavery Society. In its declaration, the new society set forth its principles and its methods for ending slavery.

More than fifty-seven years have elapsed since a band of patriots convened in this place, to devise measures for the deliverance of this country from a foreign yoke. The corner stone upon which they founded the TEMPLE OF FREEDOM was broadly this—"that all men are created equal; and they are endowed by their Creator, with certain inalienable rights; that among these are life, LIBERTY, and the pursuit of happiness." . . .

We have met together for the achievement of an enterprise, without which that of our fathers is incomplete; and which, for its magnitude, solemnity, and probable results upon the destiny of the world, . . . transcends theirs. . . .

Their principles led them to wage war against their oppressors. . . . *Ours* forbid the doing of evil that good may come, and

lead us to reject, and to entreat the oppressed to reject the use of all carnal weapons for deliverance from bondage; relying solely on those which are spiritual. . . .

Their measures were physical resistance—the marshalling in arms—the hostile array—the mortal encounter. *Ours* shall be such as only the opposition of moral purity to moral corruption—the destruction of error by the potency of truth—the overthrow of prejudice by the power of love—and the abolition of slavery by the spirit of repentance.

Their grievances, great as they were, were trifling in comparison with the wrongs and sufferings of those for whom we plead. Our fathers were never slaves. . . .

But those for whose emancipation we are striving—constituting at the present time at least one-sixth part of our countrymen—are recognized by the law, and treated by their fellow-beings, as marketable commodities, as goods and chattels, as brute beasts; are plundered daily of the fruits of their toil without redress; really enjoying no constitutional nor legal protection from licentious and murderous outrages upon their persons; are ruthlessly torn asunder—the tender babe from the arms of its frantic mother—the heart-broken wife from her weeping husband—at the caprice or pleasure of irresponsible tyrants. For the crime of having a dark complexion, they suffer the pangs of hunger, the infliction of stripes, the ignominy of brutal servitude. They are kept in heathenish darkness by laws expressly enacted to make their instruction a criminal offense. . . .

In view of the civil and religious privileges of this nation, the guilt of its oppression is unequaled by any other on the face of the earth; and therefore, . . . it is bound to repent instantly, to undo the heavy burden, to break every yoke, and to let the oppressed go free.

The masthead of William Lloyd Garrison's abolitionist newspaper the *Liberator*, started in 1840, contrasted scenes of slavery and freedom. Slavery (*left*) involved cruel whipping, the breakup of families, and the buying and selling of human beings as if they were livestock. Freedom ensured loving, intact families, and the dignity and productivity of labor.

We further maintain—that no man has a right to enslave or imbrute his brother—to hold or acknowledge him, for one moment, as a piece of merchandise—to keep back his hire by fraud—or to brutalize his mind by denying him the means of intellectual, social, and moral improvements.

The right to enjoy liberty is inalienable. To invade it, is to usurp the prerogative of Jehovah. Every man has a right to his own body—to the products of his own labor—to the protection of law, and to the common advantages of society. . . .

We further believe and affirm—that all persons of color who possess the qualifications which are demanded of others, ought to be admitted forthwith to the enjoyment of the same privileges, and the exercise of the same prerogatives, as others; and that the paths of preferment, of wealth, and of intelligence, should be opened as widely to them as to persons of a white complexion.

We maintain that no compensation should be given to the planters emancipating their slaves. . . .

Because the holders of slaves are not the just proprietors of what they claim; freeing the slaves is not depriving them of property, but restoring it to its rightful owners; it is not wronging the master, but righting the slave—restoring him to himself. . . .

We fully and unanimously recognize the sovereignty of each state, to legislate exclusively on the subject of slavery which is tolerated within its limits; we concede that Congress, *under the present national compact*, has no right to interfere with any of the slave states, in relation to this momentous subject:

But we maintain that Congress has a right, and is solemnly bound, to suppress the domestic slave trade between the several states, and to abolish slavery in those portions of our territory which the Constitution has placed under its exclusive jurisdiction.

We also maintain that there are, at the present time, the highest obligations resting upon the people of the free states, to remove slavery by moral and political action. . . . They . . . are liable to be called at any moment to suppress a general insurrection of the slaves; they authorize the slave owner to vote on three-fifths of his slaves as property, and thus enable him to perpetuate his oppression; they support a standing army at the south for its protection; and they seize the slave who has escaped into their territories, and send him back to be tortured by an enraged master or a brutal driver. This relation to slavery is criminal and full of danger; IT MUST BE BROKEN UP. . . .

We shall organize Anti-Slavery Societies, if possible, in every city, town and village, in our land.

We shall send forth agents to lift up the voice of remonstrance, of warning, of entreaty, and rebuke.

We shall circulate, unsparingly and extensively, anti-slavery tracts and periodicals.

We shall enlist the pulpit and the press in the cause of the suffering and the dumb.

We shall aim at a purification of the churches from all participation in the guilt of slavery.

We shall encourage the labor of freemen rather than that of slaves, by giving a preference to their productions; and

We shall spare no exertions nor means to bring the whole nation under a speedy repentance.

Opposition to slavery was not limited to northerners. As Nat Turner's rebellion made clear, there were slaves who were willing to stake their lives against the institution. Many non-slaveholding white southerners also hated it. The residents of western Virginia, a hilly and mountainous region with few slaves, had a long history of conflict with the great planters of the East. In the wake of Nat Turner's rebellion, political leaders in western Virginia began a campaign to abolish slavery in the state. Thomas Jefferson Randolph, a representative of Albemarle County in the state legislature, proposed a plan to free all slave children born after July 4, 1840, when they reached adulthood. His bill also provided that all free African Americans in the state be removed "beyond the limits of the United States." The supporters of Randolph's bill gave several different arguments for abolishing slavery, and the speech of George W. Summers, from the western county of Kanawba, summarized many of them.

I will not advert to the great principles of eternal justice, which demand at our hands the release of this people. . . . I am no fanatic or philanthropic enthusiast, anxious only to better the condition of the blacks. On the contrary, I believe that . . . the situation of the Virginia negro, so far as regards mere animal comfort, may be well compared with that of a large portion of the laboring classes of other countries, particularly in the severer governments of Europe. . . . It is to better our own condition, to arrest the desolating scourge of our country . . . that we are now called upon to act. . . .

As a question of political economy, the removal of this population, is justified; nay imperiously recommended. Slaves add nothing to the true wealth of any community. Their labor, when the cost of raising, and the necessity of continual subsistence . . . are taken into account, costs more than free labor. . . .

A slave population exercises the most pernicious influence upon the manners, habits and character, of those among whom it exists. Lisping infancy learns the vocabulary of abusive epithets, and struts the embryo tyrant of its little domain. The consciousness of superior destiny, takes possession of his mind at its earliest dawning, and love of power and rule, "grows with his growth and strengthens with his strength." . . .

Habits of idleness, and their usual accompaniment, dissipation, are seldom avoided in a slave-holding community. Men in all ages have been found to seek sensual indulgences and to acquire a fondness for luxuries, whenever placed within their reach. . . . Men seldom labor when they can avoid it—labor becomes dishonorable because it is the business of the slave—and when industry is made dishonorable, virtue is attacked in her strongest citadel. But, Sir, those whom interest or want would prompt to industry, rarely find employment in a dense slave population, for the field is occupied. . . . Is not this truth practically taught, in the stream of emigration from among us, annually swelling in volume, and pouring on to the unpeopled regions of the West? These, too, are the men who form the "bone and sinew" of every country.—These are they whom the government should protect. . . .

It will not be denied, I think, that slavery tends to diffuse ignorance among those more immediately in contact with it. . . . I . . . ask you to compare the general distribution of elementary education in the non-slaveholding with that in the slaveholding States. In a document recently examined, the number of persons in the State of Connecticut, unable to read, is stated at about thirty. I blush to see the catalogue of my own state. . . .

Where slavery prevails, the spirit of free inquiry and adventurous enterprize, is much repressed in the class to which I have alluded.—The difference is manifest even between the Eastern and Western parts of this Commonwealth. . . . In that quarter [western Virginia], there is more equality, more freedom of thought and expression, more boldness of investigation, with the laboring class of our free population, than in the East. The poorest individual, if he has but a trusty rifle, a log cabin, and a "patch of corn," is the most independent of men. He knows nothing of slavery, scarcely even by example—he contributes his mite cheerfully to support his country in peace, and has a heart and an arm to aid her in the hour of danger.

But, Sir, the evils of this system cannot be enumerated. . . . They glare upon us at every step. . . . Contrast the condition of the

Southern States, with that of those of the North and Middle. . . . Examine them, in relation to general education, the state of their agriculture, manufactures, foreign and domestic commerce. . . . Upon the one hand is a country furnishing all the evidences of national prosperity, and still advancing in its onward course;—on the other, is one almost stationary in every department of political improvement. . . .

The . . . black race . . . multiply with more rapidity and for longer periods than the whites. . . .

With these facts before us, can we say that the peace and tranquility of society is not threatened? . . . We see a domestic enemy increasing every day in strength, and in disposition to do mischief. . . .

The dangers to be apprehended from this population are multiplied by the increasing intelligence among them. . . . Men, to remain slaves, must remain ignorant. . . . Seditious publications are becoming numerous, which will find their way among the slaves, and exert their pernicious influence, in despite of the best regulated police. . . . These may do much to bring upon the Southern country, the mischiefs of revolt. . . .

Mr. Speaker, we have been told, that the sense of public security no longer exists with a portion of our people. The late occurrences in Southampton have taught them that they may be sleeping near the verge of a slumbering volcano. . . .

A Woman's Rights Movement Emerges

Much of the work of evangelical reform—conducting meetings, raising money, circulating petitions, distributing literature—was done by women. Their activism sometimes had a radicalizing effect, convincing some women of their right to participate as equals in public life and leading many to rethink women's place in society more broadly. This rethinking of women's status developed gradually, among different groups of female reformers. But until the emergence of a separate, organized women's movement in 1848, the boldest assertions of women's equality came from abolitionist women, and especially from the abolitionists Angelina and Sarah Grimké. In 1838, Sarah Grimké wrote *Letters on the Equality of the Sexes*, which remained the most comprehensive and radical statement of women's rights for a decade.

We must first view woman at the period of her creation. "And God said, Let us make man in our own image, after our likeness; and let them have dominion over the fish of the sea, and over the fowl of the air, and over the cattle, and over all the earth, and over every creeping thing that creepeth upon the earth. So God created man in his own image, in the image of God created he him, male and female created he them." In all this sublime description of the creation of man, (which is a generic term including man and woman), there is not one particle of difference intimated as existing between them. They were both made in the image of God; dominion was given to both over every other creature, but not over each other. Created in perfect equality, they were expected to exercise the viceregence intrusted to them by their Maker, in harmony and love. . . .

Here I plant myself. God created us equal;—he created us free agents;—he is our Lawgiver, our King and our Judge, and to him alone is woman bound to be in subjection, and to him alone is she accountable for the use of those talents with which her Heavenly Father has entrusted her. One is her Master even Christ. . . .

Permit me to offer for your consideration some views relative to the social intercourse of the sexes. Nearly the whole of this intercourse is, in my apprehension, derogatory to man and woman, as moral and intellectual beings. We approach each other, under the constant pressure of a feeling that we are of different sexes; and, instead of regarding each other only in the light of immortal creatures, the mind is fettered by the idea which is early and industriously infused into it, that we must never forget the distinction between male and female. Hence our intercourse, instead of being elevated and refined, is generally calculated to excite and keep alive the lowest propensities of our nature. Nothing, I believe, has tended more to destroy the true dignity of woman, than the fact that she is approached by man in the character of a female. The idea that she is sought as an intelligent and heaven-born creature, whose society will cheer, refine, and elevate her companion, and that she will receive the same blessings as she confers, is rarely held up to her view. On the contrary, man almost always addresses himself to the weakness of woman. By flattery, by appeal to her passions,

A party of ladies stays seated with their wine glasses turned upside down, while their hostess empties bottles of wine out the window. Women participated in a wide variety of reform efforts, from moral reform to campaigns against Indian removal and capital punishment to abolitionism and Women's Rights, but temperance was the most popular cause of the antebellum era.

he seeks access to her heart; and when he has gained her affections, he uses her as the instrument of his pleasure—the minister of his temporal comfort. He furnishes himself with a housekeeper, whose chief business is in the kitchen, or the nursery. And whilst he goes abroad and enjoys the means of improvement afforded by collision of intellect with cultivated minds, his wife is condemned to draw nearly all her instruction from books, if she has time to peruse them. . . .

Surely no one who contemplates, with the eye of a Christian philosopher, the design of God in the creation of woman, can believe that she is now fulfilling that design. . . . I believe it will be impossible for woman to fill the station assigned her by God, until her brethren mingle with her as an equal, as a moral being; and lose, in the dignity of her immortal nature . . . the idea of her being a female. The apostle beautifully remarks, " . . . There is neither Jew nor Greek, there is neither bond nor free, there is neither *male* nor *female*; fore ye are all one in Christ Jesus." . . .

There is another way in which the general opinion, that women are inferior to men, is manifested. . . . I allude to the disproportionate value set on the time and labor of men and of women. A man who is engaged in teaching, can always . . . command a higher price for tuition than a woman—even when he teaches the same branches, and is not in any respect superior to the woman. . . . This . . . is so in every occupation in which the sexes engage indiscriminately. . . . In those employments which are peculiar to women, their time is estimated at only half the value of that of men. A woman who goes out to wash, works as hard in proportion as a wood sawyer, or a coal heaver, but she is not generally able to make more than half as much by a day's work. The low remuneration which women receive for their work, has claimed the attention of a few philanthropists, and I hope it will continue to do so until some remedy is applied for this enormous evil. . . .

There are few things which present greater obstacles to the improvement and elevation of woman to her appropriate sphere of usefulness and duty, than the laws which have been enacted to destroy her independence, and crush her individuality; laws which, although they are framed for her government, she has had no voice in establishing. . . . Woman has no political existence. With the single exception of presenting a petition to the legislative body, she is a cipher in the nation. . . .

The very being of a woman, like that of a slave, is absorbed in her master [that is, her husband]. All contracts made with her, like those made with slaves by their owners, are a mere nullity. . . .

The title of the 1835 song "I'll Be No Submissive Wife" provides evidence of a growing feminist sensibility that began to emerge in several places during the 1830s and 1840s. This new sensibility grew largely out of women's increasing political experience through evangelical reform. Even popular music expressed a growing desire for autonomy and equality.

Woman . . . is placed completely in the hands of a being subject like herself to the outbursts of passion, and therefore unworthy to be trusted with power. . . .

And farther, all the avails of her labor are absolutely in the power of her husband. All that she acquires by her industry is his; so that she cannot, with her own honest earnings, become the legal purchaser of any property. . . .

Taxation, without representation, be it remembered, was the cause of our Revolutionary war . . . yet the daughters of New England, as well as of all the other States of this free Republic, are suffering a similar injustice—but for one, I had rather we should suffer any injustice or oppression, than that my sex should have any voice in the political affairs of the nation. . . .

That the laws which have generally been adopted in the United States, for the government of women, have been framed almost entirely for the exclusive benefit of men, and with a design to oppress women, by depriving them of all control over property, is too manifest to be denied. . . .

[O]ur brethren are called upon in this enlightened age, by every sentiment of honor, religion and justice, to repeal these unjust and unequal laws, and restore to woman those rights which they have wrested from her. Such laws approximate too nearly to the laws enacted by slaveholders for the government of their slaves, and must tend to debase and depress the mind of that being, whom God created as a help meet for man . . . and designed to be his equal and his companion. Until such laws are annulled, woman can never occupy that exalted station for which she was intended by her Maker. . . .

Independent of the fact, that Jehovah could not, consistently with his character as the King, the Lawgiver, and the Judge of his people, give the reins of government over woman into the hands of man, I find that all his commands, all his moral laws, are addressed to women as well as to men. When he assembled Israel at the foot of Mount Sinai, to issue his commandments, we may reasonably suppose he gave all the precepts, which he considered necessary for the government of moral beings. Hence we find that God says, —"Honor thy father and thy mother." . . . "He that smiteth his father, or his mother, shall surely be put to death." . . . But in the decalogue, there is no direction given to women to obey their husbands: both are commanded to have no other God but Jehovah, and not to bow down, or serve any other. . . . If man is constituted the governor of woman, he must be her God; and the sentiment expressed to me lately, by a married man, is perfectly correct: "In my opinion," said he, "the greatest excellence to which a married woman can attain, is to worship her husband." . . .

This much admired sentimental nonsense is fraught with absurdity and wickedness. If it were true, the commandment of Jehovah should have run thus: Man shall have no other gods before ME, and woman shall have no other gods before MAN. . . .

According to the principles which I have laid down, that man and woman were created equal, and endowed by their Creator with the same moral responsibilities, and that consequently whatever is *morally* right for a man to do, is *morally* right for a woman to do, it follows as a necessary corollary, that if it is the duty of man to preach the unsearchable riches of Christ, it is the duty also of women. . . .

Southern Leaders Defend Slavery

Garrisonian abolitionism and Nat Turner's revolt convinced many planters and political leaders in the slave states that they were surrounded by enemies. In a letter to a political ally, Governor John Floyd of Virginia depicted the Nat Turner uprising as part of a broader pattern of subversion.

I am fully persuaded, the spirit of insubordination which has, and still manifests itself in Virginia, had its origin among, and eminated from, the Yankee population, upon their *first* arrival amongst us. . . .

The course has been by no means a direct one—they began first, by making them religious . . . telling the blacks God was no respecter of persons—the black man was as good as the white—that all men were born free and equal—that they cannot serve two masters—that the white people rebelled against England to obtain freedom, so have the blacks a right to do.

In the mean time, I am sure without any purpose of this kind, the preachers, principally Northern—were very assiduous in operating upon our population, day and night, they were at work—and religion became, and is, the fashion of the time—finally our females . . . were persuaded that it was piety to teach negroes to read and write, to the end that they might read the Scriptures. . . .

At this point, more active operations commenced—our magistrates and laws became more inactive—large assemblages of negroes were suffered to take place for religious purposes—Then commenced the efforts of the black preachers, often from the pulpits these pamphlets and papers were read—followed by the

I received this afternoon . . . the "Liberator." . . . These men do not conceal their intentions, but urge on negroes and Mulattoes, slaves and free to the indiscriminate massacre of white people.

—Virginia governor John Floyd, September 27, 1831, in a letter ignoring abolitionist pacifism incendiary publications of Walker, Garrison and Knapp of Boston, these too with songs and hymns of a similar character were circulated, read and commented upon—We resting in apathetic security until the Southampton affair.

From all that has come to my knowledge during and since this affair—I am fully convinced that every black preacher in the whole country east of the Blue Ridge was in the secret, that the plans as published by those Northern presses were adopted and acted upon by them. . . .

In the wake of the multiple attacks on slavery, slave owners and their political allies began a campaign to save slavery from its enemies. One part of that campaign was the suppression of all dissent in the South, whether it came from slaves, free African Americans, or white people. Seven months after the Turner rebellion, the Virginia legislature passed a series of laws restricting slaves, free African Americans, and dissent over slavery. The laws applied to all African Americans, regardless of their legal status. They thus tightened restrictions around free blacks, blurred the boundary between enslaved and free African Americans, and widened the chasm between whites and free blacks. The law punishing incitement to rebellion was enforced against all antislavery speech and writing.

No slave, free negro or mulatto, whether he shall have been ordained or licenced, or otherwise, shall hereafter undertake to preach, exhort or conduct, or hold any assembly or meeting, for religious or other purposes, either in the day time, or at night; and any slave, free negro or mulatto, so offending, shall for every such offence be punished with stripes . . . not exceeding thirty-nine lashes. . . .

Any slave, free negro or mulatto, who shall hereafter attend any preaching, meeting or other assembly, held or pretended to be held for religious purposes, or other instruction, conducted by any slave, free negro or mulatto preacher . . . or any slave who shall hereafter attend any preaching in the night time, although conducted by a white minister, without a written permission from his or her owner, overseer or master . . . shall be punished by stripes . . . not exceeding thirty-nine lashes. . . .

No free negro or mulatto shall be suffered to keep or carry any firelock of any kind, any military weapon, or any powder or lead; and any free negro or mulatto who shall so offend, shall . . . be punished with stripes . . . not exceeding thirty-nine lashes.

If any slave, free negro or mulatto, shall hereafter willfully and maliciously assault and beat any white person, with intention in so doing to kill such white person; every such slave, free negro or mulatto, so offending . . . shall suffer death without benefit of clergy.

If any person shall hereafter write, print, or cause to be written or printed, any book, pamphlet or other writing, advising persons of colour within this state to make insurrection, or to rebel, or shall knowingly circulate, or cause to be circulated, any book, pamphlet, or other writing, written or printed, advising persons of colour in this commonwealth to commit insurrection or rebellion; such person, if a slave, free negro or mulatto, shall . . . be punished for the first offence with stripes . . . not exceeding thirty-nine lashes; and for the second offence, . . . shall be punished, with death without benefit of clergy; and if the person so offending be a white person, he or she shall be punished on conviction, in a sum not less than one hundred nor more than one thousand dollars.

Riots, routs, unlawful assemblies, trespasses and seditious speeches, by free negroes or mulattoes, shall hereafter be punished with stripes. . . .

Another element of the defense of slavery was a propaganda war. Beginning in the early 1830s, and especially during the 1840s and 1850s, scores of southern political leaders, newspaper editors, and intellectuals joined the effort to defend slavery. In doing so, they sought to change the terms on which slavery was defended. Before the 1830s, most defended the institution as a necessary evil or denounced abolition as impracticable or as a violation of property rights. By the 1840s, however, southern intellectuals and leaders declared slavery to be the most humane labor system in history. In 1845, James Henry Hammond, a former governor of South Carolina, issued such a vindication of human bondage in a public letter to an English abolitionist.

It may be . . . a novelty to you to encounter one who conscientiously believes the Domestic Slavery of these States to be not only an inexorable necessity for the present, but a moral and humane institution, productive of the greatest political and social advantages, and who is disposed, as I am, to defend it on these grounds. . . .

American slavery is not only not a sin, but especially commanded by God through Moses, and approved by Christ through his Apostles. . . . What God ordains and Christ sanctifies should surely command the respect and toleration of Man. . . .

I endorse without reserve the much-abused sentiment of Governor M'Duffie, that "slavery is the corner stone of our Republican edifice;" while I repudiate, as ridiculously absurd, that much lauded . . . dogma of Mr. Jefferson, that "all men are born equal." No

Society has ever yet existed, and . . . none will ever exist, without a natural variety of classes. The most marked of these must, in a country like ours, be the rich and the poor, the educated and the ignorant. . . . Universal suffrage . . . seems to be in fact a necessary appendage to a Republican system. Where universal suffrage obtains, it is obvious that the government is in the hands of a numerical majority; and it is hardly necessary to say that in every part of the world more than half the people are ignorant and poor. . . . It is a wretched and insecure government which is administered by its most ignorant citizens, and those who have the least at stake under it. . . . These are rapidly usurping all power in the non-slave-holding States, and threaten a fearful crisis in Republican institutions there. . . . In the slave-holding States, however, nearly one-half of the whole population, and those of the poorest and most ignorant, have no political influence whatever, because they are slaves. Of the other half a large proportion are both educated and independent in their circumstances; while those who unfortunately are not so, being still elevated far above the mass, are higher toned and more deeply interested in preserving a stable and well ordered Government, than the same class in any other country. Hence, slavery is truly the "corner-stone" and foundation of every well-designed and durable "Republican edifice." . . .

It must be admitted that free labor is cheaper than Slave labor. It is a fallacy to suppose that ours is *unpaid labor*. . . . Besides the first cost of the slave, he must be fed and clothed—well fed and well clothed—if not for humanity's sake, that he may do good work, retain health and life, and rear a family to supply his place. When old or sick he is a clear expense, and so is the helpless portion of his family. . . . We must therefore content ourselves with our dear labor, under the consoling reflection that what is lost to us, is gained to humanity; and that inasmuch as our slave costs us more than your free man costs you, by so much is he better off. . . .

I deny that the power of the slave-holder in America is "irresponsible." He is responsible to God. . . . He is responsible to the community in which he lives, and to the laws under which he enjoys his civil rights. Those laws do not permit him to kill, to maim, or to punish beyond certain limits, or to overtask, or to refuse to feed and clothe his slave. In short, they forbid him to be tyrannical and cruel. If any of these laws have grown obsolete, it is because they are so seldom violated that they are forgotten. . . .

Slave-holders are no more perfect than other men. They have passions. Some of them . . . do not at all times restrain them. Neither do husbands, parents and friends. And in each of these relations as serious suffering as frequently arises from uncontrolled passions as ever does in that of Master and Slave, and with as little chance of indemnity. Yet you would not on that account break them up. I have no hesitation in saying that our slave-holders are as kind masters, as men usually are kind husbands, parents and friends—as a general rule, kinder. A bad master—he who overworks his slaves, provides ill for them, or treats them with undue severity—loses the esteem and respect of his fellow citizens. . . .

I believe our slaves are the happiest three millions of human beings on whom the sun shines. Into their Eden is coming Satan in the guise of an Abolitionist. . . .

I have admitted, without hesitation . . . that slaveholders are responsible to the world for the humane treatment of the fellow-beings whom God has placed in their hands. I think it would be only fair for you to admit, what is equally undeniable, that every man in independent circumstances, all the world over . . . is to the same extent responsible to the whole human family for the condition of the poor and laboring classes . . . around them. . . . If so, it would naturally seem to be the duty of true humanity and rational philanthropy to devote their time and labor . . . first to the objects placed . . . under their own immediate charge. And it must be regarded as a clear evasion and sinful neglect of this cardinal duty, to pass from those whose destitute situation they can plainly see, minutely examine, and efficiently relieve, to inquire after the condition of others in no way entrusted to their care, to exaggerate evils of which they cannot be cognizant. . . .

It is shocking beyond endurance to turn over your *Records* in which the condition of your laboring classes is but too faithfully depicted. Could our slaves but see it, they would join us in lynching Abolitionists. . . . We never think of imposing on them such labor. . . . We never put them to *any work* under ten, more generally at twelve years of age, and then the very lightest. Destitution is absolutely unknown—never did a slave starve in America; while in moral sentiments and feelings, in religious information, and even in general intelligence, they are infinitely the superiors of your operatives. When you look around you how dare you talk to us before the world of slavery? For the condition of your wretched laborers, you, and every Briton who is not one of them, are responsible before God and Man. If you are really humane, philanthropic and charitable, here are objects for you. Relieve them. Emancipate them. Raise them from the condition of brutes, to the level of human beings—of American slaves, at least. . . .

Antiabolitionism and a New Racial Regime in the North

Even as abolitionists challenged racial inequality, most white northerners (as well as most southerners) embraced more systematic ideas about white superiority. One of the ways they expressed and learned those ideas was through the minstrel show. The song "Jim Crow" was performed in minstrel shows of the late 1820s and early 1830s by the white performer T. D. Rice. This character—happy-go-lucky, sexually unfettered, lazy, childlike, poor without minding his poverty—drew on older theatrical and literary character types. Jim Crow's personality traits became inseparable from his race. When Rice performed the song in New York City in 1832, it became an immediate sensation. "Jim Crow" was a figment of a white man's imagination, but it helped shape white audiences' ideas about African Americans.

Come listen all you galls and boys,
Just from Tuckyhoe
I'm going to sing a little song
My name's Jim Crow.

Chorus:
Weel about and turn about,
And do jis so
Eb'ry time I weel about,
I jump Jim Crow.

I'm a rorer on de fiddle
And down in ole Virginny
Dey say I play de skientific
Like massa Pagganninny. (*Chorus*)

I cut so many munky shines,
I dance de galloppade;
An wen I done, I res my head
On shubble, hoe, or spade. (*Chorus*)

I met Miss Dina Scrub one day,
I gib her such a buss;
And den she turn and slap my face,
An make a mighty fuss. (*Chorus*)

The Minstrel Show
The minstrel show was a music-hall variety show in which white performers blackened their faces with burnt cork and performed what they claimed to be authentic "Ethiopian" songs and dances. First performed in 1822, blackface minstrelsy was greeted by huge and enthusiastic audiences, made up mostly of working-class white men. Combining short comic skits, song, and dance, the minstrel show was the most successful commercial entertainment in America from the 1830s through the 1890s.

Tuckyhoe
Tuckahoe was a plantation district in Virginia, near the city of Richmond.

Pagganninny
Niccolò Paganini was an Italian violinist and composer. He was perhaps the most celebrated violin virtuosi of the early nineteenth century.

Buss
A "buss" was a kiss.

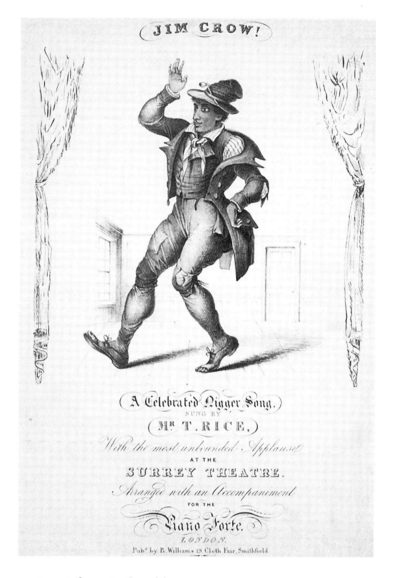

The cover for sheet music for the popular minstrel tune "Jim Crow" depicts the racialized clown that made minstrel shows a runaway success from the 1830s through the end of the nineteenth century. Lazy, sexually unfettered, carefree despite the poverty evidenced by his tattered clothes and broken shoes, Jim Crow was a character that white audiences could simultaneously love, envy for his freedom from hard work and sexual restraint, and feel superior to.

I went down to the ribber,
I didn't mean to stay;
But dare de galls dey charm me so
I cudent get away. (*Chorus*)

O den I cast de sheeps eye,
Dey all fall in lub;
I pick my choose among dem dare
An took Miss Dina Scrub. (*Chorus*)

De udder galls dey ginn to fight,
I teld them wait a bit;
I'd hab dem all, jist one by one,
As I tourt fit. (*Chorus*)

The major political parties were also major sources of new racial ideas. The abolitionist movement and the proslavery campaign created deep divisions over slavery among Democrats, and later among Whigs, threatening both parties' electoral viability and long-term survival. Most party leaders sought to quiet the growing sectional controversy, but many northern Democrats and Whigs worked to turn their constituents against the abolitionists. One way to do this was through racial appeals. One of the first party politicians to preach a message of white supremacy was James Kirke Paulding, the New York novelist and close friend of Martin Van Buren. In 1836, Paulding wrote *Slavery in the United States*, which employed newly systematic ideas of white superiority and black inferiority to defend slavery from the attacks of the abolitionists.

Their [Africans'] systems of government, their manners, habits, and social relations, were those of uncivilized barbarians. Those who were transported hither [as slaves] were captives in war; they possessed no civil rights at home; they brought none with them, and acquired none here. . . . The government of the United States, its institutions, and its privileges, belong of right wholly and exclusively to the white men; for they were purchased, not by the blood of the negroes, but by that of our fathers. . . .

The advocates of immediate emancipation . . . recommen[d] amalgamation; that is, indiscriminate marriages, between the whites and blacks, accompanied of course by a communion of social and civil rights. . . .

The project of intermarrying with the blacks, is a project for debasing the whites by a mixture of that blood, which, wherever it flows, carries with it the seeds of deterioration. It is a scheme for lowering the standard of our nature, by approximating the highest grade of human beings to the lowest. . . . A mongrel race would arise, of all shades and colours, each claiming under the new order of things equal social and civil rights. . . .

The experience of thousands of years stands arrayed against the principle of equality between the white men and the blacks.

Through ill-fitting genteel clothing, misshapen bodies and heads, a meeting place in a barn, one man's run-in with a cow, and the ridiculously misspelled sign (*left*), a Philadelphia artist portrayed African American Freemasons as aspiring to a dignity and status beyond their capacities. In a move that would be repeated throughout the nineteenth century, he depicted the associational life of African Americans as a grotesque parody of white associations.

Thousands, tens of thousands of the former, in all ages and nations, have overcome all the obstacles of their situation, the deficiencies of education, the prejudices of their age and country . . . and become lights of the age, leaders of the race. Has the black man ever exhibited similar energies, or achieved such triumphs in his native land or anywhere else? All that he has ever done is to approach the lowest scale of intellectual eminence. . . .

The mind of the African . . . in all circumstances, seems in a great degree divested of this divine attribute of progressive improvement. In his own country he has, for a long series of ages, remained in the same state of barbarism. . . . The wooly-headed race of Africans had the same opportunities for improvement that have fallen to the lot of the inhabitants of Asia and Europe. . . . Yet they have never awakened from their long sleep of barbarism. . . .

The freemen of the United States have been stigmatized as aristocrats. . . . They support the great and universal aristocracy of mind. They maintain the superiority, not of birth, title, or usurpation, but of intellect and civilization. They cannot be . . . bullied into such an abandonment of . . . their birthright, which is nothing less than the noble distinction which nature has bestowed on the great aristocracy of the white man. . . .

Suppose all the slaves spontaneously set free at once, or by degrees, and at the same time admitted to a participation of the social and political rights of free citizens. What may rational reflecting men anticipate as the result?

Separated as are the two races by impassible barriers; carrying in their very faces the badge of that separation, and animated as they must necessarily be by conflicting interests, there can be no doubt that the first struggle would be for ascendancy in political power, and that it would be one of far greater excitement than the ordinary contests of parties in the United States. . . . Elections would become battles; and blood, not ballots, would decide the mastery. The body politic would be rent asunder by eternal and inveterate struggles; civil strife would ensue, and a deadly war of extermination be the end of this woeful experiment. . . .

Without property, yet with equal rights and superior numbers, the blacks would wrest from their ancient masters the power of the state, and beyond doubt exercise it for the purpose of oppressing them. Without any rational ideas of government, they would aspire to govern. Without those habits and that experience, which are always indispensable to self-government, they would endeavour to modify the state to suit their own wayward purposes; and without any other religion than fanaticism, the piety of ignorance, they would become the dictators of public faith. Their ascendancy would be a despotism over white men, and the fabric of civilization and liberty, which consumed ages in its construction, would be demolished in a few years by the relentless fury of ignorant barbarians. A new Africa would spring up in the place of free and enlightened states, and the race of the white men be either forced to abandon their homes, or to level themselves with the degradation around.

During the 1840s, white supremacy gained the aura of scientific truth. During the 1830s and 1840s, scholars in the new fields of anthropology and phrenology (the study of the human skull) developed new theories that attributed differences in the habits and cultural attainments to biology rather than environment and culture. The most influential of these thinkers was Samuel George Morton, physician, naturalist, and professor of anatomy at Pennsylvania College (later the University of Pennsylvania). Trained as a physician and widely published in the fields of medicine, zoology, and paleontology, Morton collected hundreds of skulls from different parts of the world, measuring their size, shape, and brain capacity. From these measurements, he sought to provide a "scientific" basis for his own and other white intellectuals' growing beliefs about the character and intellectual capabilities of people of color. He published the results in *Crania Americana* (*American Skulls*) in 1839 and *Crania Aegyptiaca* (*Egyptian Skulls*) in 1844.

From remote ages the inhabitants of every extended locality have been marked by certain physical and moral peculiarities, common among themselves, and serving to distinguish them from all other people. The Arabians are at this time precisely what they were in the days of the patriarchs; the Hindoos have altered in nothing since they were described by the earliest writers; nor have three thousand years made any difference in the skin and hair of the Negro. . . .

The Caucasian Race . . . is distinguished for the facility with which it attains the highest intellectual endowments. . . . In their intellectual character the Mongolians are ingenious, imitative, and highly susceptible of cultivation. . . . The Malay Race is active and ingenious, and possesses all the habits of a migratory, predaceous and maritime people. . . . In disposition the Negro is joyous, flexible, and indolent; while the many nations which compose this race present a

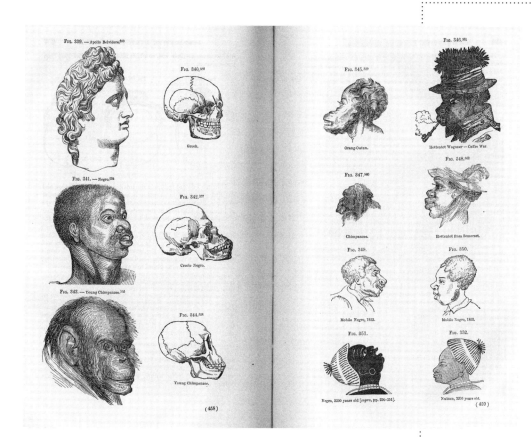

This illustration from the "scientific" treatise *Types of Mankind* compared white men to Greek gods and black men to apes.

singular diversity of intellectual character, of which the far extreme is the lowest grade of humanity. . . .

The intellectual faculties of [American Indians] appear to be of a decidedly inferior cast when compared with those of the Caucasian or Mongolian races. They are not only averse to the restraints of education, but for the most part incapable of a continued process of reasoning on abstract subjects. Their minds seize with avidity on simple truths, while they at once reject whatever requires investigation and analysis. Their proximity, for more than two centuries, to European institutions, has made scarcely any appreciable change in their mode of thinking or their manner of life; and as to their own social condition, they are probably in most respects what they were at the primitive epoch of their existence. They have made few or no improvements in building their houses or their boats; their inventive and imitative faculties appear to be of a very humble grade, nor have they the smallest predilection for the arts or sciences. . . .

However much the benevolent mind may regret the inaptitude of the Indian for civilisation, the affirmative of this question seems to be established beyond a doubt. His moral and physical nature are alike adapted to his position among the races of men, and it is as reasonable to expect the one to be changed as the other. The structure of his mind appears to be different from that of the white man, nor can the two harmonise their social relations except on the most limited scale. . . .

Morton depicted the different "races" of humanity as radically distinct, with skulls of dramatically different sizes and shapes—a purported difference that was understood to indicate unequal intelligence and capacities for "civilization." His ideas and methods quickly spread throughout the American and western European scientific communities in 1845.

On the Internal Capacity of the Cranium of the different Races of Men. Having subjected the skulls in my possession, and such also as I could obtain from my friends, to the internal capacity measurement already described, I have obtained the following results. . . .

Races	No. of skulls	Mean internal capacity in cubic inches	Largest in the series	Smallest in the series
Caucasian	52	87	109	75
Mongolian	10	83	93	69
Malay	18	81	89	64
American [Indian]	147	82	100	60
Ethiopian	29	78	94	65

Along with new ideas about racial hierarchy came increasingly violent racial practices. Between the Revolution and 1810, free African Americans had experienced discrimination, even segregation. But segregation had been partial and piecemeal; blacks and whites often lived in the same neighborhoods, worked at the same sorts of jobs, joined in public celebrations, and occasionally engaged in interracial love, sex, and marriage. After 1810, whites in the major cities fought to end racial mixing. They established a far more thoroughgoing system of segregation, excluding African Americans from most neighborhoods and jobs, creating separate "Negro" sections in theaters and on public transportation, and driving blacks away from public celebrations. They backed up this separation with violence. Frederick Douglass, a Maryland slave who later escaped north and became a renowned abolitionist, lived in Baltimore with his master when that city's whites sought to enforce the

more thoroughgoing separation of the races. In his 1845 autobiography, he tells how separation was established at his workplace.

In a few weeks after I went to Baltimore, Master Hugh hired me to Mr. William Gardner, an extensive ship-builder....

Until a very little while after I went there, white and black ship-carpenters worked side by side, and no one seemed to see any impropriety in it. All hands seemed to be well satisfied. Many of the black carpenters were freemen. Things seemed to be going on very well. All at once, the white carpenters knocked off, and said they would not work with free colored workmen. Their reason for this, as alleged, was, that if free colored carpenters were encouraged, they would soon take the trade into their own hands, and poor white men would be thrown out of employment. They therefore felt called upon at once to put a stop to it. And taking advantage of Mr. Gardner's [the shipyard owner's] necessities, they broke off, swearing they would work no longer, unless he would discharge his black carpenters. Now, though this did not extend to me in form [Douglass was a slave], it did reach me in fact. My fellow-apprentices very soon began to feel it degrading to them to work with me. They began to put on airs, and talk about the "niggers" taking the country, saying we all ought be killed; and, being encouraged by the journeymen, they commenced making my condition as hard as they could, by hectoring me around, and sometimes striking me. I . . . struck back . . . , regardless of consequences; and while I kept them from combining, I succeeded very well; for I could whip the whole of them, taking them separately. They, however, at length combined, and came upon me, armed with sticks, stones, and heavy handspikes. One came in front with a half brick. There was one at each side of me, and one behind me. While I was attending to those in front, and on either side, the one behind ran up with the handspike, and struck me a heavy blow upon the head. It stunned me. I fell, and with this they all ran upon me, and fell to beating me with their fists. I let them lay on for a while, gathering strength. In an instant, I gave a sudden surge, and rose to my hands and knees. Just as I did that, one of their number gave me, with his heavy boot, a powerful kick to the left eye. My eyeball seemed to have burst. When they saw my eye closed, and badly swollen, they left me. With this I seized the handspike, and for a time pursued them. But here the carpenters interfered, and I thought I might as well give it up. It was impossible to stand my hand against so many. All this took place in sight of not less than fifty white ship-carpenters, and not one interposed a friendly word; but some cried, "Kill the damned nigger! Kill him! kill him! He struck a white person!" . . .

Master Hugh was very much enraged. . . . As soon as I got a little the better of my bruises, he took me with him to Esquire Watson's [a lawyer] on Bond Street, to see what could be done about the matter. Mr. Watson['s] . . . answer was, he could do nothing in the case, unless some white man would come forward and testify. He could issue no warrant on my word. Of course, it was impossible to get any white man to volunteer his testimony in my behalf, and against the white young men. Even those who may have sympathized with me were not prepared to do this. It required a degree of courage unknown to them to do so; for just at that time, the slightest manifestation of humanity toward a colored person was denounced as abolitionism, and that name subjected its bearer to frightful liabilities. . . . Such was, and such remains, the state of things in the Christian city of Baltimore.

The sort of low-level violence that Frederick Douglass encountered in William Gardner's shipyard was an everyday occurrence for African Americans in antebellum America. Less frequent but more devastating were antiabolitionist and antiblack riots. Every city experienced outbreaks of such violence; Philadelphia, for example, was the site of five major riots in the 1830s and 1840s. Usually led by wealthy and prominent conservatives, antiabolitionist riots sought to intimidate and silence antislavery activists. Antiblack riots sought to intimidate local African Americans, often in order to drive them out of an area that both races frequented. Often, antiabolitionist riots became attacks on the local black community, and antiblack outbreaks morphed into attacks on white abolitionists. One such disturbance occurred in New York City in July 1834. The *New York Evening Post* described the origins of the riot, at Chatham Street Chapel on the evening of July 8.

The New York Sacred Music Society have a lease on the chapel for Monday and Thursday evenings. . . . Some person, in behalf of the blacks, had obtained from the Secretary of the Music Society permission to occupy the chapel . . . for the purpose of celebrating the postponed festival of the Fourth of July. They met and commenced their exercises. Certain members of the Music Society also arrived. . . . Their number, however, being soon augmented, by the arrival of other persons, they . . . concluded upon insisting that possession of

Destruction by Fire of Pennsylvania Hall shows a riot in 1838, when white Philadelphians burned down a newly built abolitionist meeting hall. The crowd went on to attack the Shelter for Colored Orphans and an African American church.

the chapel should be given to them. The blacks, in the meanwhile, . . . did not seem disposed . . . to break up their meeting. . . . The Sacred Music Society then took forcible possession of the pulpit, and thereupon a general battle commenced, which seems to have been waged with considerable violence on both sides. . . .

Two nights later, rioters attacked two white abolitionists: the wealthy merchant Lewis Tappan and the minister Samuel H. Cox. The *Evening Post* described the attacks.

Last night not less than three different places were the scenes of riot. . . . An impression had got abroad . . . that a meeting of the Anti-Slavery Society was to be held at Chatham Street Chapel last evening. In consequence of this impression, an immense concourse of people assembled in front of the chapel about dusk, evidently with the determination of preventing any meeting of the abolitionists. . . .

A large mob formed in front of the house of Lewis Tappan, broke open the door, entered, and commenced demolishing the furniture. . . . A party of persons then started for the dwelling of Dr. Cox, in Laight street. . . . The windows of the house were then broke; the combustible furniture dragged into the middle of the street and fired. It was supposed that the building would be set on fire, but two

Mr. Tappan's store

The building attacked was the store of Arthur Tappan, brother of Lewis Tappan and, like his brother, a wealthy merchant and a prominent white abolitionist.

Watchmen

Watchmen served as nighttime police, watching over their neighborhoods to prevent crime, catch criminals, and report fires.

Rev. Mr. Ludlow

Rev. Henry G. Ludlow was a prominent white abolitionist.

African

An "African" institution was one that was joined and controlled by African Americans.

[fire] engines arrived and began to play upon the house. The furniture is all destroyed, or so much injured as to be worthless.

Two nights later, the violence reached its peak.

For five hours our city has been the prey of an infuriated mob, or rather mobs, who have been carrying destruction before them in every direction. . . . Mr. Tappan's store was attacked at half-past nine last evening, by a number of boys and men, who fired volleys of stones and broke the upper windows, but did not attempt to force the doors. . . .

Between ten and eleven a large mob assembled at Doctor Cox's church in Laight street and smashed in the door and windows and demolished the interior of the building. From the church they proceeded to Charlton street where he resides, but a strong detachment of watchmen were placed in a line across the East end of the street and prevented all ingress to it. After remaining some time about Charlton street the mob proceeded to Spring street and attacked Rev. Mr. Ludlow's church, the doors and windows of which they began to batter in, when a small party of watchmen arrived and put a momentary stop to their proceedings, and took one or two of the ringleaders into custody. Their companions, however, soon liberated them, beat the watchmen off and maltreated some of them. They then recommenced the work of destruction, broke in the doors, shattered the windows to atoms, and entered the Church. In a short time they broke up the interior of it, destroying whatever they could. The Session House adjoining, shared the same fate. . . .

A gentleman whose name we believe is Wood . . . address[ed] the mob . . . , declaring that he would willingly cut the ears off any man who would propose to <u>amalgamate</u> a black man and white woman. . . .

Whilst this mob was spending its fury upon the churches in Laight street and Spring street, another mob assembled at the African church opposite the Opera House. They however retired after dashing a few stones into the windows. . . .

About 11 o'clock, another mob attacked St. Phillips African Episcopal church in Centre street—Rev. Peter Williams, a colored man, pastor,—and demolished it almost entirely, including a fine organ. The furniture they took out and burned in the street.

The windows of the African Baptist church in Anthony street, were broken to atoms.

The African school-house in Orange street, which is also used as a Methodist meeting house, was totally demolished.

Several houses where colored people resided, in Orange and Mulbery streets, between Anthony and Walker and about the Five Points, were greatly injured or totally destroyed. . . .

Two houses in Anthony street were attacked, and the furniture brought out into the street and burned. One or two in Leonard street shared the same fate. . . .

About 9 o'clock a detachment of the mob at the Five Points commenced an assault upon a small wooden building in Orange, new Bayard street, occupied as a barber's shop, by a colored man, named March, the front and interior of which they soon demolished. The black intrepidly kept possession of his premises, discharging a pistol three times at his assailants. . . .

A colored man, connected with one of the steamboats, was carrying a trunk for a passenger to some part of the city, ignorant of what was going on, when he was attacked by a fraction of the mob, his trunk taken from him, and he was shamefully abused. The trunk was afterwards restored. Many other blacks were injured, some of them severely.

Outside New England, law also held the new racial system in place. After about 1810, increasing numbers of legislatures began reserving certain rights to white men alone and saddling Indians and African Americans with legal disabilities. Western states and territories adopted the most restrictive laws. In 1839, the territorial legislature of Iowa passed a series of racially discriminatory laws. Laws like these were a bitter defeat for abolitionists, but not a decisive one. By the year these laws were passed, Americans had become dramatically polarized over the issues of race and slavery. A radical but growing minority agitated for racial equality and an end to slavery while southern planters and their political allies offered belligerent defenses of slavery and demanded the suppression of the abolitionists. Meanwhile, a majority of white Americans, North and South, embraced increasingly strident ideas about white supremacy and increasingly violent practices of racial subordination. This pattern of polarization would continue to deepen until it led to Civil War.

Blacks and Mulattoes

Sec. 1. . . . No black or mulatto person shall be permitted to settle or reside in this Territory, unless he or she shall produce a fair certificate, from some court within the United States, of his or

Become a charge

To "become a charge" to a county was to become poor and dependent upon the poor relief of the county.

her freedom . . . and give bond . . . of five hundred dollars, conditioned that such person shall not at any time become a charge to said county in which the said bond shall be given nor to any other county in this Territory, and also for such person's good behaviour. . . . And the conviction of such Negro or mulatto, of any crime or misdemeanor against the penal laws of this Territory, shall amount to a forfeiture of . . . such bond.

Sec. 2. If any negro or mulatto, coming into this Territory as aforesaid, shall fail to comply with the first section of this act, it shall be . . . the duty of the county commissioners . . . to summon him, her, or them, to appear before some justice of the peace. . . . And if such negro or mulatto shall fail to give the bond and security required . . . , it shall be the duty of the county commissioners of such county to hire out such negro or mulatto, for six months, for the best price in cash that can be had. The proceeds arising from such hiring shall be paid into the county treasury of the proper county, for the use of such negro or mulatto, in such manner as shall be directed by the board of county commissioners aforesaid. . . .

Sec. 4. Should any person or persons knowingly engage, or hire, or harbor, such negro or mulatto, hereafter coming . . . into this Territory, without such colored person first complying with the provisions of this act, such person or persons . . . shall pay a fine of not less than five, nor more than one hundred dollars. . . .

Sec. 6. That in case any person or persons, his or their agent or agents, claiming any black or mulatto person that now is or hereafter may be in this Territory, shall apply to any judge of the district court, or justice of the peace, and shall make satisfactory proof that such black or mulatto person or persons is or are the property of him or her who applies, . . . the said judge or justice is hereby empowered and required . . . to direct the sheriff or constable to arrest such black or mulatto person or persons, and deliver the same to the claimant or claimants, his or their agent or agents. . . .

Education

Sec. 1. . . . There shall be established a common school, or schools, in each of the counties of this Territory, which shall be open and free for every class of white citizens between the ages of four and twenty-one years.

Elections

Sec. 12. No person shall be entitled to vote at any election in this Territory who has not attained the age of twenty-one years, who is not a free white male citizen, or foreigner duly naturalized . . . , and who has not resided in this Territory for at least six months immediately previous to his application to vote.

Courts

Sec. 22. All qualified voters of the Territory, except persons of unsound mind, and those who have been convicted of a felony, shall be competent jurors in their respective counties.

Sec. 23. A negro, mulatto, or Indian, shall not be a witness in any court or in any case against a white man.

MAP OF MEXICO,
INCLUDING
YUCATAN & UPPER CALIFORNIA,
exhibiting
THE CHIEF CITIES AND TOWNS, THE
Principal Travelling Routes &c.
PHILADELPHIA:
Published by S. Augustus Mitchell
N.E. CORNER OF MARKET AND SEVENTH St.
1847.

Becoming a Continental Nation

The rebels struck on January 17. Led by a coalition of Mexican nationals and Pueblo Indians, they assembled in the central squares of several towns in northern New Mexico and quickly gained control of them. In Taos, they captured and killed Governor Charles Bent, along with other members of his "American Party," who were dedicated to supporting the American conquest. Within days, they controlled most of the towns in northern New Mexico. They issued a circular to "the Defenders of their Country" and prepared to march on Santa Fe, the territorial capital.

The insurgency took place in 1847, just five months after the United States had occupied New Mexico. The rebels certainly had their reasons. Many Mexican citizens in the territory regarded the American presence as a foreign conquest, and the occupying troops, heavy drinkers who had learned to think of Mexicans as an inferior race, frequently insulted the locals, assaulted them, and stole or damaged their property. Ironically, the Americans' treatment of the locals was much worse in other places. Along the Rio Grande, white Americans were engaging in large-scale invasions of Mexicans' farms. In the early 1850s, Anglo miners for California gold killed Mexican men, raped Mexican women, and drove all Mexicans from the mines, with the backing of the state legislature.

The U.S. Army quickly crushed the rebellion. The last group of insurgents made a final stand on February 4 in the Taos Pueblo church. The army captured them, tried them for murder and treason, and hanged them. The rebels' failure ended all efforts to drive the Americans out. Still, they had a powerful influence on the occupiers. White

This 1847 map of Mexico shows how dramatically that country's territory shrank as the result of its war with the United States. Most of the dark area labelled "Upper or New California" and the territories labelled New Mexico and Texas were part of Mexico but would soon be annexed to the United States. The new Mexico, at half its former size, would be contained in the areas to the south and west.

Americans in New Mexico learned that they could not afford to mistreat the locals. In California, where Anglos outnumbered Mexicans by wide margins, assaults, robberies, lynchings, and violent seizures of farms and mining claims continued. But Mexicans were a majority in New Mexico. The Taos rebels reminded white Americans that they were in the minority, and that violence and robbery risked violent reprisal. In that territory, they intermarried with the locals.

The Taos rebellion and its defeat were part of a broader conquest. In 1846, the United States had gone to war with Mexico. The Mexican War marked a culmination of many of the changes that had been taking place since the adoption of the federal Constitution in 1789. Although President James Polk and his Democratic allies depicted the war as a defensive one, they sought dramatic territorial concessions out of the war, and they got them. The United States seized what would later become California, New Mexico, Nevada, Utah, Wyoming, Colorado, and most of Arizona, increasing the nation's territory by a third. In doing so, it realized Thomas Jefferson's dream of becoming a continental nation. As with earlier conquests, white Americans gained a great deal in this expansion, winning hundreds of millions of acres of farmland and thousands of valuable mines. This acquisition guaranteed that independent proprietorship, and the social and political equality that went with it, would continue to be a realistic aspiration for many Americans—even as increasing numbers of them became permanent wage laborers.

N. Currier's *Battle of Buena Vista, fought Feb. 23rd, 1847* was one of many popular depictions of the war with Mexico created to satisfy Americans' nearly insatiable appetite for artistic and journalistic portrayals of the conflict. For the first time in American history, newspapers throughout the country sent correspondents to report on the action. Many Americans saw the war as proof of the United States' arrival as a power on the world stage.

As with earlier conquests, this benefit came at the expense of people of other races—most notably the Indians and Mexicans who lost their lands and mines to American intruders. As before, Americans justified this inequity with racial thinking. But they did not simply continue with old racial ideas. The Mexican War helped give rise to a new, strident racial ideology and to increasingly violent racial practices. African Americans, Indians, Mexicans, and white abolitionists opposed the new racial regime, but among the majority of white Americans white supremacy became a matter of consensus. The struggle for racial equality did not end, but it entered a new phase that was remarkably unfavorable to egalitarians.

The Mexican War sparked a new, more strident phase in another old conflict as well: the struggle over slavery. The war was extremely controversial, especially among antislavery voters and many Whigs, who saw it as an unprovoked war of aggression and part of a design to bring more slave states into the Union. The accession of half of Mexico came at a moment of increasing conflict over slavery, and political leaders of both sections, ever watchful of the balance of political power in Congress and determined that their constituents reap the benefits of conquest, battled over whether the new territory would permit slave labor. With this development, the conflict over slavery spread from the nation's meeting halls and newspapers to the main political parties and the floor of Congress. It stayed there, growing ever more violent, until the conflict erupted in civil war.

The conquest of Mexico thus represented a culmination of many of the major developments of the early American republic: conquest and the territorial expansion of the American nation, the rise of white supremacy, and conflict over slavery. This culmination transformed the United States, marking the beginning of a new era in its history. At war's end, the United States was a continental nation, a nation committed (with some vehement dissent) to white supremacy, and a nation at war with itself over the future of slavery. The conflicts of the new era would be even fiercer than those of the early republic, but they would be different conflicts.

Refiguring American Nationalism

In 1845, the United States annexed the independent Republic of Texas, where emigrants from the United States and their native Mexican allies had declared independence from Mexico in 1836. Annexation inspired anxiety among the opponents of slavery, who saw in it a new empire for American slavery and an opportunity for slave owners to consolidate their power in Congress. Among many Democrats, both northern and (especially) southern, it inspired visions of a continental empire. These Democrats embraced a new vision of American nationalism, one that celebrated territorial expansion and sought to extend the blessings of democracy, not by example and solidarity, but by absorption of new territories. In an editorial written in 1845, as Congress was debating annexation, John O'Sullivan, editor of the *United States Magazine and Democratic Review* and an influential voice among Democrats, predicted that the United States would soon become a continental nation.

Texas is now ours. . . .

Were other reasons wanting, in favor of now elevating this question of the reception of Texas into the Union, . . . it surely is to be found . . . in the manner in which other nations have undertaken to intrude themselves . . . , checking the fulfillment of our manifest destiny to overspread the continent allotted by Providence for the free development of our yearly multiplying millions. . . .

California will, probably, next fall away from the loose adhesion which, in such a country as Mexico, holds a remote province in a slight equivocal kind of dependence on the metropolis. Imbecile and distracted, Mexico never can exert any real governmental authority over such a country. . . . Already the advance guard of the irresistible Anglo-Saxon emigration has begun to pour down upon it, armed with the plough and the rifle, and marking its trail with schools and colleges, courts and representative halls, mills and meeting-houses. A population will soon be in actual occupation of California, over which it will be idle for Mexico to dream of dominion. They will necessarily become independent. All this without agency of our government, without responsibility of our people—in the natural flow of events, the spontaneous working of principles. . . . And they will have a right to independence—to self-government—to the possession of the homes conquered from the wilderness by their own labors and dangers, sufferings and sacrifices—a better and a truer right than the artificial title of sovereignty in Mexico. . . . Whether they will then attach themselves to our Union or not, is not to be predicted with any certainty. Unless the projected railroad across the continent to the Pacific be carried into effect, perhaps they may not. . . . But that great work, colossal as appears the plan on its first suggestion, cannot remain long unbuilt. . . . The day cannot be distant which shall witness the conveyance of the representatives from Oregon and California to Washington within less time than a few years ago was devoted to a similar journey by those of Ohio; while the magnetic telegraph will enable the editors of the "San Francisco Union," the "Astoria Evening Post," or the "Nootka Morning News," to set up in type the first half of the President's Inaugural before the echoes of the latter half shall have died away. . . .

Away, then, with all idle French talk of *balances of power* on the American continent. There is no growth in Spanish America! Whatever progress of population there may be in the British Canadas, is only for their own early severance of their present colonial relation to the little island three thousand miles across the Atlantic; soon to be followed by Annexation, and destined to swell the still accumulating momentum of our progress.

H. Bucholzer, *Matty Meeting the Texas Question* (1844), lampoons the explosiveness of the annexation of Texas for Democrats. In the 1844 presidential campaign, the presumptive Democratic nominee, Martin Van Buren, remained silent about whether he would support annexation, while slave-state Democrats insisted on its acceptance into the Union. The cartoon depicts the slaveholder and former president Andrew Jackson pushing his former protégé Van Buren toward Texas, which is depicted as a hideous woman. Texas is being held up by two proslavery Democrats, John C. Calhoun and Thomas Hart Benton. In the background are Van Buren's main rivals for the Democratic presidential nomination in 1844, James K. Polk and George Dallas. Polk says to Dallas, "She's not the handsomest Lady I ever saw but that $25,000 a year—Eh! It's worth a little stretching of Conscience." The president's salary was $25,000 per year. Texas holds a dagger and pistols, signifying the risk of war if the United States annexed the republic; and whips and manacles—symbols of slavery. In the year of this cartoon, southern Democrats dumped Van Buren from the presidential ticket, instead nominating the proslavery Polk.

MATTY MEETING THE TEXAS QUESTION.

Many writers and political leaders infused O'Sullivan's dream of a continental United States with white supremacist thinking. White supremacy had been growing in influence since the 1810s, but it gained unprecedented acceptance during the 1840s, largely because it purported to justify and explain Americans' conquest of Mexican territory. In an 1846 speech before the Senate, Senator Thomas Hart Benton of Missouri saw in the conquest of North America a fulfillment of Anglo-Saxons' racial destiny to conquer and civilize the continent and to uplift and reinvigorate Asia. In this speech, he offered a radical rethinking of American nationalism. Where Americans had previously placed republican or democratic principles as the focus of American unity, Benton and many like him now conceived of the United States in racial terms.

Since the dispersion of men upon the earth, I know of no human event, past or present, which promises a greater, a more beneficent change upon earth than the arrival of the van of the Caucasian race (the Celtic-Anglo-Saxon division) upon the border of the sea which washes the shore of eastern Asia. The Mongolian, or Yellow Race, is there, four hundred million in number, spreading almost to Europe; a race once the foremost of the human family in the arts of civilization, but torpid and stationary for thousands of years. It is a race far above the Ethiopian, or Black—above the Malay, or Brown (if we must admit five races)—and above the American Indian, or Red; it is a race far above all these, but still, far below the White; and, like all the rest, must receive an impression from the superior race whenever they

Just as it did in the United States, the U.S. War with Mexico elicited nationalist fervor among Mexicans. *Heroic Defense of the Gate of Belen* depicts the battle in Mexico City as an act of bravery and self-sacrifice by the Mexican troops. After the war, this sort of nationalism turned many Mexicans against the Liberal government, who many blamed for the dismemberment of the country's territory.

come in contact. It would seem that the White race alone received the divine command, to subdue and replenish the earth! For it is the only race that has obeyed it—the only one that hunts out new and distant lands, and even a New World, to subdue and replenish. Starting from western Asia, taking Europe for their field, and the Sun for their guide, and leaving the Mongolians behind, they arrived, after many ages, on the shores of the Atlantic, which they lit up with the lights of science and religion, and adorned with the useful and elegant arts. Three and a half centuries ago, this race, in obedience to the great command, arrived in the New World, and found new lands to subdue and replenish. For a long time, it was confined to the border of the new field (I now mean the Celtic-Anglo-Saxon division); and even fourscore years ago the philosophic Burke was considered a rash man because he said the English colonists would top the Alleghenies, and descend into the valley of the Mississippi. . . .

What was considered a rash declaration eighty years ago, is old history, in our young country, at this day. Thirty years ago I said the same thing of the Rocky Mountains and Columbia: it was ridiculed then: it is becoming history to-day. . . . The van of the Caucasian race now top the Rocky Mountains, and spread down to the shores of the Pacific. In a few years a great population will grow up there, luminous with the accumulated lights of European and American civilization. Their presence in such a position cannot be without its influence upon eastern Asia. The sun of civilization must shine across the sea: socially and commercially, the van of the Caucasians, and the rear of the Mongolians, must mix. . . . Moral and intellectual superiority will do the rest: the White race will take the ascendant, elevating what is susceptible of improvement—wearing out what is not.

The Red race has disappeared from the Atlantic coast: the tribes that resisted civilization, met extinction. This is a cause of lamentation with many. For my part, I cannot murmur at what seems to be the effect of divine law. I cannot repine that this Capitol has replaced the wigwam—this Christian people, replaced the savages—white matrons, the red squaws—and that such men as Washington, Franklin, and Jefferson, have taken the place of Powhattan, Opechonecanough, and other red men, howsoever respectable they may have been as savages.

Civilization, or extinction, has been the fate of all people who have found themselves in the track of the advancing Whites, and civilization, always the preference of the Whites, has been pressed as an object, while extinction has followed as a consequence of its

The philosophic Burke
Edmund Burke was an eighteenth-century Irish-born political philosopher and member of the English House of Commons. In his writings and parliamentary speeches, he articulated conservative ideas that would remain influential well into the twentieth century.

resistance. The Black and the Red races have often felt their ameliorating influence. The Yellow race . . . cannot fail to receive a new impulse from the approach of the Whites, improved so much since so many ages ago they left the western borders of Asia. The apparition of the van of the Caucasian race . . . must wake up and reanimate the torpid body of old Asia. . . . Thus the youngest people, and the newest land, will become the reviver and the regenerator of the oldest.

Anglos and Mexicans in the Conquered Territories

In the Treaty of Guadalupe Hidalgo, signed in 1848, Mexico ceded half of its territory to the United States, expanding the northern nation by one-third. The territory transferred by that treaty included what is now California, Nevada, Colorado, New Mexico, Utah, Wyoming, and most of Arizona. Despite a growing consensus among white Americans that the Mexicans who lived in that territory belonged to an inferior race, the treaty promised them citizenship and property rights.

Mexicans now established in territories previously belonging to Mexico . . . shall be free to continue where they now reside, or to remove at any time to the Mexican Republic, retaining the property which they possess in the said territories. . . .

Those who shall prefer to remain in the said territories, may either retain the title and rights of Mexican citizens, or acquire those of citizens of the United States. But they shall be under the obligation to make their election within one year from the date of the exchange of ratifications of this treaty: and those who shall remain in the said territories, after the expiration of that year, without having declared their intention to retain the character of Mexicans, shall be considered to have elected to become citizens of the United States.

In the said territories, property of every kind, now belonging to Mexicans, not established there, shall be inviolably respected. The present owners, the heirs of these, and all Mexicans who may hereafter acquire said property by contract, shall enjoy with respect to it, guaranties equally ample as if the same belonged to citizens of the United States.

The Mexicans who, in the territories aforesaid, shall not preserve the character of citizens of the Mexican Republic, . . . shall be incorporated into the Union of the United States, and be admitted, at the proper time (to be judged by the Congress of the United States) to the enjoyment of all the rights of citizens of the United States according to the principles of the Constitution; and in the mean time shall be maintained and protected in the free enjoyment of their liberty and property, and secured in the free exercise of their religion without restriction.

Wherever Anglos came to outnumber Americans of Mexican descent, the guarantees of the Treaty of Guadalupe Hidalgo became a dead letter. Armed by superior numbers, ample weaponry, a superior knowledge of American law, and a racial and nationalist ideology that imagined them to be better entitled to the land, native-born whites sought to strip Mexican property holders of their property. Mexican landowners fought back through the courts, the legislatures, and appeals to public opinion. In an 1859 petition to Congress, fifty Californios of Mexican descent described how Anglos tried to strip them of their land and the methods they used to keep their property.

During the war between the United States and Mexico the officers of the United States . . . on several occasions offered and promised in the most solemn manner to the inhabitants of California, protection and security of their persons and their property. . . .

In consequence of such promises and representations, very few of the inhabitants of California opposed the invasion; some of them welcomed the invaders with open arms. . . .

When peace was established between the two nations by the Treaty of Guadalupe Hidalgo, they joined in the general rejoicing with their new fellow countrymen, even though some—a very few indeed—decided to remain in California as Mexican citizens . . . ; [the majority] immediately assumed the position of American citizens that was offered them, and since then have conducted themselves with zeal and faithfulness and with no less loyalty than those whose great fortune it was to be born under the flag of the North American republic—believing, thus, that all their rights were insured in the treaty, which declares that *their property shall be inviolably protected and insured.* . . .

The inhabitants of California . . . , ignorant even of the law of their own country, and without the assistance of lawyers (of whom there were so few in California) to advise them on legal matters, elected from among themselves their judges, who had no knowledge of the intricate technical terms of the law and who were, of course, incompetent and ill-fitted to occupy the delicate position of forensic judicature. . . . They could hardly hope that the titles under which their ancestors held and preserved their lands . . . would be able to

As U.S. businesses moved into the territories seized from Mexico, former peasants from China migrated there as well. Fleeing famine and diminishing access to land, these migrants hoped to earn money as quickly as possible and return home to buy land. In the West, they worked primarily as common laborers.

withstand a scrupulously critical examination before a court. They heard with dismay of the appointment, by an Act of Congress, of a Commission with the right to examine all titles and confirm or disapprove them.... Though this honorable body has doubtless had the best interests of the state at heart, still it has brought about the most disastrous effects ..., for even though all landholders possessing titles under the Spanish or Mexican government were not forced by the letter of the law to present them before the Commission for confirmation, nevertheless all those titles were at once considered doubtful ... and, as a result, all landholders were ... *compelled de facto* to submit their titles to the Commission for confirmation, under the alternative that, if they were not submitted, the lands would be considered public property.

The undersigned, ignorant, then, of the forms and proceedings of an American court of justice, were obliged to engage the services of American lawyers to present their claims, paying them enormous fees. Not having other means with which to meet those expenses but their lands, they were compelled to give up part of their property, in many cases as much as a fourth of it, and in other cases even more.

The discovery of gold attracted an immense number of immigrants to this country, and, when they perceived that the titles of the old inhabitants were considered doubtful and their validity questionable, they spread themselves over the land as though it were public property, taking possession of the improvements made by the inhabitants, many times seizing even their houses . . . , taking and killing the cattle and destroying the crops; so that those who before had owned great numbers of cattle that could have been counted in the thousands, now found themselves without any, and the men who were the owners of many leagues of land now were deprived of the peaceful possession of even one vara.

The expenses of the new state government were great. . . . Onerous taxes were levied by new laws, and if these were not paid the property was put up for sale. Deprived as they were of the use of their lands, from which they had now no lucrative returns, the owners were compelled to mortgage them in order to assume the payment of taxes already due and constantly increasing. With such mortgages upon property greatly depreciated (because of its uncertain status), without crops or rents, the owners of those lands were not able to borrow money except at usurious rates of interest. . . . Hoping that the Land Commission would take quick action in the revision of titles . . . they mortgaged their lands, paying compound interest at the rate from three to ten percent a month. The long-awaited relief would not arrive; action from the Commission was greatly delayed; and, even after the Commission would pronounce judgment on the titles, it was still necessary to pass through a rigorous ordeal in the District Court; and some cases, are, even now, pending before the Supreme Court of the nation. . . . More than 800 petitions were presented to the Land Commission, and already 10 years of delays have elapsed and only some 50 patents have been granted.

The petitioners, finding themselves unable to face such payments because of the rates of interest, taxes, and litigation expenses, as well as having to maintain their families, were compelled to sell, little by little, the greater part of their old possessions. Some, who at one time had been the richest landholders, today find themselves without a foot of ground, living as objects of charity—and even in sight of the many leagues of land which, with many a thousand head of cattle, they once had called their own; and those of us who, by means of strict economy and immense sacrifices, have been able to preserve a small portion of our property, . . . see with deep pain that efforts are being made to induce those honorable bodies to pass laws

Vara

A *vara* was a measure of three feet; a league was five thousand varas.

authorizing *bills of review*, and other illegal proceedings, with a view to prolonging still further the litigation of our claims.

The Sectional Conflict Deepens

The conflict brought on by the Mexican War engulfed not only the conquered territories but the nation's capital as well. Since Texas declared independence from Mexico in 1836, northern politicians and voters had increasingly opposed opening up new territory for the expansion of slavery. President Polk's expansionist policies stoked northern fears of the institution's spread. Throughout the war with Mexico, abolitionists and antislavery Whigs had accused the Democrats of promoting a war to expand slavery. In August 1846, when Polk asked Congress for two million dollars, which everyone understood to be intended to help pay for territorial concessions, he sparked a rebellion in his own party. A dozen northern Democratic congressmen began meeting to hammer out a way to challenge the expansion of slavery. Soon after Polk's request reached the House, one of the dissident Democrats, an obscure freshman congressman from Pennsylvania named David Wilmot, proposed an amendment to the appropriations bill.

And be it further enacted, That there shall be neither slavery nor involuntary servitude in any Territory on the continent of America which shall hereafter be acquired by, or annexed to, the United States by virtue of this appropriation or in any other manner whatever, except for crimes whereof the party shall have been duly convicted; *Provided, always,* That any person escaping into such territory from whom labor or service is lawfully claimed in any one of the United States, such fugitive may be lawfully reclaimed and conveyed out of said territory to the person claiming his or her labor or service.

Wilmot's amendment, which quickly came to be known as the Wilmot Proviso, passed the House of Representatives on a sectional vote, but there was not enough time for the Senate to debate it. Wilmot reintroduced it the following February. It passed the House again but was defeated in the Senate. The stalemate would last until 1850. During this time, the controversy over the westward spread of slavery dominated national politics, dividing both major parties and public opinion along sectional lines. In a speech on the House floor, Wilmot explained the principles behind the proviso.

I stand by the Constitution. . . . I would never invade one single right of the South. So far from it, I stand ready at all times, and upon all occasions, as do nearly the entire North, to sustain the institutions of the South as they exist. . . .

But sir, the issue now presented is not whether slavery shall exist unmolested where it now is, but whether it shall be carried

THE MODERN GILPINS. LOVES LABOR LOST.

to new and distant regions, now free, where the footprint of a slave shall not be found. . . . I ask not that slavery be abolished. I demand that this Government preserve the integrity of *free territory* against the aggressions of slavery—against its wrongful usurpations. Sir, I was in favor of the annexation of Texas. . . . The Democracy of the North, almost to a man, went for annexation. Yes, sir, here was an empire larger than France given up to slavery. Shall further concessions be made by the North? Shall we give up free territory, the inheritance of free labor? Must we yield this also? Never sir, never, until we ourselves are fit to be slaves. . . .

Sir, the whole history of this question is a history of concessions on the part of the North. The money of the North was expended in the purchase of Louisiana, two-thirds of which was given up to slavery. Again, in the purchase of Florida, did slavery gain new

This 1848 cartoon lampoons the divisions in the Democratic Party over the Wilmot Proviso. Anti-Wilmot Democrats ride a sow down "Salt River Lane" (a metaphor for political oblivion) and away from the "Head Quarters of the Northern Democracy." John Van Buren tries to stop the pig, while his father Martin is up to his neck in a mud puddle. Later that year, antislavery Democrats would walk out of the Democratic National Convention when it failed to endorse the Wilmot Proviso. Many of the bolters would form the Free Soil Party and nominate Martin Van Buren as their candidate for president.

acquisitions. Slavery acquired an empire in the annexation of Texas. Three slave States have been admitted out of the Louisiana purchase. The slave State of Florida has been received into the Union; and Texas annexed, with the privilege of making five States out of her territory. What has the North obtained from these vast acquisitions? One State, sir—one: young Iowa. . . . This, sir, is a history of our acquisitions since we became a nation. A history of northern concession—of southern triumphs. . . .

I have no squeamish sensitiveness upon the subject of slavery, no morbid sympathy for the slave. I plead the cause and the rights of white freemen. I would preserve to free white labor a fair country, a rich inheritance, where the sons of toil, of my own race and own color, can live without the disgrace which association with negro slavery brings upon free labor. I stand for the inviolability of free territory. . . .

The future greatness and glory of this republic demands that the progress of domestic slavery should be arrested now and forever. Let it remain where it now is, and leave to time and a merciful Providence its results. . . .

I regard [slavery] as a great social and political evil—a blight and deadly mildew upon any country or State in which it exists. . . . Where the men who labor are slaves, you cannot place arms in their hands; and it is the free laboring man who constitutes the strength and defence of his country on the field of battle. . . .

Contrast Ohio with Kentucky. Why has the former left so far behind the latter, in the race of prosperity and greatness? It is wholly owing to slavery. . . . There is always a lack of that energy and enterprise in slave labor, which is to be found in free labor. I verily believe that the laborer of the North, who goes into the wilderness to hew himself out a home, does more work than three slaves, while he consumes or wastes less. Nothing is neglected by him; his eye sees everything that requires attention. It is the enterprise, the diligence, and the economy of free labor, that has built up new empires in the West, while the South has been falling back into decrepitude and decay. . . . Slave labor exhausts, and makes barren the fields it cultivates. That labor is only profitable to the master in the production in the staples of cotton, sugar, and tobacco. Crop follows crop, until the fertility of the soil is exhausted, when the old fields are abandoned, new and virgin soil is sought out, to be exhausted in the same manner, and in its turn likewise abandoned. Thus, sir, sterility follows its path. . . .

Southern politicians and planters saw in the Wilmot Proviso an attack on slavery and on slaveholders' position in the Union, and they predicted

that, if not defeated, it would destroy the Union. In a speech on the floor of the House of Representatives, J. A. Seddon of Virginia outlined the issues that he saw at work in the conflict. The struggle that erupted over the fate of slavery in the American West remained the centerpiece of sectional strife for the next fifteen years, contributing significantly to the outbreak of civil war in 1861.

I wish to state the estimate which I—and may I not say, we of the South . . . place upon the union of these States. I regard and venerate it as the noble work of heroic ancestry, . . . as the system under which, for sixty years, our fathers and ourselves have flourished, enjoying a government of laws, and the institutions of freedom. But . . . it should be valued and revered, not for its name nor its semblance, but for its spirit and its realities—for the Constitution on which it rests—for the solemn compromises of that sacred instrument, and the guaranties it affords to our liberties and our rights. That Constitution was designed to maintain the freedom, to guard the peace, and guaranty the rights of the people of all the States, *equally and impartially*. While it so operates, it is beyond all price. But sir, let it be perverted from its just ends of equal government, and be made the pretext and instrument of gross inequalities and favoritism—of direct attack on the institutions and peace of one-half of the States of the Union—of insult and injury, outrage and wrong on them and theirs, it becomes of less worth than the scroll on which it is written, and, like every symbol of tyranny, should be rent and scattered to the winds. . . .

The ultimate issue of the conflict may involve the dissolution of the Union. . . .

I say, sir, the proposition [to exclude slavery from the territories gained from Mexico] is grossly unconstitutional. It more than violates a single specific clause of that instrument. It outrages its whole scope and spirit, and subverts the very basis of its being. The fundamental principle of the Constitution is the perfect equality and entire reciprocity of privileges and immunities which it secures to the people of the several States. . . . The philosophy of history . . . bids us heed, that the least concession of inferiority in position or rights—the smallest provision in the framing, or action in the working of a government, by which the interests or property of one part of the people are to be less conserved or more prejudicially operated upon than those of another, in the course of events . . . would . . . be made the pretext and means of encroachments and inroads, until superiority, riches, and domination would become the arrogated possession of the favored portion, and degradation, impoverishment, and subjection, the bitter lot of the other. . . .

EIGHTH EDITION.

THE WILMOT PROVISO

IS ABOLITION, AGGRESSIVE, REVOLUTIONARY, AND SUBVERSIVE OF
THE CONSTITUTION AND ITS GUARANTIES TO THE
SLAVEHOLDING STATES.

A

VOICE FROM THE SOUTH:

COMPRISING

LETTERS FROM

GEORGIA TO MASSACHUSETTS,

AND TO

THE SOUTHERN STATES.

WITH AN

APPENDIX

CONTAINING AN ARTICLE FROM THE CHARLESTON MERCURY ON THE WILMOT PROVISO, TOGE-
THER WITH THE FOURTH ARTICLE OF THE CONSTITUTION, THE LAW OF CONGRESS,
THE NULLIFICATION LAW OF PENNSYLVANIA, THE RESOLUTIONS OF
TEN OF THE FREE STATES, THE RESOLUTIONS OF VIRGINIA,
GEORGIA AND ALABAMA, AND MR. CALHOUN'S RE-
SOLUTIONS IN THE SENATE OF THE
UNITED STATES.

BALTIMORE:

SAMUEL E. SMITH,

PUBLISHER AND BOOKSELLER,

SUN BUILDINGS,

No. 57 Baltimore street, S. E. corner of Gay.

1848.

Wilmot's Proviso brought sectional conflict to new heights. In addition to deadlocking Congress for four years, it sparked a propaganda war more widespread and bitter than had been seen in the United States. Both supporters and opponents published speeches, pamphlets, and broadsides like the anti-Wilmot pamphlet pictured here.

The proposed bill . . . proposes a prospective, permanent, fundamental law for the action of this Government in all time; . . . its clear aim is to direct the legislation, and enlist the whole influence, moral and political, of this common Union, to discountenance the institutions of the South, and to impair and restrict the rights of her people to their most valuable property; . . . these northern gentlemen . . . make it one of the chief objects of this Government to stigmatize the institutions and impair the labor and property of the people of one-half the States of the Confederacy. . . . They wholly deny to that people the equality on which is based the Constitution itself, and exclude them, with their property, from all participation in the acquisition of the common blood and treasure of the Union. . . . The gentleman from New York does, indeed, venture the assurance . . . that the Federal Government will not directly overthrow . . . the institution of slavery in the States where it exists. That is, . . . (and how gracious, indeed!) our common Federal Government will not openly plunder the people of one-half the States of their most valuable property. It will only, by its whole influence . . . undermine their institutions, and filch away, by slow degrees, their rights of property and the value of their labor. . . .

Mr. Chairman, we have had agitations and wrongs more than enough, for twelve years past, to bear from our northern fellow-citizens on this subject of slavery. Numerous societies have been tolerated among them, whose sole vocation it was to defame the character and assail the peace and property of the slaveholders of the South. Sovereign States of the North . . . have passed resolutions insulting to the feelings, and have enacted laws in direct conflict with the guaranteed rights of the people of the South. The courts of the Union . . . have in vain pronounced your laws to be unconstitutional. You repeal them not, and mobs enforce them, until it has come to such pass, that the slaveholders of the South, having their property enticed or stolen to the North, must forego the plain remedies of an acknowledged law of the Union, enacted in conformity to a solemn provision of the Constitution, and forfeit their property, rather than encounter the peril of a foul death or disgraceful imprisonment as felons. But, sir, these wrongs, gross as they are, have been all the acts of individuals or of separate States. Hard to endure as they were, we have forborne, because they could be measurably met and repelled by the associated action of our people, or by the counteracting legislation of the slaveholding states. . . . But should the offensive bill . . . pass . . . we shall be *aroused indeed and by a widely different spectacle.* The combined action of all the departments of this Government . . . with all its agencies of moral and political influence will have been enlisted in a direct attempt to subvert the fundamental equality of the Constitution—in an insidious design to undermine the institutions of one-half the States, and to stigmatize and depreciate their property and their labor. . . . The people of the South never could and never would endure it. The heritage of their fathers would be at stake—their own honor would be at hazard—the peace of their homes, the loves and the affections that cluster around their hearthstones—the security of their State and their friends—the fortunes and the lives of their wives and their families, would all be wrecked in the final issues of such agencies, unresisted and unrepelled by them. The Union would and must be first sacrificed. . . .

Fugitive Slave Laws

The Constitution of the United States and federal law guaranteed to slaveholders the right to capture and return enslaved people who had escaped to other states. In 1826, Pennsylvania passed a "personal liberty law" that forbade state officials from helping seize people accused of being fugitive slaves. Six years later, a local constable, citing that law, stopped Edward Prigg, a slave owner, from capturing Margaret Morgan, an escaped slave. The Supreme Court overturned the Pennsylvania law in 1842, declaring that states were not required to aid in capturing fugitive slaves but could not prevent slave owners or their agents from doing so. Later that year, a crowd of African Americans prevented the capture and return of a fugitive slave in Boston. Soon thereafter, several northern states passed laws, carefully crafted to conform to the Court's new doctrine, forbidding state officials from aiding in the capture of accused fugitives and outlawing the use of jails or other public property to detain them.

Timeline

1780–1799
Every northern state except Delaware abolishes slavery within its borders

1788
Federal Constitution ratified

1789
First U.S. Congress convenes

1791
Thomas Jefferson and James Madison break from the financial policies of Alexander Hamilton; Jefferson and Madison establish the *National Gazette*, the first opposition newspaper in the United States

1793
First Democratic Republican Societies, the first popular political organizations since the Revolution, are founded

1798
Congress passes the Alien and Sedition Acts; Kentucky and Virginia Resolves passed

1800
Gabriel's Rebellion, a major slave conspiracy, is discovered in Richmond, Virginia; Thomas Jefferson elected president over John Adams

1803
The United States buys the Louisiana Territory from France; Lewis and Clark expedition begins exploration of the Louisiana Territory

1805
Tenskwatawa, the Shawnee Prophet, begins public preaching

1808
Congress outlaws the Atlantic slave trade; Tecumseh begins his campaign to unite Indians of the Trans-Allegheny West against American territorial expansion

1812
War of 1812 begins, and Tecumseh and his allies side with the British

1815
War of 1812 ends, and U.S. negotiators demand millions of acres of land from England's Indian allies (and from several allies of the Americans) as a condition of peace

1815–1820
Federalist Party collapses

1819–1824
The Panic of 1819 marks the beginning of a major, five-year depression, and antibank movements and campaigns for debt relief are launched throughout the country

1819–1821
Congress deadlocks over whether to abolish slavery in the new state of Missouri

1826
Charles Grandison Finney conducts his first major religious revival in Utica, New York

1827
Freedom's Journal, the first African American newspaper, begins publication in New York City

1827
The Cherokee nation declares itself an independent nation and adopts a written constitution

1828
Andrew Jackson elected president

1829
David Walker publishes his *Appeal to the Colored Citizens of the World*; Georgia declares all Cherokee territory within state borders to be under its jurisdiction; Supreme Court issues its decision in *Cherokee Nation v. Georgia*

1830

Supreme Court issues its decision in *Worcester v. Georgia*; Congress appropriates funds to remove all eastern Indians to lands west of the Mississippi River

1831

William Lloyd Garrison begins publishing *The Liberator*; Nat Turner leads a bloody slave rebellion in Southampton, Virginia

1832

Virginia legislature debates and narrowly defeats a proposal to gradually abolish slavery in the state; Andrew Jackson vetoes the bill reauthorizing the charter of the Bank of the United States

1833

The American Anti-Slavery Society is formed

1834

The New York Female Moral Reform Society is founded; Opponents of Andrew Jackson and the Democratic Party found the Whig Party

1834–1837

Philadelphia, New York, and other cities experience a strike wave among journeyman artisans; Antiblack and antiabolitionist rioting peaks in American cities

1836

Texas declares independence from Mexico; Angelina and Sarah Grimké begin their career as abolitionist agents, speaking to large groups of men and women throughout the North, and they are met with a nationwide storm of condemnation

1837

A major financial panic occurs, sending the U.S. economy into a depression that lasts until 1843

1838

Sarah Grimké publishes *Letters on the Equality of the Sexes, and the Condition of Woman*; The eastern Cherokees are forcibly removed to Indian Territory by the U.S. Army

1840

Abolitionists found the Liberty Party; Whigs adopt the Democrats' brand of popular electioneering, and their candidate, William Henry Harrison, wins the presidency

1844

Northern and southern Democrats split over admitting Texas into the United States; James K. Polk, a proannexation Democrat from Tennessee, defeats Martin Van Buren for the presidential nomination and goes on to win the general election

1845

Congress admits Texas into the United States

1846

At President Polk's request, Congress declares war against Mexico; the Wilmot Proviso is introduced into Congress, worsening sectional divisions in and outside of Congress

1848

In the Treaty of Guadalupe Hidalgo, Mexico cedes half of its territory to the United States; First Woman's Rights Convention held in Seneca Falls, New York; Antislavery Democrats walk out of the Democratic National Convention. Later, they join with antislavery Whigs and Liberty Party activists in forming the Free Soil Party. The new party nominates Martin Van Buren as its presidential candidate.

Further Reading

Overviews

Howe, Daniel Walker. *What Hath God Wrought: The Transformation of America, 1815–1848*. New York: Oxford University Press, 2007.

Wood, Gordon S. *Empire of Liberty: A History of the Early Republic, 1789–1815*. New York: Oxford University Press, 2009.

Politics

Elkins, Stanley M., and Eric L. McKitrick. *The Age of Federalism*. New York: Oxford University Press, 1993.

Freeman, Joanne. *Affairs of Honor: National Politics in the New Republic*. New Haven: Yale University Press, 2001.

Isenberg, Nancy. *Fallen Founder: The Life of Aaron Burr*. New York: Viking, 2007.

Newman, Simon. *Parades and the Politics of the Street: Festive Culture in the Early American Republic*. Philadelphia: University of Pennsylvania Press, 1997.

Pasley, Jeffrey L. *The "Tyranny of Printers": Newspaper Politics in the Early American Republic*. Charlottesville: University Press of Virginia, 2001.

Pasley, Jeffrey L., Andrew Robertson, and David Waldstreicher. *Beyond the Founders: New Approaches to the Political History of the Early American Republic*. Chapel Hill: University of North Carolina Press, 2004.

Sharp, James Roger. *American Politics in the Early Republic: The New Nation in Crisis*. New Haven: Yale University Press, 1993.

Waldstreicher, David. *In the Midst of Perpetual Fetes: The Making of American Nationalism, 1776–1820*. Chapel Hill: University of North Carolina Press, 1997.

Watson, Harry L. *Liberty and Power: The Politics of Jacksonian America*. New York: Farrar, Straus, and Giroux, 1990.

Wilentz, Sean. *The Rise of American Democracy: Jefferson to Lincoln*. New York: W. W. Norton, 2005.

Gender and Family Relations

Boydston, Jeanne. *Home and Work: Housework, Wages, and the Ideology of Labor in the Early Republic*. New York: Oxford University Press, 1990.

Cott, Nancy F. *The Bonds of Womanhood: "Woman's Sphere" in New England, 1780–1835*. New Haven: Yale University Press, 1977.

Kerber, Linda K. *Women of the Republic: Intellect and Ideology in Revolutionary America*. New York: W.W. Norton, 1980.

Stansell, Christine. *City of Women: Sex and Class in New York, 1789–1860*. 1982. Reprint, Urbana: University of Illinois Press, 1987.

Ulrich, Laura Thatcher. *A Midwife's Tale: The Life of Martha Ballard, Based on Her Diary, 1785–1812*. New York: Knopf, 1990.

The West

Aron, Stephen. *How the West Was Lost: The Transformation of Kentucky from Daniel Boone to Henry Clay*. Baltimore: Johns Hopkins University Press, 1996.

Burlend, Rebecca, and Edward Burlend. *A True Picture of Emigration*. 1848. Reprint, Lincoln: University of Nebraska Press, 1987.

Faragher, John Mack. *Sugar Creek: Life on the Illinois Prairie*. New Haven: Yale University Press, 1986.

Gonzalez, Deena J. *Refusing the Favor: The Spanish-Mexican Women of Santa Fe, 1820–1880*. New York: Oxford University Press, 1999.

Resendez, Andres. *Changing National Identities at the Frontier: Texas and New Mexico, 1800–1850*. New York: Cambridge University Press, 2005.

Taylor, Alan. *William Cooper's Town: Power and Persuasion on the Frontier of the Early American Republic*. New York: Knopf, 1995.

———. *The Divided Ground: Indians, Settlers, and the Northern Borderland of the American Revolution*. New York: Alfred A. Knopf, 2006.

African Americans, Native Americans, and Euro-Americans

Douglass, Frederick. *Narrative of the Life of Frederick Douglass*. 1845. Reprint, New York: Dover, 1995.

Fredrickson, George M. *The Black Image in the White Mind: The Debate on Afro-American Character and Destiny, 1817–1914*. New York: Harper, 1971.

Horton, James Oliver, and Lois E. Horton. *In Hope of Liberty: Culture, Community and Protest Among Northern Free Blacks, 1700–1860*. New York: Oxford University Press, 1997.

McLoughlin, William G. *Cherokee Renascence in the New Republic*. Princeton, NJ: Princeton University Press, 1986.

Melish, Joanne Pope. *Disowning Slavery: Gradual Emancipation and "Race" in New England, 1780–1860*. Ithaca, NY: Cornell University Press, 1998.

Perdue, Theda. *Cherokee Women: Gender and Culture Change, 1700–1835*. Lincoln: University of Nebraska Press, 1998.

Perdue, Theda, and Michael D. Green. *The Cherokee Removal: A Brief History With Documents*. New York: Bedford, 1995.

Roediger, David. *The Wages of Whiteness: Race and the Making of the American Working Class*. New York: Verso, 1995.

White, Shane. *Stories of Freedom in Black New York*. Cambridge: Harvard University Press, 2002.

The Economic Transformation of the North

Balleisen, Edward. *Navigating Failure: Bankruptcy and Commercial Society in Antebellum New York*. Chapel Hill: University of North Carolina Press, 2001.

Clark, Christopher. *The Roots of Rural Capitalism: Western Massachusetts, 1780–1860*. Ithaca, NY: Cornell University Press, 1990.

Kamensky, Jane. *The Exchange Artist: A Tale of High-Flying Speculation and America's First Banking Collapse*. New York: Viking, 2008.

Laurie, Bruce. *Artisans into Workers: Labor in Nineteenth-Century America*. New York: Hill and Wang, 1989.

Mihm, Stephen. *A Nation of Counterfeiters: Capitalists, Con Men, and the Making of the United States*. Cambridge: Harvard University Press, 2007.

Wilentz, Sean. *Chants Democratic: New York City and the Rise of the American Working Class*. New York: Oxford University Press, 1984.

The South and Slavery

Berlin, Ira. *Generations of Captivity: A History of African-American Slaves*. Cambridge: Harvard University Press, 2003.

Cashin, Joan E. *A Family Venture: Men and Women on the Southern Frontier*. New York: Oxford University Press, 1991.

Glymph, Thavolia. *Out of the House of Bondage: The Transformation of the Plantation Household*. New York: Cambridge University Press, 2008.

Kaye, Anthony E. *Joining Places: Slave Neighborhoods in the Old South*. Chapel Hill: University of North Carolina Press, 2007.

Penningroth, Dylan. *The Claims of Kinfolk: African American Property and Community in the Nineteenth-Century South*. Chapel Hill: University of North Carolina Press, 2003.

Rose, Willie Lee. *A Documentary History of Slavery in North America*. New York: Oxford University Press, 1976.

White, Debora Gray. *Ar'n't I a Woman?: Female Slaves in the Plantation South*. New York: W. W. Norton, 1999.

Religion and Reform

Abzug, Robert H. *Cosmos Crumbling: American Reform and the Religious Imagination*. New York: Oxford University Press, 1994.

Boylan, Anne. *The Origins of Women's Activism: New York and Boston, 1797–1840*. Chapel Hill: University of North Carolina Press, 2002.

Butler, Jon. *Awash in a Sea of Faith: Christianizing the American People*. Cambridge: Harvard University Press, 1990.

Heyrman, Christine Leigh. *Southern Cross: The Beginnings of the Bible Belt*. New York: Knopf, 1997.

Isenberg, Nancy. *Sex and Citizenship in Antebellum America*. Chapel Hill: University of North Carolina Press, 1998.

Jeffrey, Julie Roy. *The Great Silent Army of Abolitionism: Ordinary Women in the Antislavery Movement*. Chapel Hill: University of North Carolina Press, 1998.

Laurie, Bruce. *Beyond Garrison: Antislavery and Social Reform*. New York: Cambridge University Press, 2005.

Newman, Richard S. *The Transformation of American Abolitionism: Fighting Slavery in the Early Republic*. Chapel Hill: University of North Carolina Press, 2002.

Stewart, James Brewer. *Holy Warriors: The Abolitionists and American Slavery*. New York: Hill and Wang, 1976.

Sectional Conflict

Earle, Jonathan. *Jacksonian Antislavery and the Politics of Free Soil, 1824–1854*. Chapel Hill: University of North Carolina Press, 2004.

Finkelman, Paul. *Defending Slavery: Proslavery Thought in the Old South: A Brief History with Documents*. New York: Bedford, 2003.

Freehling, William W. *The Road to Disunion. Volume 1: Secessionists at Bay, 1776–1854*. New York: Oxford University Press, 1990.

———. *The Road to Disunion. Volume 2: Secessionists Triumphant, 1855–1861*. New York: Oxford University Press, 2008.

Websites

General

The First American West: The Ohio River Valley, 1750–1820,
http://memory.loc.gov/ammem/award99/icuhtml/fawhome.html

Voluminous documents from the American Memory Project at the Library of Congress explore an early phase of American territorial expansion.

Historical Census Browser, the University of Virginia
http://fisher.lib.virginia.edu/collections/stats/histcensus/

Presents state- and county-level census data, 1790–1970. Viewers can create their own charts and maps and measure changes over time.

Library Company of Philadelphia
www.librarycompany.org/collections/exhibits/index.htm

Provides a long list of excellent online exhibitions on a number of topics in U.S. history, from Benjamin Franklin to popular medicine. Most exhibitions concern the early republic. Each exhibition contains an introduction to the topic and images of prints, paintings, documents, and objects.

Government

American President: An Online Reference Resource
www.millercenter.virginia.edu/academic/americanpresident

Sponsored by the Miller Center of Public Affairs at the University of Virginia, this site provides basic information, essays on special topics, and documents concerning each president.

A Century of Lawmaking for a New Nation: U.S. Congressional Documents and Debates
http://memory.loc.gov/ammem/amlaw/lawhome.html

Digitized and searchable versions of the journals and debates of both houses of Congress during the early republic, provided by the American Memory Project at the Library of Congress.

The George Washington Papers
http://gwpapers.virginia.edu/documents/index.html

Contains a variety of documents from Washington's presidency, as well as from other periods in his life. Presents essays, news articles, recommended websites, and online exhibitions about Washington.

A New Nation Votes
http://elections.lib.tufts.edu/aas_portal/index.xq

A database of local returns for 17,263 state, local, and federal elections in the United States, 1787–1825, searchable by candidate, office, year, and state.

Thomas Jefferson Digital Archive
http://etext.lib.virginia.edu/jefferson

From the University of Virginia, this site archives more than 1,700 transcribed and fully indexed documents written by or to Jefferson, as well as alphabetical compendia of his quotations.

Thomas Jefferson Papers
http://memory.loc.gov/ammem/collections/jefferson_papers

This section of the American Memory Project contains digitized versions of 27,000 documents in the Library of Congress.

Slavery

African American Odyssey
http://memory.loc.gov/ammem/aaohtml/exhibit/aointro.html

A small but remarkable collection of documents on African Americans' "quest for equality," starting with slaves and free blacks in the early republic, from the American Memory Project at the Library of Congress.

The Atlantic Slave Trade and Slave Life in the Americas
http://hitchcock.itc.virginia.edu/Slavery/index.php

The University of Virginia provides 1,200 visual images documenting the slave trade and slave life in Africa and the Americas, organized by topic.

Frederick Douglass Papers
http://memory.loc.gov/ammem/doughtml/doughome.html

Provides digitized images of all 7,400 documents in the papers of Frederick Douglass, one of the most important leaders of the abolitionists and northern African Americans.

From Slavery to Freedom: The African American Pamphlet Collection
http://memory.loc.gov/ammem/aapchtml/aapchome.html

Contains 396 pamphlets by and about African Americans, many from the early republic.

The Geography of Slavery in Virginia
www.vcdh.virginia.edu/gos

Contains a searchable database of thousands of runaway slave advertisements, along with laws, diaries, newspaper entries, and other documents regarding slavery in Virginia up to 1803.

Women

Do History
http://dohistory.org

Contains the diary of Martha Ballard, a Maine midwife, medical practitioner, and farmer, as well as other documents about her town. Guides viewers in constructing their own interpretations of the documents.

Women and Social Movements in the United States
http://womhist.alexanderstreet.com

Includes extensive compilations of documents on a wide variety of antebellum women's movements.

Women in America, 1820–1842
http://xroads.virginia.edu/~HYPER/ DETOC/FEM/home.htm

Transcriptions of the accounts of eighteen travelers to the United States regarding American women's status, experience, and activities.

Text Credits

Main Text

ix: Boston *Chronicle*, 9 Oct. 1794, reprinted in Connecticut *Courant*, 3 Nov. 1794.

13–14: Charles Francis Adams, ed., *The Works of John Adams, Second President of the United States: With a Life of the Author, Notes and Illustrations* (Boston: Little, Brown, 1854), 10 vols., 9: 375–78.

14–15: Thomas Jefferson, *Notes on the State of Virginia* (Richmond, VA: J.W. Randolph, 1853), 173–75.

15–16: Ibid., 148–55.

16–17: *The Pennsylvania Packet* (Philadelphia), July 10, 1788.

17–18: Charles William Janson, *The Stranger in America, 1793–1806* (1907; reprint, New York: Press of the Pioneers, Inc., 1935), 85–88.

19–20: William Blackstone, *Commentaries on the Laws of England* (London: Printed by A. Strahan for T. Cadell and W. Davies, 1803), 442–44.

20–22: "A Lady," "On the Supposed Superiority of the Masculine Understanding," *Universal Asylum and Columbian Magazine* (July 1791), 9–11.

23–24: *Digest of the Laws of Pennsylvania: From the Year One Thousand Seven Hundred, to the Thirteenth Day of October, One Thousand Eight Hundred and Forty, Laws, Etc.* (Philadelphia: M'Carty & Davis, 1841), 788–89.

24: Absalom Jones and Richard Allen, *Narrative of the Proceedings of the Black People During the Late Awful Calamity in Philadelphia in the Year 1793, and a Refutation of Some Censures Thrown Upon Them in Some Late Publications: Afro-American History Series* (Philadelphia: William W. Woodward, 1794), 23–24.

25: William Cabell Bruce, *John Randolph of Roanoke: 1773–1833: A Biography Based Largely on New Material* (1922; reprint, New York: Octagon Books, 1970), 2 vols., 1:104–5.

29–30: *The Federalist: A Commentary on The Constitution of the United States, Being a Collection of Essays Written in Support of the Constitution Agreed Upon September 17, 1787 by The Federal Convention* (New York: G. P. Putnam's Sons, 1894), 204–6.

31: John C. Hamilton, ed., *The Works of Alexander Hamilton: Comprising His Correspondence and His Political and Official Writings, Exclusive of the Federalist, Civil and Military* (New York: C. S. Francis, 1851), 388–90, 394.

32–33: *The Writings of Thomas* Jefferson, ed. Andrew A. Lipscomb and Albert Ellery Bergh (Washington, D.C.: Thomas Jefferson Memorial Association, 1903), 3:144–49.

33–34: Henry Cabot Lodge, ed., *Works of Alexander Hamilton* (New York: G. P. Putnam's Sons, 1904), 3:444–51.

34–35: *National Gazette* (Philadelphia), March 15, 19, 22, April 4, 1792.

36: Ibid., April 13, 1793.

37–39: *American Minerva* (New York), May 15, 1794.

39: Ibid., July 17, 1795.

40–41: Ibid., July 28, 1795.

41–44: George Washington, *The President's Address to the People of the United States, September 17, 1796, Intimating His Resolution of Retiring from Public Service, When the Present Term of Presidency Expired* (Philadelphia: W. Young, Mills & Son 1796), 12–23.

44–46: *Laws of the United States of America* (Philadelphia: Richard Folwell, 1799), 4 vols., 3:596–97.

46–48: *Debates in the Several State Conventions on the Adoption of the Federal Constitution as Recommended by the General Convention at Philadelphia in 1787: Together with the Journal of the Federal Convention, Luther Martin's Letter, Yates's Minutes, Congressional Opinions, Virginia and Kentucky Resolutions of '98–'99, and Other Illustrations of the Constitution, Vol. 4 Elliot's Debates* (Philadelphia: Lippincott, 1907), 528–29.

50–51: *Addresses and Messages of the Presidents of the United States from 1789 to 1839* (New York: McLean & Taylor, 1839), 8, 90–92.

55–56: Lipscomb and Bergh, 10:406–10.

56–57: Lipscomb and Bergh, 10:369–71.

57–59: Benjamin Hawkins and Charles L. Grant, *Letters, Journals, and Writings of Benjamin Hawkins, Selections* (Savannah, GA: Beehive Press, 1980), 122, 129, 140, 156, 172–73, 184–86, 189, 197.

59–60: Benjamin Drake, *Life of Tecumseh and of His Brother the Prophet: With a Historical Sketch of the Shawanoe Indians* (Philadelphia: Quaker City Publishing House, 1856), 86–89.

60–61: Samuel G. Drake, *The Book of the Indians or, Biography and History of the Indians of North America from its First Discovery to the Year 1841* (Boston: Antiquarian Institute, 1841), 121–22.

61–62: H. B. Cushman, *History of the Choctaw, Chickasaw and Natchez Indians* (Greenville, TX: Headlight Printing House, 1899), 311–12.

63–64: John Ridge to Albert Gallatin, February 27, 1826, Payne Papers, Newberry Library, Chicago. Reprinted in Michael D. Green and Theda Perdue, *The Cherokee Removal: A Brief History with Documents* (Boston: Bedford Books of St. Martin's Press, 1995), 34–43.

65–66: *The Cherokee Nation v. The State of Georgia 30 U.S. 1 (1831)* [Electronic Resource] via FindLaw: http://caselaw.lp.findlaw.com/scripts/getcase.pl?court=us&vol=30&invol=1.

66–68: James D. Richardson, ed., *Compilation of the Messages and Papers of the Presidents* (New York: Bureau of National Literature, 1917), 20 vols., 3:1019–22, 1083–86.

68–69: "Extracts from Letters of Mr. Jones." *The Baptist Missionary Magazine 18* (September 1838), 237–38.

69–70: Clarence Edwin Carter, *The Territorial Papers of the United States* (Washington, DC: United States Government Printing Office, 1934), 26 vols., 2:542, 548–49.

70–71: Ibid., 2: 638–39.

72–77: Rebecca Burlend and Edward Burlend, *A True Picture of Emigration: Or Fourteen Years in the Interior of North America* (London: G. Berger, 1831), 58–59, 64–67, 70–73, 78–80, 86–91, 106–9, 112–15, 124–29, 150–53.

77–79: Willie Lee Rose, *A Documentary History of Slavery in North America* (New York: Oxford University Press, 1976), 157–62, 346–54.

80: Ibid., 153.

81–82: The Journals of the Lewis and Clark Expedition (http://lewisandclarkjournals.unl.edu).

82–83: Stephen F. Austin, *Translation of the Laws, Orders, and Contracts on Colonization, from January, 1821, up to This Time: In Virtue of Which Col. Stephen F. Austin Has Introduced and Settled Foreign Emigrants in Texas: With an Explanatory Introduction* (San Filipe de Austin, TX: Godwin B. Cotton, 1829), 48–50.

84–85: Documents of Early Texas website (http://www.lsjunction.com/docs/tdoi.htm).

89–91: William Coventry Diary, 1798, New York State Historical Association, Cooperstown, NY.

91–92: Cynthia MacAlman McCausland and Robert R. McCausland, eds., *The Diary of Martha Ballard, 1785–1812* (Camden, ME: Picton Press, 1992), 273–75.

93–95: *George Holcomb Diary, 1840* (transcript), New York State Library, Albany, NY.

96: Hamilton D. Hurd, *History of Worcester County, Massachusetts: With Biographical Sketches of Many of Its Pioneers and Prominent Men* (Philadelphia: J. W. Lewis & Co., 1889), 1716.

97–99: Frances Milton Trollope, *Domestic Manners of the Americans* (London: Whittaker, Treacher & Co., 1832), 2 vols., 1:99–111

100: Paul E. Johnson, *A Shopkeeper's Millennium: Society and Revivals in Rochester, New York, 1815–1837, American Century Series* (New York: Hill and Wang, 1978), 110–11.

100–102: A. J. Graves, *Woman in America: Being an Examination into the Moral and Intellectual Condition of American Female Society* (New York: Harper and Brothers, 1843), 143–44, 156–58, 163–64.

103: Delores Bird Carpenter, ed., *The Selected Letters of Lidian Jackson Emerson* (Columbia, MO: University of Missouri Press, 1987), 46–47.

103–106: T. W. Dyott, *An Exposition of the System of Moral and Mental Labor Established at the Glass Factory of Dyottville, in the County of Philadelphia: Embracing a Description of the Glass Factory, Together with the System of Industry Therein Pursued, with the Report of the Committee Chosen to Investigate the Internal Regulations of the Place* (Philadelphia: n.p., 1833), 1–4, 7, 9, 10–12, 14, 21–22.

106–107: Ibid., Appendix C.

108–110: *New York Tribune,* August 20, September 20, November 29, 1845.

110–111: John Rogers Commons, Ulrich Bonnell Phillips, Eugene Allen Gilmore, Helen Laura Sumner, and John Bertram Andrews, *Documentary History of American Industrial Society* (Cleveland: A. H. Clark Company, 1910–11), 10 vols., 5:84–87.

111–112: Ibid., 5:303–5.

112–113: New York *Daily Sentinel* June 25, 1831. Reprinted in Nancy Cott, Jeanne Boydston, Ann Braude, Lori D. Ginzberg, and Molly Ladd-Taylor, eds., *Root of Bitterness: Documents of the Social History of American Women,* Second Edition (Boston: Northeastern University Press, 1996), 120–22.

113–114: Thomas Dublin, *Farm to Factory: Women's Letters, 1830–1860* (New York: Columbia University Press, 1981), 100–107.

115–116: Wolfgang Johannes Helbich, Walter D. Kamphoefner, and Ulrike Sommer, *News from the Land of Freedom: German Immigrants Write Home, Documents in American Social History* (Ithaca: Cornell University Press, 1991), 83–86.

117: *Farmer's Cabinet,* July 5, 1849.

121–122: Johann David Schoepf, *Travels in the Confederation [1783–1784],* Alfred J. Morrison, trans and ed. (Philadelphia: W. J. Campbell, 1911), 98–100.

122–124: Agustin Smith Clayton, *A Compilation of the Laws of the State of Georgia Passed by the Legislature Since the Political Year 1800, to the year 1810, Inclusive* (Augusta, GA: Adams and Duyckinck, 1812), 27, 133, 173, 332–35, 369, 462–63.

124–127: Willie Lee Rose, *A Documentary History of Slavery in North America* (New York: Oxford University Press, 1976), 346–54.

127: Peter Randolph, *Sketches of Slave Life, or, Illustrations of the "Peculiar Institution"* (Boston: Published for the author, 1855), 32.

128: Ibid., 30–31.

128–130: Thomas Anderson, *Interesting Account of Thomas Anderson, a Slave: Taken from His Own Lips* (1854). Transcribed in *Documenting the American South* (Chapel Hill: Academic Affairs Library, University of North Carolina at Chapel Hill, 2000), 1–4.

130–131: Henry B. Bibb and Lucius C. Matlack, *Narrative of the Life and Adventures of Henry Bibb, An American Slave* (New York: Published by the Author, 1849), 38–43.

132–133: Harriet A. Jacobs, *Incidents in the Life of a Slave Girl* (Boston: Published for the Author, 1861), 44–51.

133: Commons, Phillips, et al., 2:38.

133–134: Austin Steward and John Chester Buttre, *Twenty-Two Years a Slave and Forty Years a Free Man: Embracing a Correspondence of Several Years While President of Wilberforce Colony, London, Canada West* (Rochester, NY: William Alling, 1857), 30–32.

134–135: Randolph, 27–29.

135–136: Joseph Taper to Joseph Long, November 11, 1840, in Joseph Long Papers, Duke University Special Collections Library, Durham, NC.

136: *Republic* (Baton Rouge, LA), reprinted in Commons, Phillips, et al., *Documentary History of American Industrial Society,* 2:120–21.

137–139: Nat Turner and Thomas R. Gray, *The Confessions of Nat Turner* (1831; reprint, Berlin, VA: R. M. Stephenson, 1881), 10–15.

150–152: Virginia Constitutional Convention, *Proceedings and Debates of the Virginia State Convention of 1829–1830: To Which Are Subjoined, the New Constitution of Virginia, and the Votes of the People* (Richmond, VA: Ritchie & Cook, 1830), 25–30.

152–153: Charles Hale and Nathan Hale, trans., *Journal of Debates and Proceedings in the Convention of Delegates: Chosen to Revise the Constitution of Massachusetts, Begun and Holden at Boston, November 15, 1820, and Continued by Adjournment to January 9, 1821* (Boston: Daily Advertiser, 1853), 247–48.

153–154: Francis Newton Thorpe, *The Federal and State Constitutions, Colonial Charters, and Other Organic Laws of the State, Territories, and Colonies Now or Heretofore Forming the United States of America* (Washington, DC: Government Printing Office, 1909), 2642–43.

154–155: Martin Van Buren to Thomas Ritchie, January 13, 1827, Martin Van Buren Papers, Library of Congress, Washington, DC. Reprinted in Robert V. Remini, *The Age of Jackson* (New York: Harper and Row, 1972).

157–159: Democratic Republican General Committee, "Plan of Organization," Miscellaneous Broadsides, American Antiquarian Society, Worcester, MA.

159–162: *Annual Messages, Veto Messages, Protest, &c. of Andrew Jackson, President of the United States* (Baltimore: E. J. Coale, 1835), 231–45.

162–164: "Introduction," *United States Magazine and Democratic Review* 1 (October 1837), 2–9.

164–167: Horace Greeley, *Why I Am a Whig; Reply to an Inquiring Friend* (New York: New York Tribune, n.d.). 1–2, 5–8,12–13.

168–169: Margaret Prior, *Walks of Usefulness* (New York: Am. F. R. Society, 1848), 202, 203, 206.

173–176: David Walker, *Walker's Appeal, in Four Articles; Together with a Preamble, to the Coloured Citizens of the World, But in Particular, and Very Expressly, to Those of the United States of America* (3rd ed., Boston: The Author, 1830), 2, 14–15, 22, 24, 33–37, 78–79.

176–179: *Constitution of the American Anti-Slavery Society: With the Declaration of the National Anti-Slavery Convention at Philadelphia, December, 1833 and the Address to the Public* (New York: American Anti-Slavery Society, 1838), 6–9.

179–181: *Richmond Enquirer,* February 14, 16, 1832.

181–185: Sarah Moore Grimké, *Letters on the Equality of the Sexes, and the Condition of Woman. Addressed to Mary S. Parker* (Boston: Isaac Knapp, 1838), 22–25, 50–51, 54–55, 66–91, 98-106, 115–27.

185–186: Henry Irving Tragle, *The Southampton Slave Revolt of 1831; a Compilation of Source Material* (Amherst, MA: University of Massachusetts Press, 1971), 275–76.

186–187: *Acts Passed at a General Assembly of the Commonwealth of Virginia Begun and Held at the Capitol in the City of Richmond On Monday, the Fifth Day of December, In the Year of Our Lord, One Thousand Eight Hundred and Thirty-One, And of The Commonwealth the Fifty-Sixth* (Richmond, VA: Thomas Ritchie, 1832), 20–22.

187–190: James Henry Hammond, *Selections from the Letters and Speeches of the Hon. James H. Hammond, of South Carolina* (New York: J. F. Trow & Co., Printers, 1866), 114–15,118–19, 124–59, 164–65, 168–70.

190–191: S. Foster Damon, comp., *Series of Old American Songs, Reproduced in Facsimile from Original or Early Editions in the Harris Collection of American Poetry and Plays, No. 15 Jim Crow.* (Providence, RI: Brown University Library, 1936), n.p.

192–194: James Kirke Paulding, *Slavery in the United States* (New York: Harper & Bros., 1836), 41–42, 61, 64, 66, 70, 73, 79, 82.

194–196: Samuel George Morton and George Combe, *Crania Americana; or, a Comparative View of the Skulls of Various Aboriginal Nations of North and South America* (Philadelphia: J. Dobson, 1839), 1–3, 6, 21, 82, 86, 260.

197–198: Frederick Douglass, *Narrative of the Life of Frederick Douglass, an American Slave* (Dublin: Webb and Chapman, 1845), 93–98.

198–201: *New York Evening Post ,* July 9, 11, 13, 1834.

201–203: *Statute Laws of the Territory of Iowa* (Dubuque, IA: Russell & Reeves, 1839), 55–56, 111, 180–81, 188, 379.

207–208: "Annexation," *United States Magazine and Democratic Review* 17 (July–August 1845), 5–11.

210–212: *Congressional Globe,* 29th Congress, 1st Session (1846), 917–18.

212–213: J. C. Bancroft Davis, comp., *Treaties and Conventions Concluded between the United States of America since July 4, 1776* (Washington, DC: U.S. Government Printing Office, 1873), 566–67.

213–216: Robert Glass Cleland, *Cattle on a Thousand Hills* (San Marino, CA: Huntington Library Publications, 1951), 238–41.

216: *Congressional Globe,* 29th Congress, 2nd Session (1847), 318.

216–218: *Ibid.,* 317–18.

218–221: *Ibid.,* 917–18.

Sidebars

18: Francis Hawkins and Charles Moore, eds., *George Washington's Rules of Civility and Decent Behaviour in Company and Conversation* (Boston: Houghton Mifflin, 1926), 6–9.

20: "On Matrimonial Obedience." *The Lady's Magazine, and Repository of Entertaining Knowledge* (July 1792), 64–67.

34: Alexander Hamilton to Edward Carrington, May 26, 1792, in Harold C. Syrett et al., eds., *The Papers of Alexander Hamilton* (New York: Columbia University Press, 1961–87), 27 vols., 11:426–45. Reprinted in Noble E. Cunningham Jr., ed., *Jefferson vs. Hamilton: Confrontations That Shaped a Nation* (New York: Bedford/St. Martin's, 2000), 87–93.

40: *Aurora General Advertiser* (Philadelphia), August 11, 1795.

50: Thomas Jefferson to Spencer Roane, September 6, 1819, in Merrill D. Peterson, ed., *The Portable Thomas Jefferson* (New York: Penguin, 1975), 562.

57: Burlend and Burlend, 75–76.

65: *Worcester v. State of GA.,* 31 U.S. 515 (1832).

89: William Coventry Diary, Appendix B.

97: Paul E. Johnson, *A Shopkeeper's Millennium: Society and Revivals in Rochester, New York, 1815–1837,* American Century Series (New York: Hill and Wang, 1978), 108.

116: Helbich, Kamphoefner, and Sommer, 108.

122: Privy Council, Adele Stanton Edwards, South Carolina Department of Archives and History, *Journals of the Privy Council, 1783–1789* (Columbia, SC: Published for the South Carolina Dept. of Archives and History by the University of South Carolina Press, 1971).

125: Edwin Adams Davis, ed., *Plantation Life in the Florida Parishes of Louisiana, 1836–1846, as Reflected in the Diary of Bennet H. Barrow* (New York: Columbia University Press, 1943), 406–7.

129: Randolph, 29–32.

151: Francis Newton Thorpe, comp., *The Federal and State Constitutions, Colonial Charters, and Other Organic Laws of the State, Territories, and Colonies Now or Hertofore Forming the United States of America* (Washington, DC: Government Printing Office, 1909), 25-30.

152: Nathaniel H. Carter and William L. Stone, trans., *Reports of the Proceedings and Debates of the Convention of 1821 Assembled for the Purpose of Amending the Constitution of the State of New York: Containing All the Official Documents Relating to the Subject, and Other Valuable Matter* (Albany, NY: E. and E. Hosford, 1821), 180–81.

168: *Advocate of Moral Reform,* June 1, 1840, p. 82, reprinted in Daniel Wright and Kathryn Kish Sklar, *What Was the Appeal of Moral Reform to Antebellum Northern Women, 1835–1841?,* in *Women and Social Movements in the United States, 1600–2000* (Electronic Resource)

185: John Floyd to J. C. Harris, September 27, 1831, reprinted in Henry Irving Tragle, *The Southampton Slave Revolt of 1831* (Amherst, MA: University of Massachusetts Press, 1971), 274–76.

Photo Credits

Cover: Illustration of Scene on Erie Canal [1825]; image © Bettmann/Corbis Collection; ii: Library of Congress, cph 3a07353; iii: Library of Congress, cph 3a05553; vi: Collection of the Supreme Court of the United States; Library of Congress, LC-USZ62-50852 ; vii: National Archives, RG11; British Library, Cott. Vit. A XV f. 187 8152109; © Victoria and Albert Museum, London; ix: Library of Congress, LC-DIG-pga-03891; x: Library of Congress, LC-DIG-ppmsca-19468; 2: Anne S.K. Brown Military Collection, Brown University Library; 3: The New York Public Library, Prints Collection, the Miriam and Ira D. Wallach Division of Art, Prints and Photographs, Astor, Lenox, and Tilden Foundations; 4: In private collection, image courtesy of Nathan Liverant & Son; 7: The Collection of the New-York Historical Society, negative no. 44642; 10: The Granger Collection, New York, 4E36.06; 13: The Collection of the New-York Historical Society, accession no. 1876.1; 14: Courtesy of the Maryland Historical Society, 1960-108-1-3-21; 16: The Collection of the New-York Historical Society, accession no. 1903.12; 19: The Henry Francis du Pont Winterthur Museum; 21: Library of Congress, LC-DIG-ppmsca-02951; 23: American Philosophical Society, apsimage1694; 24: Moorland-Spingarn Research Center, Howard University; 25: The Historical Society of Pennsylvania (HSP), Breton, Bb 862 B756 #44; 26: The Collection of the New-York Historical Society, negative no. 2737; 29: American Philosophical Society, APSdigobj3555; 31: National Numismatic Collection, Smithsonian Institution; 32: Beinecke Rare Book and Manuscript Library, Yale University; 33: The New York Historical Society, negative no. 43339; 36: Print and Picture Collection, Free Library of Philadelphia; 37: Kilroe Collection 1796 T15, Rare Books and Manuscripts Library, Columbia University; 40: From the Collection of the York County Heritage Trust, York, PA; 42: The Historical Society of Pennsylvania (HSP), Bb 612 Se31; 44: Library of Congress, LC-DIG-ppmsca-19356; 45: © American Antiquarian Society; 46: © American Antiquarian Society; 47: The New York Public Library, Early American Imprints, series 1, no. 36857, 49: Library of Congress; 51: Library of Congress, LC-USZ62-78126; 52: Chicago History Museum, 56: Jefferson National Expansion Memorial/National Park Service; 56: Jefferson National Expansion Memorial/National Park Service; 59: Benjamin Hawkins and the Creek Indians, c. 1805, oil on canvas, H. 35-⅞ × W. 49-⅞", Greenville County Museum of Art; 60: National Portrait Gallery, Smithsonian Institution / Art Resource, NY; 61: Library of Congress, LC-USZC4-3616; 62: Library of Congress, LC-USZC4-509; 63: Library of Congress, LC-USZC4-3158; 66: Library of Congress, LC-USZC4-2566; 69: Fenimore Art Museum, Cooperstown, New York; 69: National Archives & Records Administration, Loc: vault, 18/15/05, box 37; 71: Illinois Township Surveys, Illinois State Archives; 73: The Collection of the New-York Historical Society, accession no. 1953.240; 74: New York State Library, BRD 0649; 76: Library of Congress, LC-USZ62-2028; 78: Library of Congress, LC-USZ62-108055; 80: Sabin Americana. Gale, Cengage Learning. Document # CY3808112573; 80: Sabin Americana. Gale, Cengage Learning. Document # CY3808112573; 86: The Newark Museum / Art Resource, NY; 88: The Collection of the New-York Historical Society; 89: Collection of the York County Heritage Trust, York, PA; 92: © The Shelburne Museum, Shelburne, Vermont; 93: Erie Canal, New York by John William Hill, 1831, Courtesy of the Union College Permanent Collection; 94: Sinclair Hamilton Collection No. 1424. Graphic Arts Division. Department of Rare Books and Special Collections. Princeton University Library.; 98: The Collection of the New-York Historical Society, negative no. 26275; 100: The Church of Jesus Christ of Latter-Day Saints, Church History Library; 101: Friends Historical Library of Swarthmore College; 104: Yale University Art Gallery; 107: Yale University Art Gallery, The Mabel Brady Garvan Collection; 108: The Collection of the New-York Historical Society; accession no. 1980.33; 111: The New York Public Library, KSC 1836; 115: Courtesy of The Historic New Orleans Collection, Leonard Huber Collection MSS 465, Folder 176; 117: Library of Congress, LC-USZ62-916; 118: Library of Congress, LC-USZ62-76081; 120: Library of Congress, LC-USZ62-10293; 121: Library of Congress, LC-USZ62-31864; 123: The Colonial Williamsburg Foundation, # DS95-590; 127: Burke Library, Union Theological Seminary, E443 .R19; 131: "The Broomstick Wedding," www.slaveryimages.org, sponsored by the Virginia Foundation for the Humanities and the University of Virginia Library; 134: Library of Congress, lhbcb 34319; 136: Library of Congress, LC-USZCN4-225; 138: Library of Congress, LC-USCZ62-38902; 140: Library of Congress, LC-USZ62-64427; 142: Courtesy of Wethersfield Historical Society; 143: National Gallery of Art, 1953.5.49; 143: Print and Picture Collection, Free Library of Philadelphia; 144: The Library Company of Philadelphia; 144: The Library Company of Philadelphia; 145: J. Paul Getty Museum, Los Angeles, CA. Father, Daughters, and Nurse, photograph by Thomas Martin Easterly, 84.XT.1569.1; 145: Library of Congress, Voyage dans l'intérieur de l'Amérique du Nord; 146: Mexican Family, unknown photographer. Daguerreotype, quarter-plate, c. 1847. P1981.65.18 Amon Carter Museum, Fort Worth, Texas; 146: Rare Book and Manuscript Library, Columbia University, Call no. B326.4 L524; 147: Library of Congress, LC-USZC4-5950; 147: Library of Congress, LC-USZC4-3263; 148: Library of Congress, cph 3a05553; 156: Library of Congress, LC-USZ61-1464; 157: Library of Congress, LC-USZ62-40740; 160: Library of Congress, LC-USZ62-809; 161: Library of Congress, LC-USZ62-9646; 164: © American Antiquarian Society; 167: Edwin Patrick Kilroe Collection, Rare Book and Manuscript Library, Columbia University; 170: Fugitive Slave Law Convention, Cazenovia, New York by Ezra Greenleaf Weld, daguerreotype,1850, J. Paul Getty Museum, Los Angeles, CA; 174: Image Courtesy of Accessible Archives, Inc. ©, a Pennsylvania Corporation providing electronic resources in 18th- and 19th-century publications; 177: © American Antiquarian Society; 182: © American Antiquarian Society; 184: Lester Levy Collection, Special Collections, Johns Hopkins Libraries; 191: Lester Levy Collection, Special Collections, Johns Hopkins Libraries; 192: Courtesy of the Boston Public Library, no. 93743; 195: Phoenix Collection, Rare Book and Manuscript Library, Columbia University; 199: The Library Company of Philadelphia; 204: Fray Angelico Chavez History Library, New Mexico History Museum; 206: Library of Congress, LC-USCZC4-2957; 209: Library of Congress, LC-USZ62-791; 210: Institute of Texan Cultures, UTSA, #076-0009, Source: Michaud y Thomas, Julio Album pintoresco de la Republica Mexicana Mexico, Julio Michaud-Thomas (1818); 214: Denver Public Library, Western History and Genealogy Department; 217: Library of Congress, LC-USZ62-17296; 220: Library of Congress, rbaapc 16300; 222: Library of Congress, LC-DIG-ppmsca-19468; 222: Chicago History Museum; 223: Yale University Art Gallery; 223: Fugitive Slave Law Convention, Cazenovia, New York by Ezra Greenleaf Weld, daguerreotype,1850, J. Paul Getty Museum, Los Angeles, CA

Acknowledgments

Over twenty years of writing history, I have found that none of my books or articles comes out of my own efforts or ideas alone. Much—perhaps most—of what I write emerges out of a process of talking to colleagues and students, reading their work, sharing ideas, and listening to their criticism—and then thinking and writing some more. Even when I don't take their advice, I often change what I write in response to it. After a while, the ideas are not mine or theirs, but something created by the interaction of the two. This book is no different. I've been working on it for about a decade, which is plenty of time to accumulate intellectual debts.

Several colleagues generously suggested documents to include in this book, some of them digging through their files to find them for me. I'm grateful to Peter Wood, Thavolia Glymph, Alan Taylor, Bruce Laurie, Jack Wilson, Carol Sheriff, and Sally Deutsch for this help. Innumerable librarians have helped me find materials for the book as well. I am not exaggerating when I say that without them, this book would have been impossible. I'm indebted to the staff at the University of Arizona Library; the librarians at College of the Holy Cross; Joanne Chaison and the gang at the American Antiquarian Society; and the staff at the New York State Historical Association. Most recently, Margaret Brill, Kelley Laughton, and Carson Holloway and their co-workers at Duke University Library have provided me with indispensible help. I also extend my thanks to Carol Karlsen and five anonymous readers for Oxford University Press, who provided thorough and helpful comments on the entire manuscript.

I have discussed the documents in this book most frequently with my students at College of the Holy Cross, the University of Arizona, and Duke University. Their interpretations and ideas have deeply influenced this book. I'm equally indebted to Clark Pomerleau, Paula Hastings, Orion Teal, Karlyn Forner, Michael Stauch, and Amish Sheth, who did yeoman work as research assistants, ferreting out documents, tracking down citations, and proofreading.

While I was researching and writing this book, colleagues at several institutions—College of the Holy Cross, the University of Arizona, and Duke University—have provided a warm and stimulating intellectual environment. The same goes for my colleagues at the Society for Historians of the Early American Republic. I can't think of better intellectual communities in which to work. Frankly, I don't remember whether or not David Waldstreicher suggested specific documents to me, but he probably did. I do know that he has always been an extraordinarily stimulating intellectual companion and a good friend. He has long been my "go to" person on the history of the early American republic, and his imprint is upon this book. In the same vein, Gunther Peck and David Ortiz have provided both challenge and support, intellectual and emotional, over the past decade and a half.

This book would never have been produced without the work of several editors and other creative workers at Oxford University Press. My greatest debt is to my editor, Nancy Toff, who has been patient and good-humored at my frequent delays and has responded with insight, precision, and (again) humor when I finally produced something. Nancy's assistant, Sonia Tycko, shepherded the book through the publication process and resolved endless technical problems with efficiency and good cheer. Karen Fein did a terrific job in editing the manuscript. Chloe Smith found numerous illustrations, and Jennifer Bossert saw the manuscript through the production process. Along with the others, Susan Ferber, my other editor, has made working with Oxford fun and intellectually rewarding.

I owe a debt of another sort to Sally Deutsch and Isaac Deutsch Huston. Endlessly interested in history, willing to think stuff through with me, they have left the imprint of their ideas on this book. In daily, imperceptible increments, they have fastened an even deeper imprint upon me.

232

Index

References to illustrations and their captions are indicated by page numbers in **bold**.

About the Author

Reeve Huston teaches history at Duke University. He is the author of *Land and Freedom: Rural Society, Popular Protest, and Party Politics in Antebellum New York*, which won the Dixon Ryan Fox Prize from the New York State Historical Association and the Theodore Saloutos Prize from the Agricultural History Society. He is currently writing a book about the ways in which American political practices were changing in the decade and a half before Andrew Jackson's presidency.